LAW'S INFAMY

Law's Infamy

Understanding the Canon of Bad Law

Edited by

Austin Sarat, Lawrence Douglas, *and* Martha Merrill Umphrey

NEW YORK UNIVERSITY PRESS

New York

NEW YORK UNIVERSITY PRESS
New York
www.nyupress.org

References to Internet websites (URLs) were accurate at the time of writing. Neither the author nor New York University Press is responsible for URLs that may have expired or changed since the manuscript was prepared.

Library of Congress Cataloging-in-Publication Data
Names: Sarat, Austin, editor. | Douglas, Lawrence, editor. | Umphrey, Martha Merrill, editor.
Title: Law's infamy : understanding the Canon of bad law / edited by Austin Sarat, Lawrence Douglas, and Martha Merrill Umphrey.
Description: New York : New York University Press, [2021] | Includes bibliographical references and index.
Identifiers: LCCN 2021014001 | ISBN 9781479812080 (hardback) | ISBN 9781479812097 (paperback) | ISBN 9781479812103 (ebook) | ISBN 9781479812110 (ebook other)
Subjects: LCSH: Justice, Administration of—United States. | Judicial process—United States. | Political questions and judicial power—United States. | United States. Supreme Court. | Law reform—United States. | Constitutional law—United States—Cases.
Classification: LCC KF8700 .L377 2021 | DDC 347.73/12—dc23
LC record available at https://lccn.loc.gov/2021014001

New York University Press books are printed on acid-free paper, and their binding materials are chosen for strength and durability. We strive to use environmentally responsible suppliers and materials to the greatest extent possible in publishing our books.

Manufactured in the United States of America

10 9 8 7 6 5 4 3 2 1

Also available as an ebook

To Ben (A.S.)

CONTENTS

Telling the Story of Law's Infamy

An Introduction

AUSTIN SARAT, LAWRENCE DOUGLAS, AND
MARTHA MERRILL UMPHREY WITH RYAN KYLE

This book takes up the question of whether and how to tell the story of the law's infamy. Who tells that story? And for what purpose? Is it a consoling story of progress and redemption or a piercing story of law covering the tracks of its complicity with evil? *Law's Infamy* examines when and why the word "infamy" should be used to characterize legal decisions or actions taken in the name of the law. It does so while acknowledging that law's infamy is by no means a familiar locution. More commonly, the stories we tell of law's failures talk of injustices, not infamy.[1] Labeling a legal decision as "infamous" suggests a distinctive kind of injustice, one that is particularly evil or wicked. Doing so means that such a decision cannot be redeemed or reformed; it can only be repudiated.

We are writing this book at a time when Americans are telling and hearing many stories of injustice. In the United States and elsewhere, the confident proclamation of the triumph of liberal values and the "end of history"[2] has given way to postliberalism and authoritarianism. The federal government has been boldly restricting political rights or penalizing those who seek to exercise them. Citizens' life chances now are shaped by great and seemingly intractable disparities in income and wealth. And from the murder of George Floyd in 2020 to the systematic dismantling of voting rights since the election that November, legal institutions are implicated in these injustices.

Narratives of law's complicity in miscarriages of justice are hardly new. They are a repeated staple of our history. From the largely unknown Tulsa Race Riot of 1921, to the 1930s case of the Scottsboro Boys, to the lynching of the African American teenager Emmitt Till, to the 1983 case of Rolando Cruz, to countless other instances of police brutality against black men, the twentieth and twenty-first centuries have witnessed more than their share of miscarriages of justice. Faulty eyewitness identifications, false confessions, and biased juries—as well as the politicization of prosecution and the pervasive fact of racial bias in the criminal justice system—make error a legal commonplace throughout the legal system.[3]

As a result, political theorist Judith Shklar argues that, in our stories of law, "injustice should not be treated intellectually as a hasty preliminary to the analysis of justice."[4] According to Shklar, "the real realm of injustice is not in an amoral and prelegal state of nature. It does not appear only on those rare occasions when a political order wholly collapses. It does not stand outside the gate of even the best known states. Most injustices occur continuously within the framework of an established polity with an operative system of law, in normal times."[5]

Yet the language of infamy rarely appears in stories of law's miscarriages of justice, as bad as they may be. To offer but one example, law professor Jamal Greene labels a few of the most odious Supreme Court decisions—*Dred Scott v. Sanford, Plessy v. Ferguson, Lochner v. New York,* and *Korematsu v. United States*—"anti-canonical," not infamous.[6] Greene's analysis is empirical rather than normative. And there is more that could be said about the injustices for each of those cases represents and signifies but also masks. Thus, for example, as one of the reviewers of this book noted: "The slavery/Jim Crow anti-canon includes no lynching cases, no death penalty cases, no convict leasing cases, etc."

In Greene's analysis, cases are marked as anticanonical by the frequency with which subsequent cases and legal scholarship repudiate them. They serve as negative reference points in a narrative of constitutional progress. Their anticanonical status does not derive from the fact that they are poorly reasoned. Indeed, for Greene, identifying cases as anticanonical showcases the ease with which reasonable judges can perpetrate constitutional wrongs.[7]

While the language of infamy seems a bit odd, out of date, a leftover from a different time, it is not completely foreign to American law. In various places, infamy is part of the story law tells about citizens' conduct rather than the stories citizens and scholars tell about the law. This book, *Law's Infamy*, seeks to alter that course by making legal actions and decisions the subject of a story about infamy.

Designating someone or something as infamous can be traced back to ancient Greece and Rome, where *infamia* was used to describe certain dishonorable behavior.[8] That designation could be based on a legal finding, usually attendant to conviction for committing a crime. Alternatively, it could be based on a pattern of conduct that, while not criminal, the community regarded as disreputable. But whether a legal designation or a social fact, *infamia* transformed people into social outcasts, stripping them of honor and dignity. It also deprived those so designated of the privileges of citizenship, including the right to vote or testify in court.[9]

To be infamous was to be put on the other side of a social boundary, marked as other. Infamy stigmatized. It was reserved for offenses and behaviors that went to the core of what it meant to be an upstanding person.[10] It was rooted in a society in which status and reputation mattered greatly. Scholars note that in the ancient world *infamia* was used to oppress certain groups of people and to defend the existing social hierarchy.[11]

Infamia was also important in medieval Europe.[12] Legal manifestation of "infamy" in medieval societies "was especially useful because it allowed legal professionals and communities to bridge gaps between the ephemeral, social quality of the word on the street . . . and the steely realities of one's legal status."[13] While civil jurists insisted that "legal infamy" was a narrow concept elicited only by specific crimes, religious leaders used it to label a wide range of scandalous and immoral behavior in the clergy and the larger society.[14]

For centuries, *infamia* was a designation easily alleged but hard to shed. People whose conduct or attitudes were unpopular could be made into outcasts with little or no redress. Lives and reputations were promiscuously ruined.

Criticisms of such abuses of *infamia* surfaced in several eighteenth-century theories of punishment. One of the most notable of its critics was the renowned Italian criminal legal theorist Cesare Beccaria.[15] Beccaria condemned it as an irrational categorization of conduct, one that was arbitrarily applied to conduct done by some people and withheld when the same conduct was done by others. "Infamia," he said, was "a sentiment regulated neither by laws nor by reason, but entirely by opinion,"[16] in particular by the opinions of the powerful.[17]

Fear of abuse in the designation of infamous crimes is reflected in the Fifth Amendment to the United States Constitution, which entitles persons accused of such crimes to a grand jury hearing.[18] Commentators on American criminal law at the time the Fifth Amendment was ratified in 1791 said that "an infamous offence is one involving moral turpitude in the offender, or infamy in the punishment, or both."[19] From time to time, the United States Supreme Court has stated that the nature of the *crime* is what distinguishes infamous from noninfamous offenses, but in the late nineteenth century, in *Ex parte Wilson*, the Court decided that the nature of the *punishment* for a given crime also should determine whether it was infamous.[20] As Justice Horace Gray explained:

> What punishments shall be considered as infamous may be affected by the changes of public opinion from one age to another. In former times, being put in the stocks was not considered as necessarily infamous. And by the first Judiciary Act of the United States, whipping was classed with moderate fines and short terms of imprisonment in limiting the criminal jurisdiction of the district court. . . . But at the present day either stocks or whipping might be thought an infamous punishment.[21]

Decades later in the 1950s, the era of red-baiting led by U.S. senator Joseph McCarthy brought attention to stories of infamy and their meaning in the Fifth Amendment. Thus, in 1956 in *Ullman v. United States*, the Supreme Court ruled that a person given immunity from prosecution loses their Fifth Amendment right against self-incrimination and may be compelled to testify about their association with the Communist Party. Justice William Douglas dissented, constructing a narrative of the damage that immunized testimony might do by still exposing a witness to infamy. As he explained: "The Fifth Amendment was designed to protect the accused against infamy, as well as against prosecution. . . . Beccaria and his French and English followers . . . influenced American thought in the critical years following our Revolution. They understood that the history of infamy as a punishment was notorious."[22]

Douglas's account noted that the authors of the Fifth Amendment understood that "[l]oss of office, loss of dignity, loss of face were feudal forms of punishment. Infamy was historically considered to be punishment as effective as fine and imprisonment. . . . The curse of infamy . . .

results from public opinion. . . . 'It is in the power of the mores, rather than in the hands of the legislator, that this terrible weapon of infamy rests, this type of civil excommunication, which deprives the victim of all consideration, which severs all the ties which bind him to his fellow citizens, which isolates him in the midst of society.'" He called attention to the fact that "[t]here is great infamy involved in the present case, apart from the loss of rights of citizenship under federal law which I have already mentioned. The disclosure that a person is a Communist practically excommunicates him from society."[23]

The McCarthy era also witnessed the birth of so-called badge of infamy claims in due process cases. These claims were brought by people who refused to take loyalty oaths and, as a result, were branded as disloyal in some government proceeding. In *Wieman v. Updegraff*, the Supreme Court acknowledged that a "badge of infamy" would be affixed to anyone branded disloyal by the government. But it held that that in itself was not sufficient to trigger the due process guarantees of the Fourteenth Amendment.[24]

Subsequent cases suggest that a person would be entitled to a hearing only if a badge of infamy was associated with some additional, tangible loss of employment or other opportunity. As Justice William Rehnquist noted in *Paul v. Davis*: "The Court has recognized the serious damage that could be inflicted by branding a government employee as 'disloyal,' and thereby stigmatizing his good name. But the Court has never held that the mere defamation of an individual, whether by branding him disloyal or otherwise, was sufficient to invoke the guarantees of procedural due process absent an accompanying loss of government employment."[25]

In the United States, as in the ancient world, stories of infamy work at both the social and legal levels to stigmatize and ostracize people, to mark them as irredeemably other.[26] *Law's Infamy* subjects law itself to such an examination. What stories can we tell of law's infamy? How are those stories used by legal officials? Do they support or undermine efforts to ground legal legitimacy in narratives of progress? Do stories of law's infamy misdirect our attention and in so doing help perpetuate injustices not so branded? Are there some decisions that should be branded as infamous and cast into the dustbin of history? How do law or legal decisions become infamous? Who are the actors involved in constructing stories of legal infamy? What works and what does not work in those processes? Are cultural and legal changes today undermining the power of stories of law's infamy? These are the questions the contributors to this book address.

We begin with Justin Collings's "After Law's Infamy: Judicial Self-Legitimation in the Aftermath of Judicial Evil" (chapter 1), which addresses the relationship between infamy and institutional legitimacy in Germany, Italy, and the United States. Collings contends that branding legal regimes and/or decisions as "infamous" is a tool used by legal decision makers to legitimize the institutions of which they are a part. But he also notes that recalling an infamous past also may carry a destabilizing effect. He illustrates this duality by offering a comparative analysis of courts in the trio of countries mentioned.

In Germany and Italy, the creation of a new constitutional tradition after World War II required coming to terms with the infamous history of both the prior regimes and the judiciaries that were part of those regimes. The German Federal Constitutional Court, according to Collings, positioned itself as the "antithesis of a tainted past," but it nonetheless had to reckon with past legal decisions as a source of its authority. It has been, in his account, more successful than the Italian Constitutional Court in repudiating fascist laws; as a result, the Italian court has not gained the same credibility as its counterpart in Germany.

The United States Supreme Court, Collings argues, has adopted a different strategy to maintain its legitimacy in light of its past endorsement of slavery, racial segregation, and Native American genocide. The Court constructs a story in which only four of its decisions are branded "infamous," the same cases that Green designates the "anti-canon." While the German and Italian supreme courts have acknowledged that entire eras in their countries' histories are infamous, the Supreme Court acts as if the problem of legal infamy can be laid at the feet of a few judges, not the Constitution itself. Collings concludes that this has been a successful but costly strategy, absolving the Supreme Court of having to confront "scores of equally unsavory cases."

In "'The Courts of the Conqueror': Colonialism, the Constitution, and the Time of Redemption" (chapter 2), Sherally Munshi highlights some of those unacknowledged infamous cases and challenges constitutional theorist's Jack Balkin's claim that the Supreme Court consistently redeems itself. It seeks to do so by identifying infamous cases as the touchstone against which constitutional progress can and should be measured. Munshi contends that this narrative ignores a series of cases starting in 1823 with *Johnson v. M'Intosh* and extending through 2018 with *Trump v. Hawaii*. These cases, she contends, have granted—and continue to grant—the government unilateral authority to deprive foreigners of constitutional rights based on the United States' inherent "sovereignty." In her view, they are every bit as infamous as the cases identified in Greene's anticanon.

Chief Justice John Marshall's opinion in *Johnson v. M'Intosh* allowed the U.S. government to seize Native land by acknowledging the extralegal prerogatives of sovereignty. Marshall granted the government a dangerous extraconstitutional power that, Munshi notes, the Court has been unable or unwilling to check in subsequent cases. Though Marshall attempted to absolve the Court of blame by claiming Native dispossession was "inevitable," Munshi insists that it was not.

She contends that Marshall's decision deserves to be recognized as infamous and responsible for the development, as well as the abuses, of the "plenary power doctrine," which provided the underpinnings of President Donald Trump's Muslim ban. She notes that, in *Trump v. Hawaii*, Chief Justice John Roberts condemned *Korematsu*, one of Greene's anticanonical cases, only for its endorsement of racial discrimination. He did not challenge the US government's unilateral authority over foreigners. Seeing the legacy of *M'Intosh* played out in the Trump case is, Munshi notes, a reminder that infamy is a social and legal construction, not an objective fact. She urges her readers to attend to the processes through which law's infamy is constructed and concludes that Greene's anticanon lets the Supreme Court off the hook for other decisions that merit being labeled infamous.

Chapters 3–5 each takes up Munshi's invitation to examine the processes through which stories of law's infamy are constructed. In "Supreme Court Precedent and the Politics of Repudiation" (chapter 3), Robert L. Tsai challenges the notion that Supreme Court cases become infamous only when the Supreme Court overturns one of them. He calls our attention to the "politics of repudiation," or the process of constructing stories to delegitimize a case. The politics of repudiation require creating a sense that an infamous decision no longer aligns with the culture.

Tsai discusses the way in which the power of the politics of repudiation worked in the case of *Dred Scott v. Sanford*. In his account, *Dred Scott*, long before it was repudiated in law, had come to be regarded as infamous in the country at large because of the efforts of President Abraham Lincoln's Republican Party. He sees a similar process of political change leading the way for legal change in the stories that conservatives have told about *Roe v. Wade*. Today, large segments of the country see it as an exemplar of law's infamy even though the Supreme Court has not repudiated it.

Elites can and do play a substantial role in constructing persuasive stories about law's infamy. A few well-positioned people, according to Tsai, can persuade the Supreme Court that a precedent no longer fits with American society. He argues that this pattern of elite action played a key role in constructing a persuasive story of *Plessy v. Ferguson's* infamy and in paving the way for its repudiation in *Brown v. Board of Education*. Particularly important in this regard was the work of the Department of Justice in showing how racial segregation contradicted American values and damaged the country in its Cold War competition with the Soviet Union.

Tsai concludes by examining how stories of infamy constructed by social movements and among elites paved the way for Chief Justice Roberts to repudiate *Korematsu* in *Trump v. Hawaii*. Whatever one thinks of the adequacy of that repudiation, Tsai contends that it offers yet another example of the political and cultural work that is necessarily a part of the construction of accounts of law's infamy.

Following Tsai's emphasis on the construction of stories of infamy in several different contexts, Richard L. Abel in his contribution "Law's Infamy in the U.S. 'War on Terror'" (chapter 4) examines similar efforts in the context of the war against global terrorism. He focuses on various lawyers' roles in perpetuating and combatting threats to the rule of law in the context of the trials of Guantánamo detainees during the George W. Bush administration. While some lawyers lend themselves to the work of providing legal cover for torture, Abel is particularly interested in the efforts of other lawyers to expose the infamy of what the United States was doing.

Abel contends that lawyers are as likely to lend themselves to infamy as oppose it and to suffer few adverse consequences for doing so. This is, in part, because judgments of law's infamy are generally retrospective judgments, made long after the particular injustice that the law condoned. But he says it is the work of other lawyers who see and stand up to the evil that law does or condones that is crucial to Tsai's politics of repudiation. Abel highlights the work of five military lawyers—Matthew Diaz, Stephen Abraham, Morris "Moe" Davis, William Kuebler, and Darrel Vandeveld—who worked to preserve the rule of law in the conduct of the "war on terror" and to help others see law's complicity in the injustices of that war. Doing so required them to flout the normal routes of protest and to risk their careers in the military.

Abel stresses that the politics of repudiation requires heroic action and individual sacrifice. Calling out law's infamy is never easy. It requires that those who do so to both memorialize the evil they witness and address an indeterminate future with the hope that it can and will heed stories of law's infamy that may not be hearable in the present moment.

In "Law's Infamy: *Ashker v. Governor of California* and the Failures of Solitary Confinement Reform" (chapter 5), Keramet Reiter addresses herself to another example of law's infamy—the use of solitary confinement in American prisons—and examines the work of activists trying to end it. She examines the case of *Ashker v. Governor of California*, a class-action lawsuit filed on behalf of 500 prisoners in California who had each been housed continuously in solitary confinement for ten years or more. She considers whether the case repudiated the practice of solitary confinement, "consigning it to legal infamy."

She documents the failure of the case to effectively end solitary confinement in part because it has not been able to overcome resistance to the politics of repudiation. Reiter reminds us that stories of law's infamy often provoke resistance, led by people who have a stake in the perpetuation of the evil and by others who are not persuaded that law is implicated in it. She shows how defenders of solitary confinement resisted the legal infamy story by demonizing the reformers and activists who were seeking to bring about its end and by turning social science studies seemingly critical of solitary confinement into defense of that practice—what Reiter labels "co-opting knowledge production into a tool of legitimation."

Reiter's contribution shows that the construction of stories of law's infamy is seldom linear. Such stories provoke counternarratives that may neutralize and hinder reform efforts. Her chapter suggests that enlisting courts as allies in the effort to repudiate other legal practices is subject to the same limitations that have been amply demonstrated in scholarship on the implementation of routine judicial decisions.

The last contribution to *Law's Infamy*, "Fame, Infamy, and Canonicity in American Constitutional Law" (chapter 6), by Paul Horwitz, suggests that stories of law's infamy may be losing their purchase at a time characterized by cultural fragmentation and polarization. Such stories can work only when the legal community and broader society embrace narrow and generally agreed on definitions of "fame" and "infamy" to establish and maintain a reputable canon and anticanon. It is, Horwitz suggests, the very democratization of culture that undermines the ability of lawyers, judges, political parties, or social movements to identify elements that all would recognize as branding a legal decision as "infamous." What may be obvious to all who saw the killing of George Floyd may not be obvious when what is at issue is the moral content of a judicial decision.

Horwitz contends that stories of infamy depend on the kind of complex temporality highlighted by Abel (chapter 4) and Reiter (chapter 5). But in all cases, those stories depend on the passage of time and culture change. Horwitz suggests that American culture's increasing obsession with immediacy has transformed "fame" and "infamy" into broader and less meaningful concepts. More specifically, he claims that Americans' fierce attachment to the present has motivated them to assign the labels "famous" and "infamous" to practically everything—a practice that has subsequently made its way into the legal community.

Neither that community nor the society it serves is unified or consensual. Today, the influx of new voices in law has undermined the canonical and anticanonical status of existing cases. Horwitz sees the same thing at work in the culture at large. Polarization makes it harder to construct persuasive stories of law's infamy.

Horwitz concludes his chapter by acknowledging that the increasing meaninglessness of fame, infamy, and canonicity complicates the work of those seeking to construct a new politics of repudiation or, as Munshi (chapter 2) does, to add new cases to the anticanon. Yet Horwitz suggests that it may be a sign of a growing, vibrant pluralism in which taken-for-granted conceptions of the just and the unjust are subject to healthy reexamination.

Infamy, as Sherally Munshi contends in chapter 2, is a designation of a past event as "not just wrong but so wrong that it compels repudiation." Taken together, the contributions collected in *Law's Infamy* show how legal institutions themselves encounter the complexities of constructing narratives that clearly and finally render some past event or decision "infamous" and worthy of repudiation. They show how stories of infamy are constructed and contested and how the choices of individuals run up against institutional logics and social forces that they may not be able to control. In the end, the chapters published in these pages locate a conversation about law's infamy within the broader conversation about the construction of history and memory as they relate to law.

NOTES

1 Austin Sarat, Lawrence Douglas, and Martha Umphrey, eds., *Law's Mistakes* (Boston: University of Massachusetts Press, 2016).

2 Francis Fukuyama, *The End of History and the Last Man* (New York: Free Press, 2006).

3 Charles Ogletree and Austin Sarat, eds., *When Law Fails: Making Sense of Miscarriages of Justice* (New York: New York University Press, 2009).

4 Judith Shklar, *The Faces of Injustice* (New Haven: Yale University Press, 1990), 12.

5 Ibid., 24.

6 Jamal Greene, "The Anticanon," 125 *Harvard Law Review* (2011): 380.

7 Ibid., 405.

8 Sarah Bond, "Altering Infamy: Status, Violence, and Civic Exclusion in Late Antiquity," 33 *Classical Antiquity* (2014): 1–30.

9 Ibid., 6–7.

10 Mitchell Franklin, "Romanist Infamy and the American Constitutional Conception of Impeachment," 23 *Buffalo Law Review* (Winter 1974): 313–42, https://heinonline.org.

11 Ibid.

12 The majority of scholarship on medieval infamy seems to revolve around European medieval societies. However, Jan Abbink's article on the "infamous" Beta Esra'el, a small Jewish minority in northwestern Ethiopia, seems to suggest that the "infamy" idea transcended medieval Europe. Jan Abbink, "A Socio-Structural Analysis of the Beta Esra'el as an 'Infamous Group' in Traditional Ethiopia," 37 *Sociologus*, New Folge/New Series (1987): 140–54, www.jstor.org.

13 Jeffrey Bowman, "Infamy and Proof in Medieval Spain," in *Fama: The Politics of Talk and Reputation in Medieval Europe*, ed. Thelma Fenster and Daniel Lord Smail (Ithaca: Cornell University Press, 2003), 96, www.jstor.org.

14 Justin Steinberg, "Dante and the Laws of Infamy," 126 *PMLA*, Special Topic: Celebrity, Fame, Notoriety (Oct. 2011): 1119–20, www.jstor.org.

15 Mitchell Franklin, "The Encyclopediste Origin and Meaning of the Fifth Amendment," 15 *Lawyers Guild Review* (Summer 1955): 43, https://heinonline.org.

16 Cesare Beccaria, "Of Torture," in *Of Crimes and Punishments* (Philadelphia: Philip H. Nicklin, 1819), www.laits.utexas.edu, cited in Franklin, "Encyclopediste," 43.

17 Franklin, "The Encyclopediste," 61.

18 Ibid., 44. Additionally, the Founders invested the power of infamy based on "fact" in the people through impeachment, which further undermined the state's claim to that power. Franklin, "Romanist Infamy," 314.

19 Discussed in Reuben Oppenheimer, "Infamous Crimes and the Moreland Case," 36 *Harvard Law Review* (1923): 310, www.jstor.org.

20 Ex parte Wilson, 114 U.S. 417 (1885). See also Gabriel J. Chin and John Ormonde, "Infamous Misdemeanors and the Grand Jury Clause," 102 *Minnesota Law Review* (May 2018): 1931, https://heinonline.org.

21 Ex parte Wilson, 422.

22 Ullman v. United States, 350 U.S. 422, 435 (1956).

23 Ibid., 441.

24 Wieman v. Updegraff, 344 U.S. 183 (1952).

25 Paul v. Davis, 424 U.S. 693, 714 (1976).

26 Chin and Ormonde, "Infamous Misdemeanors."

1

After Law's Infamy

Judicial Self-Legitimation in the Aftermath of Judicial Evil

JUSTIN COLLINGS

Introduction

Law legitimates power,[1] and tradition legitimates law. Students of judicial legitimacy suggest that law's traditional symbols shield courts' legitimacy—defined sociologically as diffuse support or public acceptance of courts as institutions—against popular dissatisfaction with their rulings.[2] Exposure to judicial symbols, they argue, neutralizes disappointment with particular decisions.[3] More than fifty years ago, Walter Murphy underscored the almost mystical power of what he called the "cult of the robe."[4] Some of that power stems from the sense of mystery that surrounds the "law," but some stems from law's longevity. The symbols of judicial authority highlight the virtues of venerability. Courts lose legitimacy when citizens perceive judges as mere "politicians in robes,"[5] but courts benefit, by contrast, from their ties to tradition—from citizens' sense that courts belong to a broader narrative and, thanks to such belonging, take a longer view. Professor Dieter Grimm, a former justice of the German Federal Constitutional Court (Bundesverfassungsgericht; abbreviated as BVerfG), has contended that constitutional justice enhances democracy because judges can look beyond looming elections and orient politics toward enduring principles.[6] Positivity theorists posit that citizens view courts through the lens of preexisting stores of legitimacy.[7] People inherit, in other words, much of what their forebears thought about courts. This means that popular perceptions of courts are often refracted through the prism of the past.

But for many courts, the past is a risk as well as a resource. The risk arises when the judiciary generally or the relevant court specifically was complicit in some past wrong—some widescale injustice or institution-alized evil. Law's current legitimacy is then threatened by its past in-famy. For courts, that earlier infamy can be either general (i.e., the court loyally served an infamous regime), particular (the court itself issued infamous judgments), or personal (sitting judges either served an infa-mous regime or issued infamous judgments themselves). This chapter will discuss all three: regime infamy, judgment infamy, and personnel infamy, but with different emphases at different points. The problem can be captured in a series of pointed questions: Why should anyone accept the rule and rulings of tribunals that once used their power to iniquitous ends? Might they not do so again? Why obey courts that once obeyed tyrants? Why embrace law's rule in the aftermath of law's infamy?

Courts in general, and apex courts in particular, are attentive to their own legitimacy. They recognize the need to have themselves and their judgments accepted by both politicians and the public. Sometimes courts reflect openly about that need, but many published judgments include arguments and observations that are hard to explain other than as appeals for acceptance addressed to one or more of the court's mul-tiple audiences. Apart from the most conclusory per curiam, most judg-ments of most apex courts are acts of judicial self-legitimation. This is just another way of saying that they are exercises in persuasion.

Although it is rarely possible to say with certainty which audience a court is addressing at what points of which opinions, I think it is safe to say that when courts expatiate broadly about the national past, the pol-ity's ethical commitments, or the underlying values of the constitutional order, they are speaking to a broad audience. Whether they reach that audience is, of course, a very different question. But it is often possible to recognize a court seeking recognition. Apex courts seem especially concerned about their own legitimacy—especially eager to solicit politi-cal or popular acceptance—and as such are especially attentive to ques-tions raised in response to their earlier infamy. Such courts must either answer those pointed questions persuasively or suppress them entirely. In either case, the past poses a real risk.

However, it provides a powerful resource. The past, after all, is pro-tean. Judges can invoke it in myriad ways to multiple ends. Courts can marshal the past's lessons to bolster decisions of every imaginable sort.

And they can make the most of their own continuity, real or imagined, with a real or imagined past. As suggested earlier, many of the legitimating symbols of judicial power and much of the iconography of justice—robes and gavels, benches and bars, statues and friezes, columns and panels—connote continuity. They signal law's antiquity and perdurance. Because Lady Justice is blind, she can take the long view. Also, judges can make the most of any past instances when they saw more (or more clearly) than politicians or the public did. They can wrap themselves in the mantle of judicial landmarks ostensibly more just than the society that spawned them. In all of these ways, the past gives judges a vigorous, versatile resource.

This chapter addresses how judges balance the two—resource and risk—and how they unite them. It focuses on two jurisdictions: Germany and the United States; and on two different dynamics: how courts position themselves vis-à-vis their own past infamy and how new courts asserts themselves vis-à-vis the earlier infamy of the judiciary at large. Both positions present challenges. A veteran court can ground its legitimacy in tradition, but it must bear the past's burdens as well as its honors. It must confront the past's crimes as well as bask in its glories. A new court, by contrast, can define itself in opposition to a tainted past. But if it does so too forcefully, it risks cutting itself off from the legitimating resources of tradition. New or old, courts seek to claim the past's legitimating force and to distance themselves from its delegitimating infamy. They thus invoke the past to underwrite their power in the present. It is a delicate dance. Different courts have undertaken it in very different ways.

In the United States, for instance, the Supreme Court has adopted two principal strategies for addressing its complicity with historic evils. The first and predominant approach has been silence. Most monstrous precedents are quietly buried or simply ignored. Sometimes they linger on for decades with an ambiguous status—discredited, embarrassing, but never formally interred. This was the case most famously—until 2018—with *Korematsu v. United States*. Other times, infamous precedents persist as the law of the land, but with no mention of the noxious ideologies that informed them or the noxious language that befouled them. This is the case, to cite one ignoble example, with most of federal Indian law. In that realm, the Court has often reversed course, but it never forcefully repudiated even its most obnoxious earlier decisions. Indeed, some of the most offensive language in the field appears in its seminal cases.

The second approach has been to craft a narrow anticanon of exceptionally awful cases—awful, sometimes, for their putative technical incompetence and awful, more often, for their presumptive moral malodor.[8] That they are ostensibly *exceptional* is key. The Court has presented the problem as one of isolated apostasy by misguided or morally myopic judges rather than as a deeper rot in the Court's jurisprudence or the country's constitutional tradition. Conversely, the Court has loudly trumpeted countervailing acts of judicial statesmanship and virtue, presenting these as the broad highway of our constitutional past—the straight and narrow path from which the anticanonical cases departed and that the current Court is committed to resume. Thus, to take just one example, *Plessy v. Ferguson* gets cast as an outburst of stupendous iniquity—"wrong the day it was decided"—whereas the first *Brown v. Board of Education* opinion (*Brown I*) gets held up as an emblem of judicial virtue—the essence of the Court's tradition and the fount of its modern legitimacy (in a moral as well as a sociological sense). Never mind that without *Plessy* there was no need for *Brown*. *Plessy* stands as an exceptional departure from the true path, *Brown* as an act of grace that covers a multitude of sins.

Germany

Germany has witnessed similar efforts to cordon off an evil past and mark it as exceptional. And it has witnessed similar efforts at silence and elision. But it has also witnessed more forthright, if often delayed, efforts to come to terms with the past. Especially in recent decades, Germany's apex-court judges have been more willing than their American counterparts to grapple with historic evil—their country's and their courts'.

One obvious difference between the two countries is that Germany's highest court, the Federal Constitutional Court, was founded only in 1951—six years after Hitler's subterranean suicide and the collapse of his millennial Reich—whereas the U.S. Supreme Court operated alongside (and often abetted) constitutionally countenanced slavery for seventy-seven years and legally entrenched segregation for nearly ninety more. The German Constitutional Court is a designedly *post-*

Fascist court and an avowedly *anti*-Fascist court. The U.S. Supreme Court is not *post*-slavery or *post*-apartheid in any similar way. But this obvious difference conceals similarities. Germany, after all, has more than one apex court. Its professional judiciary is headed by five federal supreme courts of specialized jurisdiction.[9] The most prominent of the five is the Federal Court of Justice (Bundesgerichtshof, or FCJ), the court of final appeal in civil and criminal cases. For seven decades, the Federal Court of Justice and the Federal Constitutional Court—both of which sit in the sleepy southwestern city of Karlsruhe—have nurtured a sometimes fraught, sometimes fruitful relationship. They have been, by turns, both colleagues and rivals. The rivalry was sharpest early on. Part of that rivalry stemmed—ideologically, jurisprudentially, and personally—from the two courts' different postures toward the Nazi past and different perceptions of the judiciary's role and responsibility within that past.

Both courts were ostensibly new. But they were new in different ways. The Constitutional Court was new in fact and deed. The Court of Justice was new in name only. In reality, it was the rebaptized successor to the Imperial Supreme Court (Reichsgericht), which had been founded in 1879 as the court of final appeal in Bismarck's Reich and dissolved, following Germany's unconditional surrender, in 1945. The Supreme Court had served Hitler's Reich from beginning to end. Its record during that period might euphemistically be described as "problematic." But after the passage of three-fourths of a century, there is no need for euphemism. The court's Third Reich record was dark and often murderous.[10] As its postwar successor, the Federal Court of Justice had powerful reasons to sanitize and soft-pedal that past while still drawing on—indeed, participating in—the Supreme Court's venerable tradition and prestige. That effort brought the Court of Justice into early conflict with the Constitutional Court, which had equally powerful reasons to define itself in pointed opposition to the past.

The clash was stupendous. The junior court prevailed. The upshot was an eventual and tacit compromise by which the Court of Justice drew its legitimacy primarily from the postwar, anti-Nazi constitution but by which the Constitutional Court also relied significantly on the legacy of pre-1933 German judicial traditions.[11] How this came about constitutes the first portion of our tale.

As noted earlier, the Court of Justice and the Constitutional Court are siblings, almost twins. Both sit in Karlsruhe. Both were born half a decade after World War II. The Court of Justice opened its doors in October 1950. The Constitutional Court began its work eleven months later, in September 1951. The Constitutional Court comprised two chambers (officially, "Senates") of a dozen (later eight) justices each. The Court of Justice encompassed many chambers, both civil and criminal, and was presided over by a "Grand Chamber" for civil cases and another for criminal ones. As often happens with a narrow gap in age, there soon developed a serious sibling rivalry.

The Court of Justice did its best to present itself as the successor of the Imperial Supreme Court, to draw on that court's proud tradition and drape itself in the legacy of the pre-1933 accomplishments that won the Supreme Court domestic prestige and international renown.[12] No one did more in this regard than Hermann Weinkauff, the FCJ's first president.[13] A strong and forceful judicial personality, Weinkauff himself had sat on the Supreme Court during the Nazi era. His record there was far from glorious. Some of the worst has been unearthed only recently.[14] Perhaps the very worst is not yet known. The very fact of Weinkauff's earlier activity highlighted the precarious side of his appeal to tradition. One could not draw on pre-1933 prestige without risking a post-1933 taint.

From the outset, Weinkauff introduced many Supreme Court practices, as well as its particular style of judgment, into the work of the Court of Justice. He presented his tribunal as a veteran court with a proud tradition. Some FCJ judges looked down on the justices of the Constitutional Court with the condescension of experienced professionals regarding the work of embattled amateurs. The Constitutional Court, for its part, had no tradition to invoke. Apart from fledgling experiments at the state (Land) level soon after the war, there was no prior experience of constitutional justice in Germany. The justices had to remake their world anew. They presented their institution as the antithesis of a tainted past and the guardian of a new dispensation.

Lacking tradition posed challenges, but it also meant that the Constitutional Court was unburdened by participation in Nazi misrule and complicity in Nazi misdeeds. This was true both of the Constitutional Court as an institution and, in most cases, of the individual justices. Few founding justices had prior judicial experience. A majority had been punished, personally or professionally, by the Nazi regime. Some had spent the war in exile. The several justices of Jewish descent were the highest-ranking Jews in the postwar German state.

All of this made the Constitutional Court a happy outlier in the post-war judiciary. Other German courts were staffed overwhelmingly by judges who served the Nazi state. And the courts of that earlier era had much for which to answer.

The historical evidence has long been irresistible. Nazi-era judges were not passive victims of oppressive laws, forced by fear of reprisal to apply wicked laws against their will. A courageous few resisted the regime. Most advanced its aims actively, even eagerly.[15] Nearly every branch of the judiciary—trial courts as well as appellate, civil courts as well as criminal—proved all too willing to support and further the Nazi tyranny. "The German judiciary," writes one historian, "assimilated itself within a system of institutionalized lawlessness and state-sanctioned ca-price and thereby made itself an instrument of the legally unhindered implementation of the Regime's power interests and by so doing became its henchman."[16]

Between 1933 and 1945, German courts issued at least 50,000 death sentences,[17] likely more. More than 90 percent of those capital sentences came in the latter years of the war, from 1941 to 1944.[18] During that period, the German criminal justice system executed more than 8,000 people per year, or 160-plus per week.[19] Throughout the Nazi era, Ger-man courts implemented Nazi racial laws with preemptive alacrity and immoderate zeal. They read laws with almost ludicrous expansiveness. A ban on "sexual relations" (Geschlechtsverkehr) between Jews and "Aryans," for instance, was extended to kisses and hugs.[20] Eugenic laws requiring compulsory sterilization for persons with "major hereditary physical deformities" were extended to "such disorders as hemophilia, harelip, cleft plate, muscular dystrophy, and dwarfism."[21] The same was true of laws requiring sterilization for "congenital feeblemindedness."[22] Across all courts and fields of law, the dominant mode of interpretation was purposive and teleological. The purposes were those of the Nazi party; the end served was the establishment of Hitler's racial empire.

Such energetic service to the regime was by no means limited to the judicial backwaters. It suffused the Supreme Court itself. By the end of

1943, more than 2,000 men had been convicted of "racial defilement" (Rassenschande), a crime the Supreme Court construed capaciously.[23] In a broad range of cases, the Supreme Court led the way for other courts with "creative" interpretations of already harsh regulations.[24] During the war, the Supreme Court adopted as its own the extreme interpretations of the "special courts" (Sondergerichte) and urged those courts toward even harsher implementation.[25] A special panel of the Supreme Court was convoked to hear "extraordinary appeals" lodged "on behalf of the Führer." Such appeals allowed the chief prosecutor to ask the Supreme Court to annul trial decisions. The Supreme Court did so consistently and with a vengeance. Extraordinary appeals were comparatively rare, but from the twenty-one appeals lodged, the Supreme Court's special panel converted fourteen prison sentences into death sentences.[26] More common were "pleas of nullity," which showed in their thousands how willing the Supreme Court was to defer to the regime's wishes.[27] It was, according to one leading historian, "extremely rare" for the Supreme Court to thwart the prosecutor's will.[28]

Many of those sent to their deaths by German judges had committed only petty crimes—minor theft or deeds of vice. Many judges tortured precedential texts to cover the case at hand. Many went out of their way to impose capital sanctions with no textual basis at all. As one historian concludes: "The balance shows clearly: the German judiciary was at all levels and in all forms burdened in the most serious way with crimes cloaked in legal garb. . . . [T]he judiciary as such had become part of the system of state injustice."[29] The judges' robes were stained in blood. There were many murderers among them.

Very few were called to account after the war in any meaningful way. Sixteen German jurists were convicted at Nuremberg. In nearly every case, the sentence was later softened or the conviction overturned.[30] The postwar courts of West Germany were exquisitely lenient toward the judges in their docks. As of 1968, there had only been fifteen criminal cases, and only seven convictions, involving illegal death sentences.[31] In total, the 50,000-plus death sentences issued between 1933 and 1945 gave rise to only fifteen convictions.[32] The lion's share of judicial criminality was never subject to postwar prosecution.[33] Not a single judge from the ordinary German judiciary was convicted after the war by West German courts for Nazi-era judicial crimes.[34] Most Nazi-era judges returned to the bench after the war. The remaining jurists, by and large, retired in peace and died in their beds.

Shut down when the war in Europe ended, courts in the Western occupation zones reopened by June 1945.[35] Within a year, all restrictions on the reentry of former judges had been dropped, provided the applicant had been through a denazification procedure.[36] Soon, thousands of former Nazi jurists—including judges from the notorious special courts and members of the SA (the Brownshirts)—were flooding the courts and the civil administration.[37] An amnesty law of May 1951 (discussed below) opened the way for thousands more. During the first half of the 1950s, reckons one historian, the number of former Nazi party members on some courts exceeded the comparable figure from 1939.[38]

Nazi-era judges were as prevalent on the Federal Court of Justice as on any other court. By the mid-1950s, some 80 percent of the FCJ's judges had been active in the Nazi-era judiciary.[39] Unsurprisingly, perhaps, those sitting on the Court of Justice led the way in the lenient treatment of their former colleagues. Only four of the eighteen Nazi judges tried before the FCJ were convicted.[40] None of these was a career judge of the ordinary judiciary.[41] Even more importantly, as one historian notes, the FCJ's "judges crafted a criminal law doctrine that operated as a sort of 'permanent firewall' against the prosecution of judicial murder."[42] The FCJ never questioned the Nazi judiciary's "nearly boundless expansion of the crime of high treason,"[43] and it uncritically accepted the Nazi regime's legality claims.[44] In one of its most notorious early decisions, the FCJ's first criminal chamber absolved Walter Huppenkothen, the judge who condemned to death the resistance fighters Wilhelm Canaris, Hans Oster, Karl Sack, and Ludwig Gehre, as well as Dietrich Bonhoeffer, the heroic pastor of the Confessing Church, and his best friend, brother-in-law, and erstwhile Supreme Court judge, Hans von Dohnanyi.[45]

Postwar courts' anemic response to the past highlighted for many minds the troubling continuity of their personnel. So, too, did a propaganda campaign initiated in East Germany. At the formal request or with the financial backing of the East German government, gadflies in West Germany published lists of the "blood judges" (Blutrichter) from the Nazi era that were still active on the newly founded benches of the neophyte Federal Republic of Germany. The ensuing outcry put judges on the defensive. They knew that their honor and their legitimacy were both at stake. Even earlier, sensibilities about institutional reputation and popular acceptance stirred an unprecedentedly intense battle among courts.

* * *

As president of the Court of Justice, Hermann Weinkauff proved to be one of the most forceful apologists for the Nazi-era judiciary. This put him at striking odds with some of his counterparts on the Constitutional Court. Indeed, the politics of the past lay at the heart of a stupendous early jurisdictional clash between the two courts.

Things had begun amicably enough. There were, after all, some personal ties between the two institutions. The Federal Constitutional Court Act of 1951 (FCCA) required that a third of the Constitutional Court's justices be drawn from the specialized supreme courts.[46] For the first cohort of justices, the vast majority came from the Court of Justice—in part because of the FCJ's prominence and links to the Reichsgericht, but largely because at the time only two of the five supreme courts had been set up. (Some of the first justices were appointed to another court, only to be immediately transferred to the Constitutional Court.) Strikingly, some judges even worked for both courts simultaneously. The most dramatic example was Willi Geiger, who for more than a decade served as both a judge on the Court of Justice and a justice of the Constitutional Court. Tellingly, perhaps, no justice in the Constitutional Court's history has had a past as compromised as Geiger's.[47]

The main point of jurisdictional contact was through Article 100 of the Basic Law, which required ordinary courts to refer constitutional questions to the Constitutional Court. If, in the course of a legal proceeding, a court concluded that a law or regulation germane to resolving the case was unconstitutional, it must stay the proceeding, refer the constitutional question to the Constitutional Court, and finally, after receiving the Constitutional Court's answer, resume the case and decide it in a manner consistent with that answer. In its original form, the FCCA clarified that all such referrals must be routed through the relevant supreme court of subject-matter jurisdiction.

From the beginning, the referrals started coming. Many referrals included an advisory opinion from the forwarding supreme court. These opinions outlined the relevant issues and sometimes proposed a resolution. The court most active in submitting such opinions was the Federal Court of Justice. The opinions were the work of Hermann Weinkauff. Even in criminal matters, the referrals—and the advisory opinions— came from Weinkauff's First Civil Senate. Some opinions had the look of full-fledged judgments. Some were even published in the FCJ's official reports.

Initially, the Constitutional Court welcomed and encouraged the practice. In a circular of 7 November 1951—two months into the Court's existence—Chief Justice Hermann Höpker-Aschoff noted that, when the Supreme Federal Courts forwarded a lower-court referral to the Constitutional Court, they had the option of appending their own opinion on the matter.[48] "Whether the federal supreme courts wish to take advantage of this opportunity," the chief justice added, "lies within their own discretion. But their opinion is in all events desirable."[49] Later, in a formal judgment of 4 March 1953, the Court's First Senate (over which Höpker-Aschoff presided) noted that the FCCA required referral by way of the federal supreme courts in part "to give these courts the opportunity to give their own opinion" on the matter referred.[50] In time, however, the Constitutional Court would change its tune. That happened in response to the FCJ's increasingly aggressive referrals and in response to a spectacular clash between the two courts. Things came to a head with a particularly prickly controversy, the substance of which was, for the veteran judges of the other apex courts, deeply personal.

The underlying issue was how to treat Nazi-era bureaucrats who wished to return to the civil service after the war. The issue was explosively controversial—so much so that the Basic Law's drafters conspicuously kicked the can down the road, deferring the matter for future parliamentary resolution. Article 131 of the Basic Law stated simply that the legal status of those who lost their posts on 8 May 1945 (the date of unconditional surrender) were to be "regulated by federal law."[51]

Parliament responded to this charge in May 1951. The "131 Law," named for the constitutional clause that required it, gave civil servants generous terms—a sweeping right to reinstatement that only excluded members of the Gestapo. But the civil servants remained unsatisfied. In their view, they had a right to automatic reentry and to full back payment, as their legal status had never changed. Unconditional surrender did not alter their relations with the enduring German state. For the law's civil servant detractors, this was a matter of principle. A legal entitlement was involved, not merely a question of legislative largesse. Affected civil servants formalized these claims in a constitutional complaint. They asked the Constitutional Court to quash the offending portions of the otherwise lavish law.

The Court answered these claims with a bombshell. Its judgment was long—104 printed pages flanked by seventeen headnotes, one of which had six subheadings.[52] But the Court answered the key question in single short sentence: Alle Beamtenverhältnisse sind am 8. Mai 1945 erloschen—"All civil service ties were abolished on 8 May 1945," the date of unconditional surrender. The implications were as dramatic as they were obvious. Nazi-era civil servants lost their jobs when Germany lost the war. Their claims dissolved when the state collapsed. On that state's successor they had no claims at all. Those dismissed at war's end had not been indefinitely suspended; they had been terminated for good and all. Whatever they received from the new Federal Republic, in the way of recompense or reinstatement, they received only by Parliament's grace.

The Court's path to this stark conclusion was relentless, thorough, and (for the complainants, anyway) devastating. The conclusion rested on crucial observations about the Nazi state and its ties with the civil service.

Those relations, the justices held, were revolutionary. The Nazis had transformed the bureaucracy beyond recognition. National Socialism aimed definitively to crush the traditional, nonpartisan state.[53] It saw the state as "an apparatus of power in the service of 'the People' [das Volk]," and it equated the people's will with the Nazi party.[54] That the state was subservient to the people and that the people were embodied in the party led naturally to a conception of the state as the instrument (Werkzeug) of the party—the instrument, in practice, of the Führer's unfettered rule.[55] Legislation, administration, and even adjudication all centered on the Führer, as articulated in Carl Schmitt's 1934 article (which the justices cited), "The Führer Protects the Law."

"Thus," the Court observed, "the State became a dictatorship in which the Party Führer, endowed with limitless power which he at once stretched to its utmost technical possibilities, arbitrarily set in motion the state power apparatus toward the fulfillment of his plans."[56] The state, in short, became Hitler's state—a "centralized power state" (zentraler

Machtsstaat) that allowed the Führer to "pursue his political goals in the War against nearly every Great Power of the world."[57]

This was the state that collapsed on 8 May 1945, and its collapse was total—militarily, financially, and economically.[58] (The Court might have added "morally" as well.) The debacle was so dramatic as to raise doubts whether the German Reich continued to exist.[59] Even assuming that it did, there were compelling reasons to conclude that the status of its civil servants did not.

Those civil servants, moreover, took their oath of loyalty not to the German Fatherland but to the person of Adolf Hitler. They swore they would "be faithful and obedient to the Führer of the German Reich and [German] People, Adolf Hitler; honor the laws; and conscientiously fulfill the duties of my office, so help me God."[60] That oath suggested, in the Court's view, that civil servants' status was "utterly dependent on the continuance of the National Socialist form of rule embodied in Hitler."[61] This suggestion was amply confirmed by Nazi-era civil service legislation, all of which stressed the civil servant's duty to serve the party-state.[62] At the time, some legal scholars had taken a similar view, and the Court collected quotations to that effect.[63] The same was true of the Nazi-era judiciary.[64] The Court concluded that the civil servants' legal status had morphed from partisan neutrality and loyalty to the state to "personal loyalty to Hitler and . . . dependence on the NSDAP."[65] It followed that their official status and legal rights endured only as long as Hitler remained in power and his party ruled the state. It followed, in other words, that their offices and rights were abolished on 8 May 1945. Q.E.D.

The judgment elicited howls of protest from many quarters. Press coverage was overwhelmingly hostile. Scholarly condemnation was almost universal. In its sweeping indictment, the Court had spared no branch of the civil service. But universities came in for special censure,[66] and legal scholars, stung to the quick, attacked the judgment with full-throated ferocity. So did prominent judges. Judges and jurists were among the civil servants whose allegiance to Hitler the Court had denounced. From elsewhere in the judiciary there sounded tones of truculent defiance. The loudest of these came from the neighboring Court of Justice.

In May 1954—less than four months after the Constitutional Court's *Civil Servants* decision—the FCJ, through Weinkauff's First Civil Senate, ruled that the judgment was wrong and need not be followed.[67] As an initial matter, the Court of Justice contended that ordinary courts are bound only by the Constitutional Court's disposition of a given case, not by its rationale. This was so even when the Constitutional Court itself thought the rationale was essential to its holding. In the *Civil Servants* judgment, this meant that the Court of Justice was bound only by the Constitutional Court's holding that the 131 Law was not unconstitutional. For the rest, the Court of Justice was free to reach its own conclusions.

In reaching those conclusions, Weinkauff and his colleagues rejected the Constitutional Court's reasoning out of hand. The German state, they argued, had not ceased to exist with the unconditional surrender of 8 May 1945; it had merely altered form.[68] As for the civil service, its essential functions were administrative and judicial, not political in the formal sense. These were functions "that the State as such always performs," functions largely independent of the state's shifting external forms and the political forces expressed through such shifts.[69] Political regimes might rise and fall. But the state and its civil service endured forever, perpetually bound to one another.[70]

The Court of Justice objected even more passionately to the Constitutional Court's specific observations about the Nazi-era civil service. The Constitutional Court's conclusion that Nazi-era civil servants had transferred loyalty from the eternal German state to the person of Adolf Hitler was, in the FCJ's view, "an historical value judgment" rather than a legal conclusion.[71] And the Constitutional Court had gotten its history dead wrong. In the FCJ's contrary assessment: "The overwhelming majority of German civil servants—despite the abusive, illegal pressures that weighed upon them—still felt themselves primarily bound to the State and its legitimate functions, and they conceived of their office in this sense."[72] They swore their initial oath to Hitler only in the sense that he was the supreme organ of the state, and then to the Nazi Party only out of respect for a political decision made by a majority of the nation.[73] "But as the criminal aims and methods of National Socialism were gradually exposed," the court concluded, "this imposed allegiance was overwhelmingly tolerated only unwillingly, with keen internal rejection, and in the face of the severest terror."[74]

Weinkauff and his colleagues were clearly defending the honor of their jurists' guild and of the German civil service writ large. Weinkauff's defiant judgment was a frontal challenge to the Constitutional Court's authority and to its legal craftsmanship. But it was also a challenge to its implicit claim to a legitimacy untainted by the recent past. Whereas the Constitutional Court claimed the mantle of a constitutional new beginning, the Court of Justice sought to rehabilitate the tradition of which it saw itself as the post-Fascist extension.

Weinkauff made this explicit in a contemporaneous speech honoring the seventy-fifth anniversary of the Supreme Court's founding.[75] He began by noting the universal human need for an internal bond to a common past.[76] In Germany, alas, such a bond was complicated. "To our misfortune," he said, "we do not have that impartial, self-evident relationship to our history—that simple accord with it and that serene pride in it—that other, happier peoples have."[77] But the Supreme Court provided, on the whole, a proud tradition on which the postwar judiciary could build and draw. The Supreme Court, Weinkauff maintained, had been overwhelmingly successful in its mission to create a German legal consciousness and to provide a symbol for the rule of law in Germany.[78] Staffed for the most part by strong and independent personalities—by men of "comprehensive and even musical culture"[79]—the Supreme Court had swiftly assumed its rightful and honored place "within the circle of the supreme courts of civilized peoples."[80] Now the Federal Court of Justice had assumed the Supreme Court's "legacy" (Erbe) and mantle.[81]

Weinkauff acknowledged that the Supreme Court's role during the Nazi era marked a tragic chapter in its history. The court had succumbed, in part, to massive efforts to bend its jurisprudence to the rulers' will. The judges hadn't been perfect. But, during those turbulent times, who had been? Let him that is without sin, Weinkauff admonished, cast the first stone.[82]

In any case, the real problem lay less with the sitting judges than with the regnant legal philosophy. Legal positivism, in Weinkauff's view, had left the Supreme Court unequipped to respond to profound injustices in positive law and vulnerable to colonization by an evil regime. What was needed, in Weinkauff's view, was a court willing to resume the Supreme Court's noblest traditions but immunized by principles of natural law against material injustices imposed by positive law. That was Weinkauff's vision for the Federal Court of Justice—a vision underwritten by his sense that the noble traditions of an honorable past could be bracketed off from history's unsavory chapters. The lofty dream of a unitary rule of law in Germany could be unproblematically resumed, with sensible adjustments, in the aftermath of Nazi misrule.

Following its 1954 judgment on the 131 Law, Weinkauff's chamber continued to issue advisory opinions on the constitutional questions that the FCJ referred to the Constitutional Court. To some constitutional justices, the FCJ's frequent and extensive advisory opinions felt increasingly like the patronizing oversight of veteran judges to novices in need of help. Such patronizing interference, together with the FCJ's truculence on jurisdictional questions, did much to sour the Constitutional Court's relations with the other federal supreme courts. In time, the constitutional justices responded by lobbing an interpretive grenade to their peers.

It exploded in an otherwise unremarkable judgment of 30 November 1955. With little warning, the First Senate announced that "advisory opinions of the forwarding court . . . are inadmissible."[83] Despite what the Court or its chief justice might have said earlier, the practice of appending advisory opinions was valid only if expressly authorized by statute.[84] Accordingly, the FCCA's silence on the matter must be construed as proscribing the practice—a view affirmed, the Court argued, by the relevant legislative history.[85] Advisory opinions, moreover, might undermine the rule of law. Should the Constitutional Court disagree with the advisory opinion, the public would be faced with clashing assessments from multiple apex courts. Such disharmony would undermine citizens' faith in the courts specifically and in the law more generally. It was a striking decision, not only because it flatly contradicted what the Court had said before but also because the case at hand involved neither a referring court nor an advisory opinion.[86]

The supreme courts' judges were shocked and hurt. Their presidents responded unitedly and promptly. In a step unusual in the history of German law,[87] they wrote a joint statement of dissent and published it in a leading legal periodical.[88] The statement spoke for all five courts. But the voice was clearly Weinkauff's.

The presidents noted that their courts had been appending advisory opinions with the Constitutional Court's explicit encouragement for more than four years.[89] The Constitutional Court's decision reversing

course was arrant *obiter dictum*. It made a mash of statutory interpretation and badly abused the legislative history.[90] These were pointed
criticisms—eminent professionals bashing the craftsmanship of those
they deemed amateurs. More fundamentally, the presidents accused the
Constitutional Court of institutional arrogance and presumption. "The
new decision of the Federal Constitutional Court," they wrote, "does not
accord with the structure of our judiciary. The Federal Constitutional
Court is not the pinnacle toward which all other parts of the judiciary
flow. Rather, it is entrusted only with very specific questions, namely the
essential questions of constitutional law."[91]

There was, the presidents noted, no tradition of constitutional justice in Germany upon which the Constitutional Court could draw.
Why, then, would the justices cut themselves off from the insight and
expertise of judges more familiar than they with the underlying areas of
substantive law? The opinions, after all, were nonbinding. The Constitutional Court needn't follow them. And if it chose not to follow them,
why worry about the split? Clashing views were a feature, not a bug.
Only through "the continuing contest of opposing views" and the "can-
did, common contest of minds" could "the best solution be developed"
within a jurisprudence worthy of the public's fealty and trust.[92]

To the Constitutional Court's concern that waiting for advisory opinions might unduly slow its docket, the presidents responded, cheekily,
that the Constitutional Court often waited years to decide a case. Why
worry about a few months' delay for an advisory opinion?[93] The presidents concluded, however, with their biggest concern. The Constitutional Court's decision, they wrote, would bring the apex federal courts
"into the unworthy position of being silenced with respect to all fundamental legal questions in which the constitution is implicated. This
situation," they protested, "must not endure."[94] In fact, by and large, it
endures to this day.[95]

The Constitutional Court bided its time before responding to its
academic critics and judicial rivals. Some of the delay resulted from a
cause célèbre that dominated the First Senate's docket—a case involving
a government petition to ban the German Communist Party (KPD). In
August 1956, the Court did ban the KPD with a ruling that fills 308 pages
of the Court's official reports.[96] That judgment defined the postwar constitutional order as not only fundamentally anti-Nazi but also antitotali-

tarian. The Court thus fused the constitution's aversive posture toward the Nazi past with the geopolitical imperatives of the Cold War present.

Six months after its KPD judgment, the First Senate returned to the question of Nazi-era civil servants.[97] This time the complaint came from a former member of the Gestapo—the one group denied reentry in the postwar civil service—who wished to become a policeman. The First Senate rejected the complaint and reaffirmed the essentials of its earlier *Civil Servants* judgment. Along the way, the justices responded to that earlier decision's many critics. The Senate answered some critics by citing their own Nazi-era publications against them.[98] This was strong medicine, but so was the Constitutional Court's response to the Federal Court of Justice. The constitutional justices wrote that, when Weinkauff and his colleagues concluded that the overwhelming majority of Nazi-era civil servants still felt primarily bound to the enduring state and its legitimate purposes, they were not engaged in legal factfinding but merely offering "a political hypothesis."[99] But such a hypothesis was neither here nor there. It had no bearing on the central issue. The fact remained that any civil servant who didn't act as though bound to prosecute the aims of the Nazi regime whenever they collided with the state's legitimate functions was sure to be fired or worse.[100] And, as the justices went on to demonstrate in remorseless detail, the Nazi-era civil servants, with appallingly few exceptions, pursued with undiminished zeal the inhumane objectives of the regime to which they pledged their loyalty.

The justices explained that they would not discuss the Final Solution and would give "only a small extract of the arbitrary measures against Jews and foreign ethnic groups."[101] But even that small extract was horrific and, for the self-serving claims of the Constitutional Court's detractors, annihilating. The justices chronicled a pattern of systematic persecution that permeated the entire civil service and encompassed agencies of every conceivable sort. The Senate enumerated these examples of oppression in a smaller font that filled page after page after page. The cancer had spread, malignant and swift, through all levels of the judiciary, infecting judges, prosecutors, clerks, registrars, and other officers of the court.[102] It contaminated agencies responsible for tax collection, municipal affairs, property appraisal, youth matters, social security, labor, trade, education, health, medicine, food, traffic, customs, and more.[103]

Perhaps, the justices continued, such systematic persecution could co-incide with some normal functions of the state.[104] Perhaps there were isolated acts of decency by which individual civil servants did their best to soften the sting of unjust decrees.[105] Perhaps some judges of the special tribunals (Sondergerichte) sometimes gave softer sentences than they might have. Perhaps they even acquitted some defendants.[106] But none of that, in the Court's view, altered the inescapable conclusion that, if the civil servants of the Nazi era had really thought themselves exclusively bound to serve the people and the state by upholding the rule of law, then they must inevitably have drawn the attention of their overseers to the irreconcilable conflicts between prevailing law and their official duties.[107] The fact was that the National Socialist state did not tolerate apolitical or objective administrators.[108] There was nothing normal about its civil service. The salient fact was not that some individuals tried to make the best of a bad situation. The salient fact was that every Nazi-era civil servant remained active within a unitary civil service that devoted itself—body and soul, heart and mind—to the monstrous aims of a murderous regime.[109] By populating that regime's institutions, Nazi-era civil servants had forfeited any claim that might survive the Nazis' rule.

It was a powerful judgment, relentless in its candor about the recent past and, especially, the judiciary's active role in subverting the rule of law. In a separate judgment announced the same day, the Constitutional Court finally responded to the FCJ's decision of May 1954.[110] The Court rejected the FCJ's position for the simple and sufficient reason that the FCJ had no jurisdiction over constitutional questions. The justices said nothing at all about the merits of the FCJ's position or about the circular paper signed by the supreme court presidents. The Constitutional Court asserted the supremacy and exclusivity of its constitutional jurisdiction simply by presuming it. The Constitutional Court's hand had been strengthened in the meantime by an FCCA amendment that dropped the requirement that trial courts route constitutional referrals through the relevant supreme court. Lower courts could now refer constitutional questions directly to the Constitutional Court.

The *Gestapo* judgment and its partner marked the Constitutional Court's decisive triumph in its early clash with the specialized courts. It also coincided with foundational fundamental rights decisions that consolidated that triumph. In the *Elfes* judgment of January 1957, the

Court ruled that the constitution's promise of the free development of one's personality (Article 2 GG) comprised a "general liberty of action" (allgemeine Handlungsfreiheit) that provided a measure of constitutional protection against government infringement to every imaginable human act or omission.[111] A year later, in its landmark *Lüth* judgment, the Court ruled that fundamental rights are not only subjective shields against state encroachment but also objective *values* that infuse all law and permeate all legal relationships, even those between private parties.[112] (As it happened, *Lüth* also played out against the politics of the past. The losing party was Veit Harlan, the Nazi regime's star filmmaker; the case's eponymous hero was Erich Lüth, an engaged citizen who had called for a boycott of Harlan's first postwar film.)

The upshot of these holdings was clear: All law was now constitutional law, and every case raised the possibility of referral to the Constitutional Court. The federal supreme courts might have seen this as an irreparable blow to their authority—their definitive subordination to the newfangled Constitutional Court. In a way, it was. But the process of referring (or not referring) cases to the Constitutional Court also allowed the ordinary courts to develop a constitutional jurisprudence of their own. And no Court did so with quite as much creativity and zeal as did the Federal Court of Justice.

* * *

Weinkauff's presidency of the FCJ ended on 1 March 1960. He devoted his retirement to directing a project exploring the history of the Nazi-era judiciary. The labor was large, the harvest meager. Weinkauff himself produced only one volume, a slender apologia on behalf of himself and his guild.[113] Weinkauff repeated at length his familiar arguments that legal positivism had left German judges unequipped to counter Nazism's lawlessness masked in legal forms and that a solid grounding in natural law was the only bulwark against another judicial collapse.

Weinkauff's successors did not obey his summons. Instead, they followed the Constitutional Court's lead in grounding the postwar rule of law in the positive provisions of an anti-Nazi constitution. Beginning around 1960, the Federal Court of Justice began to develop a constitutional jurisprudence of its own. It did so in the process of weighing how constitutional provisions influenced subconstitutional norms and whether to refer constitutional questions to the Constitutional Court. The FCJ's referrals were rare—only eleven between the Constitutional Court's founding in 1951 and the fall of the Berlin Wall in 1989.[114] But the Court of Justice also developed a robust rights jurisprudence, including doctrines dealing with the general personality right and freedom of speech that at some points were just as creative and expansive as those of the Federal Constitutional Court.[115] One judge who served for many years on both courts characterized their relations as marked by "some dissensus, but also much agreement."[116] Sometimes the disagreements have been sharp—as with conflicts between personal honor and freedom of speech in the mid-1990s—but on the whole the Court of Justice has increasingly grounded its claim to legitimacy in its role in the postwar constitutional order than in its ties to a deeper past.

Indeed, the Court of Justice's posture toward the past has shifted over time, albeit very slowly. Its early, astonishing leniency toward judges accused of Nazi crimes persisted. Sometimes, to be sure, the court took a sterner stance. "The accused is a fully qualified lawyer," the Court explained in one case, "from whom can be expected a sense of whether a punishment stands in intolerable disproportion to the seriousness of the offense and the guilt of the offender."[117] But the accused in that case was not a full-fledged career judge. In 1968, the Court of Justice remanded the conviction of Hans-Joachim Rehse, a quondam judge of the incarnadined People's Court (Volksgerichtshof), where he took part in more than 230 death sentences, often for petty or political crimes.[118] According to one historian, Rehse was "after Roland Freisler, . . . the most incriminated judge at the People's Court."[119] The Court of Justice's remand was accompanied by an "undisguised recommendation to find for acquittal, which the lower court duly did."[120] As one journalist scathingly observed: "Judge Rehse of the People's Court could not have committed murder, for this would have meant that the West German judicial system had been established by murderers in the hundreds."[121]

Coming to terms with the judiciary's role in the Nazi terror was a glacially slow process. This was true among postwar academics as well as among judges. Law professors, much like judges, had zealously supported the regime between 1933 and 1945 and had unabashedly resumed their positions after the war. They were hardly the ones to scrutinize the judiciary's past. With plenty of skeletons in their own closets, such jurists were loath to pry open the closets of others. Likewise, neither was their first generation of postwar students. Postwar professors promoted their most pliant pupils—those least likely to question their mentors' past. That was left to a later generation of jurists.

The effort began in the late 1950s. High-profile trials of SS commandos (the Nazi paramilitary) and concentration-camp henchmen focused the public gaze on widescale wartime crimes. A spate of anti-Semitic vandalism rattled nerves and raised worries that the past wasn't quite dead. Then, in 1959, a traveling exhibition titled "Unexpiated Nazi Justice: Documents on the National Socialist Judiciary" (Ungesühnte Nazijustiz—Dokumente zur NS-Justiz) began its three-year tour in, of all places, Karlsruhe.[122] The exhibit documented the Nazi-era crimes of scores of active judges. Despite dismissals of the exhibit as paltry propaganda promoted by communist East Germany, it prompted a wave of revisionist research that reshaped views of the German judiciary and its past. (That research did, in fact, receive an impetus, and some funding, from East Germany, which had published lists of the Blutrichter [blood judges] still active in the Federal Republic.) Revisionist scholars completely discredited the positivist alibi set forth by Weinkauff and others. As noted earlier, Weinkauff published his own history of the Nazi-era judiciary in 1968, in which he argued once again that it had been a helpless victim of Nazi exploitation and that its helplessness stemmed from its embrace of legal positivism.[123] Weinkauff's thesis met with some skepticism upon its first appearance.[124] Among a later generation of scholars, it met with angry rejection. As Udo Reifner put it in the early 1980s: "Judges and prosecutors, administrative jurists and law professors . . . out of personal conviction and with professional self-evidence took part in the construction of the 'Third Reich' and to that end abused the institution of the legal system."[125] In 1987, Ingo Müller published his pathbreaking book *Furchtbare Juristen: Die unbewältigte Vergangenheit unserer Justiz* (Terrible Jurists: Our Judiciary's Unmastered Past),[126] an unsparing account of both the judiciary's and legal professoriate's zealous participation in Nazi misrule and of their wholesale reintegration after the war. Müller paved the way for more detailed studies, including in 2005 a relentlessly damning history of the early Federal Court of Justice.[127]

Eventually these trends reached the Court of Justice itself, which began, several decades on, to take stock of its own ignoble past. By the mid-1990s, the FCJ, now asked to sit in judgment on crimes committed by functionaries of the defunct East German state, stressed the need to honor Gustav Radbruch's distinction between positive law and material justice.[128] And at the turn of the twenty-first century, the FCJ's president, Günter Hirsch, seized on the centennial of Hans von Dohnanyi's birth to say strong things about his own court's past.[129] Von Dohnanyi was a former Supreme Court judge, Hirsch noted, and thus a colleague and forebear of the Federal Court of Justice. "He was murdered," Hirsch continued, "by criminals who called themselves judges."[130] The 1956 FCJ judgment exonerating von Dohnanyi's murderers was, in Hirsch's view, "a slap in the face"[131]—a judgment for which "one must be ashamed."[132] The postwar judiciary had failed as a whole to come to terms with the Nazi past—including its own Nazi past—and to do justice to Nazism's victims, judicial and otherwise. "This failure of the postwar judiciary," Hirsch said, "is a dark chapter in German legal history and will remain such."[133] Hirsch and his court viewed the centennial of von Dohnanyi's birth as "an occasion to present the darker side of the court's past in order to underscore its responsibility in the present."[134]

Hirsch's speech could hardly have been more different from Weinkauff's speech half a century earlier honoring the Imperial Supreme Court on the seventy-fifth anniversary of its founding. Weinkauff sought to position the Court of Justice as the Supreme Court's successor—or as the same court with a new name—and to claim for the FCJ the Supreme Court's legitimacy (i.e., popular approval) and prestige, albeit with a promise and a plea to do some things differently, lest the postwar judiciary prove as vulnerable as its forebear to lawless external pressures. Hirsch, by contrast, spoke as the confident president of a court firmly embedded within the liberal-democratic postwar constitutional order—a court, indeed, that had helped to forge that order and had helped it flourish. Hirsch's Court of Justice had a history of its own. Its public acceptance stemmed more from its association with a beloved constitution than from its ties to a venerable past. In fact, Hirsch regarded the FCJ's early refusal to confront the judiciary's tainted past as a serious stain on its postwar record. The twenty-first-century court's willingness to confront *that* tainted past was a symbol, for Hirsch, of its contemporary accountability. The court's new posture toward the past was part of its present bid for legitimacy, its yearning for acceptance.

The modern Court of Justice, like the modern Constitutional Court, sees itself as defined by a systemic rupture with and response to a dark and dismal past.

This new attitude came late—too late, for some observers. Many see the decades-long failure to address the crimes of German judges as a stark contrast to commendable efforts to come to terms with the past (Vergangenheitsbewältigung) in other spheres. The Federal Constitutional Court, as I have argued elsewhere,[135] did define itself in strong opposition to the Nazi past, but the Constitutional Court itself had no preconstitutional past and had little occasion or inclination to revisit the role of Nazi-era judges. It drew with some frequency on pre-1933 German legal traditions,[136] but it routinely skipped over the judiciary's part in the horrors and crimes of 1933–1945. The constitutional justices regularly invoked the Nazi past to underwrite their interpretations of the anti-Nazi constitution. But although they won their early jurisdictional row with the Court of Justice, their 1950s judgments discussing the role of Nazi-era jurists had few successors.

In the end, the postures toward the past of Germany's two most powerful courts have substantially converged. Initially, the Constitutional Court sought popular and political acceptance by defining itself in stark opposition to the Nazi past and the Nazi-era judiciary. The early Federal Court of Justice, by contrast, grounded its claims to legitimacy in its ties to the pre-Nazi past. Over time, however, the FCJ's personal links to the Nazi-era judiciary subsided, and the Court became increasingly embedded in the postwar constitutional order. Once the FCJ had a liberal-constitutional history of its own, it could afford to train a critical gaze on the history of its pre-1945 predecessor—and on its own earliest years.

United States

The United States Constitution (1787) both accommodated and, in some respects, unwittingly strengthened slavery. The same is true, in spades, of the antebellum Supreme Court. After the American Civil War (1861–1865), the Court eviscerated statutory and constitutional protections for black people and upheld legislative measures openly designed to subordinate them. The Court was also a passive and active participant in the oppression of Native American people and often described them in shamefully racist terms. One could surely enumerate other examples of the Court's implication in law's infamy—from its endorsement of compulsory sterilization in the 1920s to its approval of the internment of Japanese Americans in the 1940s.

All of this poses a legitimacy challenge for the modern Court—the challenge of getting its adjudications and authority accepted by politicians and publics painfully aware of the Court's earlier, inglorious interventions. Unlike the German Federal Constitutional Court, which opened its doors six years after the Nazis fell, or the German Federal Court of Justice, which was the successor to the Imperial Supreme Court and assumed some of its personnel, the relevant infamy in the American case is the infamy of the very same institution—the same court with the same name. How can the highest court in the land solicit the allegiance of citizens and successfully assert its authority to provide equal justice under law when it has sometimes failed spectacularly to do so in the past? What is a court of last resort to do in the aftermath of law's infamy when that infamy is of its own making?

Sometimes, the Court's response has been to pile infamy upon infamy. For half a century after the Civil War, its main response to historical evil was to resume the evil, passively or actively, in altered guise. Having taken a serious institutional drubbing in the aftermath of *Dred Scott v. Sanford* and its forerunners, and having been severely chastened by the Reconstruction Congress, the Court cultivated the support, wittingly or unwittingly, of a powerful new constituency: the rising might of American capital.[137] At the same time, the Court was deaf to the pleas of racial and other minorities and ignored the spirit and letter of the most recent constitutional amendments.

Decades passed before the Court would address these new infamies, the bulk of which long remained effective law. Redress required overruling, and the Court was often slow to take that step. The persistence of new infamies, moreover, prevented overt responses to the old ones. The justices, for instance, rarely had a harsh word to say about *Dred Scott* before the 1950s. Some justices even cited it approvingly. In a 1934 dissent, Justice George Sutherland quoted the *Dred Scott* majority opinion in support of what would now be called an originalist methodology.[138] *Dred* didn't become an anticanonical antiprecedent until a century after it was decided.

Things changed, of course, after *Brown v. Board of Education*. After *Brown*, the justices began the collective work of crafting an anticanon of (purportedly) exceptionally awful cases. The anticanon began small and has remained small. According to a leading article by Jamal Greene, it consists of only four cases: *Dred Scott, Plessy v. Ferguson, Lochner v. New York*, and *Korematsu v. United States*. These four antiprecedents have been cited in a multitude of contexts and in a host of ways. They have been invoked by justices of very different persuasions toward very different ends. That, Greene argues, is the point. The anticanon is useful precisely for what Greene calls its "pluripotency."[139] Anticanonical cases can be adduced in support of a dizzying array of arguments. From them can be drawn various and sometimes wildly clashing lessons.

Before turning attention to those putative lessons, it's worth noting that citations to the anticanon represent virtually the only time the Court acknowledges its earlier work as truly bad. But many students of the anticanon and its constituent parts conclude that the four cases central to the anticanon are *not* exceptionally bad—neither in terms of conventional legal reasoning nor in moral terms. Each was of its time; each had many peers. For each anticanonical case, professor Greene identifies a rough contemporary—part of a "shadow anticanon"—that is arguably as bad or worse, both morally and jurisprudentially.[140] But condemning a narrow set of cases as exceptionally bad serves an important psychological and symbolic purpose. Mark Graber argues that bashing *Dred Scott* serves to sanitize our constitutional tradition and spare us the anguish of confronting the problem of constitutional evil.[141] Greene adds that "*Dred Scott* does not gnaw at us because it misused syllogism or invented constitutional rights; we hate it because it abided constitutional evil."[142] Jack Balkin observes that we wish *Plessy* to have been exquisitely wrongly decided because "we do not want to be the sort of country in which *Plessy* could have been a faithful interpretation of the Constitution."[143]

Lochner, by contrast, has received so much revisionist treatment[144] and so many efforts at rehabilitation that its long-term anticanonical status is in question—if that status hasn't been already shaken. One difference, perhaps, is that at a distance of more than a century, *Lochner* strikes many readers as less morally reprehensible than *Korematsu* or *Plessy* or *Dred Scott*. This raises the interesting possibility that enduring antiprecedents must prompt moral revulsion. Judicial infamy, perhaps, requires ethical iniquity, not just ghastly judicial craft. In any case, far fewer constitutionalists are willing to say that *Lochner* was "wrong the day it was decided" than are willing to say the same of *Dred Scott* or *Plessy* or *Korematsu*.[145] It is perhaps ironic, then, that since 1955 *Lochner* has been cited just as often as its anticanonical peers—sixty-one times as against sixty-two citations to *Plessy* and twenty-six to *Dred Scott*. (There have been forty-nine citations to *Korematsu* during that period, but the tally is misleading, as most have cited *Korematsu* as a seminal articulation of the strict scrutiny standard, not as an execrable icon of the anticanon.) *Lochner* is, moreover, the only anticanonical case whose name is regularly foisted on an entire age. The justices have referred fifteen times to the "*Lochner* era." By contrast, there has been only one reference to the "*Plessy* era" and none at all to a "*Dred Scott* era" or a "*Korematsu* era." Thus, the anticanonical case that now garners the least moral opprobrium is the only one consistently presented as typical of its time.

According to professor Greene, the supreme service of the anticanon is that, on the one hand, it helps maintain faith in a "perfect" Constitution;[146] on the other, "[p]retending that judges rather than the Constitution are always responsible for the most objectionable results reinforces judicial supremacy and discourages the American people from taking ownership over the Constitution."[147] "Anticanonical cases," he concludes, "are vilified out of proportion to their conventional errors in order to save us all from ourselves."[148]

Greene's point about judicial supremacy is a powerful one. In the hands of judges themselves, the anticanon further suggests both that the Supreme Court's infamy is limited to less than a handful of egregious judgments and that, despite intolerable delays, the Court has generally corrected its mistakes and drawn from them the appropriate lessons. In the latter regard, it is perhaps telling that the Court has cited *Dred Scott* much less often as an antiprecedent than it has *Lochner* or *Plessy*. After all, *Dred Scott* wasn't overruled by the Court but by the Thirty-Ninth Congress and by the American people. *Korematsu* has been cited as an antiprecedent less often still—and surely in part because the Court didn't formally overturn it until 2018. Akhil Amar places *Lochner*, *Plessy*, and *Dred Scott*—and not *Korematsu*—in the "lowest circle of constitutional hell."[149] *Plessy* and *Lochner* are most serviceable to the Court because the Court itself overturned them and did so in contexts that form the basis of its modern bids for legitimacy—the heart of the story the Court narrates about itself to the American people. *Lochner* was overturned in 1937, a year before the Court announced in its most momentous footnote that it was getting out of the business of reviewing socioeconomic legislation and, perhaps, getting into the business of safeguarding minority rights. *Plessy* was overturned (sort of) in 1954 in the case that every clubbable or confirmable jurist must defend to the death as rightly decided. Pointing to *Plessy* is also a way of pointing to *Brown* and to the first Justice Harlan's canonic dissent to the *Plessy* decision, in which he rejected the majority's embrace of the separate-but-equal doctrine in segregation cases. Grappling with its historic sins has also been a way of underscoring the Court's heroic virtues.

Modern justices most often invoke their forebears' infamy either to insist that they are now doing the opposite of what was done before or to accuse misguided colleagues of repeating or reviving earlier errors. Sometimes the anticanonical shorthand serves simply as a particularly crushing epithet. "I am optimistic enough," wrote Justice Antonin Scalia at the outset of one impassioned dissent, "to believe that, one day, *Stenberg v. Carhart* will be assigned its rightful place in the history of this Court's jurisprudence beside *Korematsu* and *Dred Scott*."[150] More often, however, the invocation asserts a specific lesson (beyond visceral distaste) to be drawn from the antiprecedent. Often those lessons point in opposite directions.

A common lesson taken from anticanonical cases, for example, focuses on the virtue of judicial restraint. Both *Dred Scott* and *Lochner* have been cited forcefully and frequently as exemplary and admonitory instances of what goes wrong when courts overplay their hand and try to settle torrid political controversies themselves, or when they substitute their own economic, policy, or social views for those of political actors.[151] Similarly, *Dred Scott* and *Lochner* both serve as hobgoblins that embody the ills of substantive due process.[152] Conversely, *Plessy* and *Korematsu* have been invoked just as vigorously as warnings against judicial abdication.[153] Conveniently, the anticanon is split evenly between two decisions in which the Court egregiously intervened and two in which it fecklessly stayed its hand. Half the anticanon counsels activism, the other half deference. There is usually in the anticanon ready support for whatever a given justice wants to do.

Justices eager to overturn precedent often invoke the whole of the anticanon. Rigid adherence to precedent, after all, would leave anticanonical cases still standing.[154] As Justice Neil Gorsuch put it in a dissenting opinion in 2019: "[B]lind obedience to *stare decisis* would leave this Court still abiding grotesque errors like *Dred Scott v. Sandford*, *Plessy v. Ferguson*, and *Korematsu v. United States*."[155] (Note, however, *Lochner*'s telling absence.) Thus, the very existence of precedents that might undermine the Court's moral legitimacy or imperil its popular acceptance are invoked to defend the legitimacy of departing from precedent, which is itself a traditional and principal basis of judicial self-legitimation. Sometimes, of course, justices acknowledge the anticanon only to argue that its lessons don't apply to the case at hand. Some justices have even warned against overhasty, "apocalyptic" reliance on antiprecedent.[156]

In all of their invocations of the anticanon, the justices acknowledge that their predecessors have, at times, gotten things terribly wrong. But they have also, eventually, set things right. At bottom, as noted earlier, the anticanon reinforces judicial supremacy. The Court has thus—with help from commentators, academic and otherwise—turned one of the greatest challenges to its authority into an indirect means of asserting and affirming its authority. At the same time, invoking the anticanon provides powerful rhetorical support for just about anything a justice might be inclined to do.

The anticanon, then, is protean and pluripotent. It is versatile and flexible. It is also, one might argue, an extended exercise in subversion and containment.[157] It raises the specter of judges wielding their power to malevolent ends, only to tame that specter with the assurance that the modern Court has learned its lessons, repudiated past sins, and gloriously set things right. True, there might be a legitimacy risk when justices accuse their colleagues of reviving the ghosts of evils past.[158] Dissenting opinions might adduce anticanonical lessons in order to assert legitimating values against majority departures from those values, but the empirical evidence on whether dissenting opinions enhance or erode legitimacy is rather mixed.[159] It is quite possible that the increasingly acerbic dissents in recent decades have impaired legitimacy by fostering perceptions of judges as partisans in robes.[160] One might certainly wonder whether it helps the Court's legitimacy to accuse one's colleagues of reviving errors that crippled the Court's legitimacy in the past. But if there is a risk to the Court's legitimacy when justices invoke the anticanon against their colleagues, the risk seems slow in materializing. Perhaps such invocations are too readily dismissed as rhetorical overkill.

Beyond the anticanon's pliable pluripotency, its most salient feature is its tiny size. Compared with the Court's heroic canon, the anticanon is miniscule indeed. In the Court's self-presentation, the anticanonical cases mark aberrational departures in the stalwart, triumphant march from *Marbury* and *McCulloch* to *Barnette* and *Brown*. In this telling, infamous antiprecedents are isolated, ignoble stains on an otherwise noble tradition of interpreting a fundamentally noble constitution. It is a useful tale, and the Court has told it well. But that telling has often entailed the systematic forgetting of scores of equally unsavory cases. The Court's strategy for reconstructing its authority in the aftermath of its own infamy has been one of very selective remembrance against a backdrop of wide-ranging amnesia. The strategy seems to have worked beautifully so far. But perhaps the palpable divisions within the current Court—and the public's deepening perception that those divisions are purely partisan—will put pressure on the Court's preexisting patterns of self-legitimating self-narration.

Conclusion: A Second Infamy?

In 1987, the German writer Ralph Giordano published an essay titled "The Second Guilt or, On the Burden of Being German."[161] "Second guilt" is a Talmudic concept referring to the failure to expiate misdeeds: the original misdeed brings the first guilt, the failure to address it the second. Giordano argued that, in the early decades following World War II, West Germany as a whole had incurred a second guilt through its failure to adequately confront the Nazi past. His thesis was fiercely disputed,[162] but the notion of a second guilt raises some pointed questions regarding judges in Germany and the United States. In either of these countries, has the judiciary, and in particular the Supreme Court, adequately confronted its own complicity in past crimes? If not, what should the judges have done differently? Should judges apologize for—and not merely overrule—their own or their forebears' worst offenses? Is doing so consistent with the judicial task? Are judges equipped to discern between jurisprudential mistakes and moral misdeeds, or between enforcing unjust laws and committing independent crimes? Is there a category difference between the criminality of Nazi judging and American judges' complicity in slavery and segregation? However one answers this last question, what are its implications for contemporary jurisprudence?

Such questions reach beyond the scope of this mainly descriptive and comparative contribution to *Law's Infamy*. But the comparison does at least raise the possibility that the effort to reconstruct judicial legitimacy and power in the aftermath of law's infamy has given rise, perhaps in both countries, to a second infamy of a different sort. The possibility of a "second guilt" also highlights an additional dilemma of judicial Vergangenheitsbewältigung. On the one hand, courts might be motivated to come to terms with their own past by a perceived need to shore up popular support for their authority and judgments in the present. On the other, that motivation is undermined if an aggressive effort to come to terms with the past might itself be unpalatable or intolerable to contemporary politicians or publics. But the German Supreme Court after Nazism and the U.S. Supreme Court after slavery and segregation have at times been caught between the need to assert their legitimacy by taking past infamy seriously and the need to render politically digestible judgments by not taking past infamy too seriously.[163] It is a delicate dance—perhaps, at times, a tragic one. The same legitimating imperative that might have led the two high courts to confront their pasts—that is to say, the need to persuade politicians and populaces to accept their institutional authority—has sometimes prompted them to stay their hands, leave the past unmastered, and thus incur a second guilt.

NOTES

1 Bruce Ackerman, *Revolutionary Constitutions: Charismatic Leadership and the Rule of Law* 1 (2019).

2 *See, e.g.*, James L. Gibson, Milton Lodge, and Benjamin Woodson, "*Losing, But Accepting: Legitimacy, Positivity Theory, and the Symbols of Judicial Authority*," 48 *Law & Society Review* 837 (2014).

3 James L. Gibson and Michael J. Nelson, "*Change in Institutional Support for the U.S. Supreme Court: Is the Court's Legitimacy Imperiled by the Decisions it Makes?*," 80 *Public Opinion. Quarterly* 622 (2016).

4 Walter Murphy, *Elements of Judicial Strategy* 13 (1964). The phrase pre-dates Murphy. *See* Jerome Frank, "The Cult of the Robe," *Saturday Review of Literature*, Oct. 13, 1945.

5 See James L. Gibson and Gregory A. Caldeira, *Citizens, Courts, and Confirmations: Positivity Theory and the Judgments of the American People* (2009).

6 See Dieter Grimm, "*Europe Needs Principles, Not Pragmatism*," in Dieter Grimm, *The Constitution of European Democracy* 233 (Justin Collings, trans., 2017).

7 James L. Gibson and Michael J. Nelson, "*Reconsidering Positivity Theory: What Roles do Politicization, Ideological Disagreement, and Legal Realism Play in Shaping U.S. Supreme Court Legitimacy?*," 14 *Journal of Empirical Legal Studies* 592, 595 (2017).

8 On the notion of the anticanon, see especially Richard A. Primus, "Canon, Anti-Canon, and Judicial Dissent," 48 *Duke Law Journal* 243 (1998); and Jamal Greene, "*The Anticanon*," 125 *Harvard Law Review* 379 (2011).

9 The five courts deal with labor law (Bundesarbeitsgericht), welfare matters (Bundessozialgericht), taxation and finance (Bundesfinanzhof), administrative law (Bundesverwaltungsgericht), and civil and criminal appeals (Bundesgerichtshof).

10 For an extended account, not exclusively focused on the Supreme Court, see Ingo Müller, *Hitler's Justice: The Courts of the Third Reich* (Deborah Lucas Schneider, trans., 1991). For the original, see Ingo Müller, *Furchtbare Juristen: Die unbewältigte Vergangenheit der deutschen Justiz* (1987).

11 On this last point, see this exhaustive study: Alexander Blankenagel, *Tradition und Verfassung: Neue Verfassung und alte Geschichte in der Rechtsprechung des Bundesverfassungsgerichts* (1987).

12 See Hans Joachim Faller, *Bundesverfassungsgericht und Bundesgerichtshof*, 115 *Archiv des öffentlichen Rechts* 185, 187–88 (1990).

13 On Weinkauff, see Daniel Herbe, *Hermann Weinkauff (1894–1981): Der erste Präsident des Bundesgerichtshofs* (2008); Klaus-Detlev Godau-Schüttke, *Der Bundesgerichtshof: Justiz in Deutschland* 21–108 (2005).

14 See Klaus Godau-Schüttke, "*Blut und Roben*," *Die Zeit* (Sep. 18, 2015).

15 Stephan Alexander Glienke, "*Der Dolch unter der Richterrobe. Die Aufarbeitung der NS-Justiz in Gesellschaft, Wissenschaft und Rechtsprechung der Bundesrepublik*," *Zeitgesichte-online* (Dec. 2012), https://zeitgeschichte-online.de.

16 *Ibid.*

17 Joachim Rückert, "*Strafrechtliche Zeitgeschichten: Vermutungen und Widerlegungen*," 84 *Kritische Vierteljahresschrift für Gesetzgebung und Rechtswissenschaft* 223, 224 (2001); Axel von der Ohe, "Der Bundesgerichtshof und die NS-Justizverbrechen," in *Erfolgsgeschichte Bundesrepublik? Die Nachkriegsgesellschaft im langen Schatten des Nationalsozialismus*, ed. Stephan A. Glienke, Volker Paulmann, and Joachim Perels, 293, 294 (2008).

18 Bernd Diestelkamp, *Die Justiz nach 1945 und ihr Umgang mit der eigenen Verantwortung*, in *Justizalltag im Dritten Reich* 131, 132 (Michael Stolleis, ed., 1988).

19 Ibid.
20 Glienke.
21 Müller, 121.
22 *Ibid.*, 122.
23 See Godau-Schüttke.
24 Müller, 134.
25 *Ibid.*, 130.
26 *Ibid.*, 129.
27 *Ibid.*, 129–30.
28 *Ibid.*, 130.
29 Diestelkamp, 133.
30 *Ibid.*, 134.
31 *Ibid.*, 135.
32 von der Ohe, 294.
33 *Ibid.*
34 Diestelkamp, 145.
35 Glieneke.
36 *Ibid.*
37 *Ibid.*
38 *Ibid.*
39 Joachim Feest, "Die Bundesrichter. Herkunft, Karriere und Auswahl der jurist-ischen Elite," in *Beiträge zur Analyse der deutschen Oberschicht* 95, 104 (Wolfgang Zapf, ed., 1965).
40 von der Ohe, 294.
41 *Ibid.*
42 *Ibid.*, 295.
43 *Ibid.*, 296.
44 *Ibid.*, 297.
45 On the case, see Christoph Schminck-Gustavus, *Der "Prozess" gegen Dietrich Bon-hoeffer und die Freilassung seiner Mörder* (1995); Joachim Perels, "Die schrittweise Rechtfertigung der NS-Justiz: Der Huppenkothen-Prozeß," in Joachim Perels, *Das juristische Erbe des "Dritten Reiches" Beschädigungen der demokratischen Rech-stordnung* 181 (1999).
46 BVerfGG § 4(1) (Mar. 12, 1951).
47 See Klaus-Detlev Godau-Schüttke, *Der Bundesgerichtshof: Justiz in Deutschland* 334–81 (2005).
48 The circular was later published in the *Bundesanzeiger* of March 12, 1951.
49 *Ibid.*
50 2 BVerfGE 136, 138 (1953).
51 Art. 131 GG.
52 See 3 BVerfGE 58 (17 Dec. 1953).
53 *Ibid.*, 85.
54 *Ibid.*, 86.

55 *Ibid.*

56 *Ibid.*

57 *Ibid.*

58 *Ibid.*, 87–88.

59 *Ibid.*, 88.

60 *Ibid.*, 99.

61 *Ibid.*, 101.

62 *Ibid.*, 101–03.

63 *Ibid.*, 103–08.

64 *Ibid.*, 94–95.

65 *Ibid.*, 95.

66 *Ibid.*, 141–43.

67 13 BGHZ 265 (1954).

68 *Ibid.*, 294–95.

69 *Ibid.*, 296.

70 *Ibid.*, 296–97.

71 *Ibid.*, 299.

72 *Ibid.*

73 *Ibid.*

74 *Ibid.*

75 Hermann Weinkauff, *75 Jahre Reichsgericht*, 1954 Deutsche Richterzeitung 251.

76 *Ibid.*, 251.

77 *Ibid.*

78 *Ibid.*

79 *Ibid.*, 252.

80 *Ibid.*

81 *Ibid.*, 253.

82 *Ibid.*, 252.

83 4 BVerfGE 358, 358 (1955).

84 *Ibid.*, 362–67.

85 *Ibid.*

86 See Manfred Baldus, "*Frühe Machtkämpfe*," in *Das Lüth-Urteil aus (rechts-) historischer Sicht: Die Konflikte um Veit Harlan und die Grundrechtsjudikatur des Bundesverfassungsgerichts*, ed. Thomas Henne and Arne Riedlinger, 237, 243 (2005).

87 See Hans Joachim Faller, "*Bundesverfassungsgericht und Bundesgerichtshof*," 115 *Archiv des öffentlichen Rechts* 185, 190 (1990).

88 "*Stellungnahme der Präsidenten der Oberen Bundesgerichte*," 11 JuristenZeitung 90 (1956).

89 *Ibid.*, 91.

90 *Ibid.*

91 *Ibid.*, 92.

92 *Ibid.*

93 *Ibid.*, 93.

94 *Ibid.*

95 Baldus, 245.

96 5 BVerfGE 85 (1956).

97 6 BVerfGE 132 (1957).

98 See ibid., 175 (contrasting Ernst Forsthoff's 1954 criticism with his 1934 article).

99 *Ibid.*, 179.

100 *Ibid.*

101 *Ibid.*, 185.

102 *Ibid.*, 185–92.

103 *Ibid.*, 193–95.

104 *Ibid.*, 195.

105 *Ibid.*

106 *Ibid.*

107 *Ibid.*, 196.

108 *Ibid.*, 196–97.

109 *Ibid.*, 197–98.

110 6 BVerfGE 222 (1957).

111 6 BVerfGE 32, 35–38 (1957).

112 7 BVerfGE 198, 205 (1958).

113 Hermann Weinkauff, *Die deutsche Justiz und der Nationalsozialismus* (1968).

114 Faller, 207.

115 See ibid., 197–203.

116 *Ibid.*, 209.

117 Quoted in Bernd Diestelkamp, *Die Justiz nach 1945 und ihr Umgang mit der eigenen Verantwortung*, in *Justizalltag im Dritten Reich* 131, 143 (Michael Stolleis, ed., 1988).

118 See 22 *Neue Juristische Wochenschrift* 1379 (1968).

119 Müller, 280.

120 *Ibid.*, 281.

121 In ibid.

122 On the exhibition, see Stephan Alexander Glienke, *Die Ausstellung "Ungesühnte Nazijustiz" (1959–1962): Zur Geschichte der Aufarbeitung nationalsozialistischer Justizverbrechen* (2008).

123 Hermann Weinkauff, *Die deutsche Justiz und der Nationalsozialismus* (1968).

124 *See, e.g.*, Hans Peter Bull, *"Rechtsprechung im NS-Staat,"* Die Zeit (Sep. 20, 1968); Werner Sarstedt, *"Warum wir versagt haben,"* Der Spiegel (Dec. 23, 1968).

125 Udo Reifner, *"Juristen im Nationalsozialismus: Kritische Anmerkungen zum Stand der Vergangenheitsbewältigung,"* 16 Zeitschrift für Rechtspolitik 13, 18 (1983).

126 The book was translated into English, following the tried-and-true pattern of making Hitler the titular hero of books translated from the German, as *Hitler's Justice*. See Müller. The title misdirects attention from the judges and professors who are the real villains of Müller's tale.

127 See Klaus-Detlev Godau-Schüttke, *Der Bundesgerichtshof: Justiz in Deutschland* (2005).

128 39 BGHSt 1, 15–17 (1992); 41 BGHSt 101, 105–10 (1995).

129 Günter Hirsch, *Die deutsche Justiz im Unrechtssystem und bei der Aufarbeitung von Justizunrecht*, 2002 *Die Richterzeitung* 228.

130 *Ibid.*

131 *Ibid.*, 229.

132 *Ibid.*

133 *Ibid.*

134 *Ibid.*, 230.

135 See Justin Collings, *Scales of Memory: Constitutional Justice and Historical Evil* (Oxford University Press, 2021).

136 See Blankenagel.

137 See Barry Friedman, *The Will of the People: How Public Opinion Has Influenced the Supreme Court and Shaped the Meaning of the Constitution* 137–66 (2009).

138 Home Bldg. & Loan Ass'n v. Blaisdell, 290 U.S. 398, 450 (1934) (Sutherland, J., dissenting).

139 Greene, 460.

140 *Ibid.*, 427–34.

141 Mark Graber, *Dred Scott and the Problem of Constitutional Evil* (2006).

142 Greene, 411.

143 Jack Balkin, "'Wrong the Day it Was Decided': *Lochner* and Constitutional Historicism," 85 *Bost. University Law Review* 677, 710 (2005).

144 *See, e.g.*, David Bernstein, *Rehabilitating* Lochner: *Defending Individual Rights against Progressive Reform* (2011).

145 See Balkin.

146 *Cf.* Henry P. Monaghan, "Our Perfect Constitution," 56 *N.Y.U. Law Review* 353 (1981).

147 Greene, 472.

148 *Ibid.*, 475.

149 Akhil Reed Amar, *America's Unwritten Constitution: The Precedents and Principles We Live By* 270 (2012).

150 Stenberg v. Carhart, 530 U.S. 914, 953 (2000) (Scalia J dissenting).

151 *See, e.g.*, Williams v. State of N.C., 325 U.S. 226, 274 (1945) (Rutledge, J., dissenting) ("I am confident, however, that today's decision will no more aid in the solution of the problem than the *Dred Scott* decision aided in settling controversies over slavery."); United States v. Int'l Union United Auto., Aircraft & Agr. Implement Workers of Am. (UAW-CIO), 352 U.S. 567, 591 (1957) (Frankfurter, J.) ("The Court's failure in *Dred Scott* . . . to take the smooth handle for the sake of repose by disposing of the case solely upon the outside issue and the effects of its attempt to settle the agitation are familiar history.") (internal quotation marks omitted); Planned Parenthood of Southeastern Pennsylvania v. Casey, 505 U.S. 833, 984, 998, 1001–02 (1992) (Scalia, J., dissenting); England v. Louisiana State Bd. of Med. Ex-

aminers, 375 U.S. 411, 431 (1964) (Douglas, J., concurring); Ferguson v. Skrupa, 372 U.S. 726, 730 (1963); Moore v. City of E. Cleveland, Ohio, 431 U.S. 494, 502 (1977); Cent. Hudson Gas & Elec. Corp. v. Pub. Serv. Comm'n of New York, 447 U.S. 557, 589 (1980) (Rehnquist, J., dissenting); Indus. Union Dep't, AFL-CIO v. Am. Petroleum Inst., 448 U.S. 607, 724, 100 S. Ct. 2844, 2905, 65 L. Ed. 2d 1010 (1980) (Marshall, J., dissenting); City of Cleburne, Tex. v. Cleburne Living Ctr., 473 U.S. 432, 459–60 (1985) (Marshall, J., concurring in part and dissenting in part); Metro. Life Ins. Co. v. Ward, 470 U.S. 869, 900 (1985) (O'Connor, J., dissenting); Obergefell v. Hodges, 135 S. Ct. 2584, 2621 (2015) (Roberts, C.J., dissenting).

152 *See, e.g.*, Griswold v. Connecticut, 381 U.S. 479, 522 (1965) (Black, J., dissenting)

153 *See, e.g.*, Skinner v. Ry. Labor Executives' Ass'n, 489 U.S. 602, 635 (1989) (Marshall, J., dissenting) (*Korematsu* is an "extreme reminder[] that when we allow fundamental freedoms to be sacrificed in the name of real or perceived exigency, we invariably come to regret it."); City of Richmond v. J.A. Croson Co., 488 U.S. 469, 501 (1989) ("The history of racial classifications in this country suggests that blind judicial deference to legislative or executive pronouncements of necessity has no place in equal protection analysis. See Korematsu v. United States, 323 U.S. 214, 235–40, 65 S.Ct. 193, 202–05, 89 L.Ed. 194 (1944) (Murphy, J., dissenting)."); Goldman v. Weinberger, 475 U.S. 503, 522, 106 S. Ct. 1310, 1321, 89 L. Ed. 2d 478 (1986) (Brennan, J., dissenting) (warning against undue deference to executive or military authorities); Greene v. McElroy, 360 U.S. 474, 516, 79 S. Ct. 1400, 1423, 3 L. Ed. 2d 1377 (1959) (Clark, J., dissenting).

154 Citizens United v. Fed. Election Comm'n, 558 U.S. 310, 377 (2010) (arguing that if stare decisis were an "inexorable command," lots of bad cases, including *Plessy*, would remain good law) (Roberts, C.J., concurring).

155 Gamble v. United States, 139 S. Ct. 1960, 2005 (2019) (Gorsuch, J., dissenting).

156 *See, e.g.*, Epic Sys. Corp. v. Lewis, 138 S. Ct. 1612, 1630 (2018) (Gorsuch, J.) ("[L]ike most apocalyptic warnings, this one proves a false alarm.").

157 See Stephen Greenblatt, "Invisible Bullets," in Stephen Greenblatt, *Shakespearean Negotiations* 21 (1988).

158 See Michael J. Nelson and James L. Gibson, *"U.S. Supreme Court Legitimacy: Unanswered Questions and an Agenda for Future Research,"* in *The Routledge Handbook of Judicial Behavior*, ed. Robert M. Howard and Kirk A. Randazzo, 132, 140 (2018).

159 *See, e.g.*, Michael A. Zilis, *The Limits of Legitimacy: Dissenting Opinions, Media Coverage, and Public Responses to Supreme Court Decisions* (2015).

160 See Nelson and Gibson.

161 Ralph Giordano, *Die zweite Schuld oder Von der Last Deutscher zu sein* (1987).

162 *See, e.g.*, Manfred Kittel, *Die Legende von der "Zweiten Schuld": Vergangenheitspolitik in der ära Adenauer* (1993).

163 I am indebted to Lawrence Douglas for the formulation of this insight.

2

"The Courts of the Conqueror"

Colonialism, the Constitution, and the Time of Redemption

SHERALLY MUNSHI

Scholars of American constitutional law often find themselves confronting fundamental questions about the legitimacy of our government. For some, the crisis of legitimacy stems from the perception that the Constitution has been rendered meaningless in the hands of judges who have shown too little fidelity to the words on the page or the intentions of founders who drafted it. For others, the question is why Americans owe such fidelity to a 200-year-old document representing the aspirations of settlers whose vision of freedom and equality was conditioned upon racial slavery and genocidal conquest. How do Americans maintain faith in a constitutional system that has produced decisions like *Dred Scott v. Sandford*, upholding slavery and denying citizenship to black Americans, or like *Korematsu v. United States*, sanctioning the imprisonment of Japanese Americans during World War II? Jack Balkin, a leading constitutional theorist, offers an explanation that is perhaps reflective of an attitude shared by most liberal Americans. As he contends, the legitimacy of our constitutional government depends on a shared faith in the Constitution itself and, just as importantly, "its future trajectory."[1]

Attempting to reconcile the views of originalists, who would confine the Constitution to its original meaning, and living constitutionalists, who argue that the Constitution should be interpreted to reflect changing values and circumstances, Balkin writes of the "constitutional project" in distinctly temporal language, describing it as the eventual fulfillment of an original promise. "To believe in the constitutional project," he writes, "is to believe in a story," one that situates us, a national collective, along a narrative arc that "extends back into the past and forward into the future."[2] The constitutional story is not one of stasis or one of straightforward progress—or decline. Instead, in Balkin's account, the constitutional story is a story of "redemption,"

> returning the Constitution we have to its correct path, pushing it closer to what we take to be its true nature, and discarding the dross of past moral compromise. Through constitutional redemption, the Constitution becomes what it always promised it would be but never was; it changes in the direction of its correct interpretation and application.[3]

The story of redemption, Balkin insists, is not one of restoration or unending change. Instead, it is movement along a twinned axis of hope and historical reasoning. Hope, because the legitimacy of any political project requires a measure of faith—if not in our founding institutions then in some shared vision of their promise.[4] Historical reasoning is essential to achieving that promise because it allows us to make better sense of collective progress, to follow that plot, to maintain a sense of direction.

Balkin's appeal to a redemptive constitutionalism follows a broader turn toward collective memory in legal scholarship, one that investigates the relation between the nation's founding mythologies, its record of racial violence, and the demands of historical redress.[5] Redemptive approaches to constitutional memory are intended to disrupt originalist attempts to restore the Constitution to some fixed and knowable meaning while grounding liberal progressivism in a critical understanding of history.[6] Amy Kapczynski, for instance, advocates a "redemptive historicism" that reads "history against the grain," studying the past not with the longing to return to it but to render it a meaningful resource to us in the present, "to break apart traditional narratives that blind us to possibilities of both transcendence and disaster."[7]

For Balkin and others, the study of the constitutional canon, including what has emerged as the "anticanon," is essential to developing professional judgment and historical orientation. Lawyers study "great" cases like *Brown v. Board of Education*, perhaps the most celebrated case in American history, because they offer important lessons in how change is made. The study of infamous cases, such as *Dred Scott* and *Korematsu*, are as instructive, if not more so, the argument goes, because historical progress is marked by the collective condemnation of past wrongs; we move forward by putting cases like *Dred Scott* behind us, by learning from past mistakes, by vowing never to repeat them.[8] But those who study collective memory also warn that attempts to memorialize past wrongs have a way of affirming rather than unsettling narratives of national greatness. Memorials to past wrongs can themselves become markers of triumph.

In this sense, calls to redemptive constitutionalism are also repudiations of the constitutional *pessimism* expressed by race critics, ranging from Justice Thurgood Marshall to leaders of the Black Panther Party to a growing number of scholars who challenge the very racial foundations of Western liberalism.[9] Balkin acknowledges that the Constitution's compromise with slavery is a crippling defect, one that should challenge our faith in it today and one that renders strict originalism indefensible.[10] But Balkin also rejects pessimist claims that the Constitution itself is irredeemable, that it has been superseded—or should be. At an event commemorating the bicentennial of the Constitution, Justice Thurgood Marshall famously declared that the Constitution was dead; the Civil War rather than the Constitution brought an end to slavery, and the Reconstruction Amendments represent a refounding of the nation.[11] At another ceremonial address soon after, Laurence Tribe defended the Constitution against Marshall's remarks, appealing to a narrative of original promise and perfectibility. The Constitution, however flawed, has also "made it possible for the Supreme Court . . . after a century of blindness, both to see, and to make the country face, what had to be done to redeem the fourteenth amendment's promise."[12] Since the beginning, Tribe insists, "the Constitution's story . . . is a story of struggle to live by its light—to extend its writ, making rights available to groups that had once been excluded, and making responsibilities attach to individuals who had once been exempted."[13] The arc of progress, according to the redemption narrative, extends the founding promise of the Constitution to an ever-widening diversity of individuals, without distinction of race, gender, or creed. In the broadest strokes, that arc of inclusion is plotted in the movement from slavery to reconstruction, from segregation to civil rights.

Besides failing to address the concerns of racial pessimists, who trace the persistence of inequality to founding arrangements, this narrative of inclusion leaves unexamined the unreconstructed relationship between the Constitution and colonialism. What Balkin and perhaps most Americans overlook is the way in which settler colonialism has fundamentally shaped our constitutional order, with explicit and ongoing sanction from the Supreme Court, which continues to grant broad deference to the political branches in their exercise of imperial power. Even the most circumspect studies of cultural memory in law take for granted the way in which colonial conquest and Indigenous dispossession appear as the fixed backdrop against which the drama of racial inclusion unfolds.

The violence of colonialism cannot be redeemed by a politics of inclusion. To be very clear, neither can a politics of inclusion redress the extraordinary violence of slavery, which consisted of innumerable crimes at once: expropriation of labor, denial of personhood, loss of liberty, coercion and terror—none of which is adequately redressed by liberal commitments to nondiscrimination or formal equality.[14] A politics of racial inclusion is particularly inadequate to redressing the violence suffered by Indigenous peoples, for whom inclusion—particularly in the form of assimilation or imposed citizenship—has been experienced as part of a broader strategy of elimination.[15] As Joanne Barker observes, the "Indian" appears within the national imaginary as a racialized subject rather than as a foreigner, only *after* and because indigenous sovereignty has been extinguished by the settler state: "[T]he erasure of the sovereign is the racialization of the 'Indian.'"[16] Racialization and colonization are related but discrete processes, Jodi Byrd reminds us.[17] The point in distinguishing them is not to argue that one form of violence is more foundational than any other. Instead, it is to develop a critical understanding of the ways in which the settler colonial project gives rise to a multiplicity of simultaneous grievances that remain unheard and unrecognized within a legal regime, political discourse, and national imaginary thoroughly shaped by the ongoing project of settler imperialism.[18]

The United States was conceived not in the pure realm of ideals, as some constitutional scholars might have us believe, but in a fever of colonial acquisition and expansion. The ideals of freedom, equality, and self-government enshrined in our Constitution are not universal ideals but *settler* ideals, promised to a limited class of propertied white men and underwritten by the prospect of continuous growth realized primarily by stealing land from Indians and labor from enslaved Africans. The settler colonial project in the United States, as Aziz Rana contends, was organized around an essential division, between racialized "insiders" and "outsiders." The organization of sovereign power within our constitutional jurisprudence reflects and reproduces this essential division: the Constitution protects "insiders" from the abuses of sovereign power but leaves "outsiders," especially those who stand in the way of expansion, exposed to sovereign violence.[19]

This chapter seeks to shift our focus from what is often presented as the main drama in the story of constitutional redemption—the country's struggle to overcome the legacy of racism—to bring into view another set of cases that represent the unchanging architecture of colonial sovereignty, often relegated to the backdrop. These cases, beginning with *Johnson v. M'Intosh*, decided in 1823, broadly represent the Supreme Court's reconciliation of constitutionalism with colonialism. In *Johnson v. M'Intosh*, the Supreme Court effectively transferred sovereignty over the land that now comprises the contiguous United States from Indians to colonists. The Court held that Indians had neither ownership nor sovereignty over lands "discovered" by European colonizers, explaining that "discovery gave the Conqueror an exclusive right to extinguish Indian occupancy."[20] Acknowledging the irreducible tension between colonial conquest and founding principles of freedom and equality, Chief Justice John Marshall laments that the Court is simply powerless to constrain the federal government: "Conquest gives a title which the Courts of the Conqueror cannot deny."[21]

If, within redemptive constitutionalism, the stain of infamy marks a judicial decision that is not just wrong but so wrong that it compels repudiation, then a case like *Johnson v. M'Intosh* is revealing of the ways in which law places certain forms of sovereign violence beyond the realm of legal redress, national progress, or the time of redemption. *Johnson v. M'Intosh* continues to hold a privileged, if increasingly uncomfortable, place within the American legal canon.[22] It appears at the beginning of many property law casebooks, establishing the foundational principle that the federal government holds ultimate title to the land within its borders. Often taught in the first days of law school, the case is also used to introduce American law students to the distinction between natural law and positive law—Marshall laments that the "abstract principles of justice" and the "law of the nation" are seldom coterminous. But the lessons of *Johnson v. M'Intosh* far exceed the scope of either property doctrine or common law conventions. The case remains foundational not only in that it remains the basis for U.S. "possession" over Indian lands; it also demonstrates the Court's reluctance to constrain what it recognizes to be the extra-constitutional power "inherent" in national sovereignty. That unconstrained power, originating in the time of conquest, represents the ongoing life of colonialism and U.S. imperialism.[23]

In the constitutional imaginary, colonization is often presented as a regrettable prehistory to the building of a nation, an event that conditioned the founding of the revolutionary republic but is not constitutive of it. Extraordinarily, in his opinion in *Johnson v. M'Intosh*, Marshall identified the United States' authority to assert control over Indians as an *extra*-constitutional power, inherent to sovereignty and inherited from its imperial predecessors. In what follows, I offer a reading of *Johnson v. M'Intosh*, then trace the still unfolding legacy of the case in the "plenary power" doctrine, according to which the federal government holds certain powers not enumerated by the Constitution and not subject to judicial review. With explicit reference to *Johnson v. M'Intosh*, the doctrine was formalized in the late nineteenth century, a period marked by the "pacification" of Native Americans, the exclusion of Asian immigrants, and acquisition of overseas territories; it continues to define the United States' relationship to its subject subordinates—Indigenous Americans, immigrants, and colonized peoples. This line of cases represents the relative stillness of sovereignty, a power that is often taken for granted in narratives of racial redemption and constitutional perfectibility.

Johnson v. M'Intosh and the Constitution of Empire

Historians trace the tangled roots of the property dispute in *Johnson v. M'Intosh* to the chaos of the revolutionary period, when the British Empire began to lose its hold over its North American colonies and the rush to claim new lands outpaced the development of government institutions.[24] Jurisdictional confusion, the slow and uneven development of the legal system, and the lure of cheap and abundant land created a "vacuum," as one scholar writes, into which "speculation and greed became the driving forces for the . . . founders of our nation."[25] Nearly every member of the revolutionary elite participated in land speculation. John Marshall himself was hardly disinterested. His father, after joining a young George Washington on a surveying expedition, earned his living as a surveyor for a British lord and eventually acquired more than 200,000 acres of land in Virginia and Kentucky, generating tremendous wealth.[26] Decades later, in 1816, when a lawsuit involving the property reached the Supreme Court, Justice Marshall had no choice but to recuse himself, though he evidently kept a close eye over the writing of the opinion and "concurred with [its] every word."[27]

In the decades before the American Revolution, land speculation had been constrained only by war and British regulation. During the French and Indian War, France and its Indian allies had prevented British colonists from claiming lands west of the Allegheny Mountains. After the war ended, in 1763, France surrendered its vast territory to Britain, but King George III, eager to avoid another costly war on the continent, issued a proclamation prohibiting British colonists from claiming lands in the ceded territory. The Proclamation of 1763 established a fixed line of partition between Indian and settler lands, drawn along the crest of the Allegheny Mountains. Lands west of the Proclamation Line were reserved for Indian use; colonial governors were barred from surveying or granting title to the lands; and squatters who had already settled on the land were ordered "forthwith to remove themselves."[28]

Colonists were enraged by the Proclamation. Many had served as foot soldiers in the war against the French and had been promised land in exchange for their service. Others resented being constrained by a distant government. But the war left the British government in a compromised position: indebted not only to colonist-soldiers but also to several Indian nations—Iroquois, Cherokee, Choctaw, and Chickasaw—who had contributed to France's defeat. Those Indian nations lived west of the Allegheny Mountains, on lands that colonists were eager to claim for themselves. The Proclamation forbid colonial expansion, at least in part, to protect the rights of Indians who were recognized as "a new kind of colony," as Greg Grandin suggests, quite distinct from British settlers but imperial subjects invested with competing rights and interests.[29] Indians, according to the Proclamation, "live under our protection" and as such "should not be molested or disturbed in the possession of such parts of our dominion and territories."[30]

Of course, the British government was not motivated simply by its concern for Indians. By claiming for itself a preemptive, or exclusive, right to purchase land from Indians, the Crown sought to protect an established fur trade and otherwise control the spread of British colonies in North America.[31] Instead, the Proclamation spurred colonists to revolt against what they perceived as a violation of their right to claim new lands. Others, such as Benjamin Franklin, seemed to believe that colonial expansion was inevitable, anticipating that nothing would "prevent the settlement of lands over the mountains . . . neither road nor provincial proclamations, nor the dread and horror of savage war."[32] Settler militias moved forward in defiance of the Proclamation, often terrorizing the Indians from whom they seized land. More elite speculators also viewed the Proclamation as little more than a "temporary expedience to quiet the mind of Indians," bound to be revoked sooner or later, as George Washington wrote. A veteran of the French and Indian War, Washington instructed his surveyors "to secure some of the most valuable lands in the King's part," west of the Proclamation Line, "under the guise of hunting game," to avoid scrutiny.[33]

The Proclamation prohibited the purchase of Indian lands without permission from the Crown, but speculators sought to purchase lands from Indians anyway, anticipating that their purchases would eventually gain legal recognition, transforming their lawless ventures into enormous windfalls. *Johnson v. M'Intosh* involved such purchases. The plaintiffs, land speculators organized as the United Illinois and Wabash Land Companies (the "Companies"), purchased several large tracts of land, first from the Piankeshaw in 1773, then from the Illinois in 1775. Both purchases were made a decade after the Proclamation in clear violation of its terms.

Incredibly, an agent for the Companies, to avoid the scrutiny of British officials charged with enforcing the Proclamation, produced a forged document—a doctored copy of a twenty-year-old judicial opinion governing land purchases in British India. The 1757 opinion, often referred to as the Camden-Yorke opinion, declared that representatives of the British East India Company could purchase lands directly from "the Mogul or any of the Indian princes or governments," even without permission from royal officials.[34] The doctored opinion eliminated references to "the Mogul," creating the impression that royal permission was no longer required for purchasing land from "Indian princes" and that the Proclamation had been revoked.

Under the false impression that the Proclamation had been super-seded by the Camden-Yorke opinion, British officials in North America allowed the Companies to make purchases from Indian tribes, but as news of the purchases reached London, they were declared "void and fraudulent." Under ordinary circumstances, such a declaration would have extinguished the purchaser's claim, but the dissolution of the Brit-ish Empire gave rise to new jurisdictional questions and, for the Compa-nies, reason to persist in legalizing the purchases. For the next thirty-five years, from 1775 to 1810, the Companies pursued the colony of Virginia, the Continental Congress, and eventually the United States Congress for recognition of title to the lands, but each to no avail. If the United States retained the exclusive right to purchase Indian lands, then it had little to gain by recognizing these purchases.[35]

Eventually, United Illinois and Wabash turned its attention away from Congress and toward an increasingly powerful Supreme Court. But to obtain a judgment from the Court, the Companies would have to manu-facture a dispute, positioning itself as the plaintiff. In his remarkable history of the murky events leading up to the case, Lindsay Robertson demonstrates, as many others have suspected, that there was no real dis-pute in *Johnson v. M'Intosh*. Instead, the case was the result of collusion. William M'Intosh—himself an ambitious speculator—held a competing claim to land within the original purchase, but he held no real grievance against the Companies. He was approached by the plaintiff's lawyer who, for some time, had been searching for a suitable defendant to sue for ejectment. As Robertson suggests, M'Intosh's interests happened to be aligned with those of the plaintiff: as a speculator with interests in other lands, he may have benefited from a ruling in favor of the Companies; he may have been offered a share in the Companies themselves; and a ruling in favor of the Companies may have given M'Intosh the priceless satisfaction of settling a personal vendetta having little to do with the case.[36] When the Companies brought the original suit for ejectment be-fore a district court in Illinois, M'Intosh agreed entirely to the plaintiff's statement of the facts, raising no counterarguments and confining the question before the court to whether the land purchases would be le-gally recognized even though they violated the Proclamation of 1763. In a brief opinion, the district court answered unequivocally: they did not.

When *Johnson v. M'Intosh* reached the Supreme Court in 1821, it was essentially a title dispute, one that could have easily been put to rest in a few short paragraphs or by affirming the lower court's decision. Instead, in the hands of Chief Justice Marshall, a feigned controversy—grounded in no factual disagreement, generating no meaningful counterargument, and orchestrated only to secure judicial recognition of an unlawful purchase—would yield a doctrine that would dispossess millions of the lands on which they had lived for centuries. A case that otherwise might have disappeared into obscurity would become catastrophic for Indians and remain foundational to the nation because Justice Marshall reframed the question before the Court.

The real question, as Marshall put it, was whether Indians had "the power . . . to give . . . a title which can be sustained in the Courts of this Country."[37] Having so dramatically reframed the question, Marshall opened his answer by reviewing the history of European colonization in the Americas. Upon "discovery" of the continent, he explained, European powers were so eager to appropriate for themselves as much land as they could, to avoid war and conflicting settlement, that they needed to devise a principle according to which they determined who owned what. This principle is known as the "discovery doctrine": "discovery gave title to the governments by whose subjects or by whose authority it was made—against all other European governments."[38]

But the discovery doctrine itself does not answer Marshall's question; it does not tell us whether Indians have the power to transfer title. An honor among thieves, the discovery doctrine defines rights and duties among conquering powers, but it says nothing about the relationship between conquerors and the conquered. The discovery doctrine itself, in other words, does not necessarily divest conquered peoples of their right to land. To the contrary, as Marshall acknowledged, under existing "international" law recognized by European imperial powers, conquered peoples generally retained such rights.[39] "[U]sually, they are incorporated with the victorious nation, and become citizens" of the conquering power. "Where this incorporation is impracticable, humanity demands, and a wise policy requires, that the rights of the conquered to property should remain unimpaired."[40]

But in the Americas, Marshall claimed, European nations followed a different practice. "All of the nations of Europe, who have acquired territory on this continent, have asserted in themselves, and have recognized in others, the exclusive right of the discoverer to appropriate the lands occupied by the Indians."[41] In Marshall's analysis, European powers uniformly claimed for themselves "an exclusive right to extinguish Indian occupancy," not as a matter of discovery itself but as a matter of sovereign prerogative. The question that Marshall then put before himself was whether the United States had "rejected or adopted" this principle.[42] Though *Johnson v. M'Intosh* has become notorious for its constitutionalization of the imperial discovery doctrine, perhaps the more astonishing turn in the decision is Marshall's claim that the United States would inherit from its imperial predecessor the sovereign prerogative to assert authority over others.

In language that is in turns chastising and resigning, Marshall attempts to reconcile a founding myth of the United States—the notion that the American Revolution established a sharp break with the illiberal traditions of imperial Europe—with its embrace of imperial power. Rhetorically, Marshall distances the revolutionary United States from the arrogance of its imperial predecessors even while affirming that the new nation, a reluctant successor in conquest, inherited from the British Empire a sovereign right to assert dominion over Indians and their lands. Marshall is ironic, for instance, when he writes that "the potentates of the old world found no difficulty in convincing themselves that they made ample compensation to the inhabitants of the new, by bestowing upon them civilization and Christianity, in exchange for unlimited independence."[43] With mock deference, he suggests that while "they may find some excuse, if not justification, in the character and habits of the people whose rights have been wrested from them . . . we do not mean to engage in the defense of those principles which Europeans may have applied to Indian title."[44]

But while condemning the arrogance of European empires, Marshall engages in a deft sleight-of-hand, attributing to Europe a history of Indian erasure that is one of his *own* invention. The actual history of European engagement with Indians in North America was far more varied, nuanced, and contested than Marshall's lament would suggest; his representation of European custom was belied by centuries of treaty-making—a history that evidenced European recognition of Indian sovereignty and a history with which Marshall was surely familiar.[45] Marshall's assertion that "discovery gave the Conqueror an exclusive right to extinguish Indian occupancy" was not exactly set forth in international treaties, nor was it clearly established by European custom. To be very clear, it was not set forth by the Constitution. In a decision remarkably uncluttered of citations, the power recognized in *Johnson v. M'Intosh*—the power of the federal government to assert sovereignty over Indigenous people—is an extra-constitutional power rooted in sovereignty itself.

All but acknowledging that the colonial foundations of the settler nation were morally indefensible, Marshall declined to offer a moral defense. Instead, he seemed to suggest that it would be impractical for the Court to unsettle the foundations of the settler colonial nation:

> However extravagant the pretensions of converting the discovery of an inhabited country into conquest may appear; if the principle has been asserted in the first instance, and afterwards sustained . . . it becomes the law of the land, and cannot be questioned. So, too, with respect to the concomitant principle, that the Indian inhabitants are to be considered merely as occupants. . . . However this restriction may be opposed to natural right, and to the usages of civilized nations, yet, if it be indispensable to that system under which the country has been settled . . . [it] certainly cannot be rejected by Courts of justice.[46]

Among the achievements for which Marshall is most celebrated is his bold articulation of the principle of judicial review—the authority of the Supreme Court to declare acts of Congress and the president unconstitutional. In perhaps his most canonical opinion, *Marbury v. Madison*, decided in 1803, Marshall asserted that the Constitution formed "the fundamental and paramount law of the nation" and that "[i]t is emphatically the province and the duty of the judicial department to say what the law is."[47] That is to say, the Constitution is a legal rather than a political document, and the Court is the final authority on matters of interpretation. These principles, taken for granted today, were less firmly established before Marshall's tenure. But in *Johnson v. M'Intosh*, stunningly, Marshall maintains that the Court is powerless to intervene in the irreversible and inevitable progress of colonial conquest. Regardless of the "original justice of the claim which has been successfully asserted," Marshall explained, "[c]onquest gives a title which the Courts of the conqueror cannot deny."[48]

As Philip Frickey has observed, Marshall's opinion in *Johnson v. M'Intosh* is organized around a conceptual distinction between colonialism and constitutionalism. "Colonialism," in Frickey's reading of the case, "raises almost exclusively nonjusticiable, normative questions beyond judicial authority and competence. Colonialism was thus prior to, and the antithesis of, constitutionalism, which involves justiciable, *legal* questions about the judicially enforceable limits on governmental action."[49] Colonialism and empire—the exercise of sovereignty in relation to outsiders—raised political rather than legal questions. To extend Frickey's analysis, Marshall's opinion participates in the construction of a distinctly settler-colonial narrative of national progress, one in which the colonial violence that enables the founding of the nation is cast beyond the realm of legal redress, constitutional review, and thus the plot of redemption.

This temporal construction of colonialism, in which colonial violence appears as a regrettable precondition to the creation of an exceptional nation, distorts our understanding of the relationship between colonialism and constitutionalism in at least two ways. First, the sequential ordering of colonial founding and constitutional progress obscures the way in which colonialism is constitutive of our constitutional republic and, as I demonstrate in the next section, has persisted within narratives of constitutional progress. Second, the sequential ordering of colonialism and constitutionalism creates the impression that conquest is over and complete. In Marshall's characterization, conquest is not only beyond judgment; it is irreversible. The language of "inevitability" permeates his account:

> Was this the *inevitable* consequence of this state of things? The Europeans were *under the necessity* of either abandoning the country, and relinquishing their pompous claims to it, or of enforcing those claims by the sword, and by the adoption of principles adapted to the condition of a people with whom it was impossible to mix, and who could not be governed as a distinct society. . . . Frequent and bloody wars, in which the whites

were not always the aggressors, *unavoidably* ensued. European policy, numbers, and skill, prevailed. As the white population advanced, that of the Indians *necessarily* receded. . . . The game fled into thicker and more unbroken forests, and the Indians followed. . . . That law [of assimilation] which regulates, and ought to regulate in general, the relations between the conqueror and the conquered, was incapable of application. . . . The resort to some new and different rule . . . was *unavoidable*.[50]

Marshall follows a familiar historical script, according to which settlers "advance" and Indians "necessarily recede," as if by some unyielding organic process rather than as a result of concerted national policy.[51] Marshall obscures the role that he and the Court would play in all but assuring the removal and elimination of Indians. At the time of his writing, continental conquest was hardly a foregone conclusion. To the contrary, Marshall's opinion in *Johnson v. M'Intosh* provided the legal foundation for Indigenous dispossession not only in the United States as it continued to expand westward but also in other parts of the white settler world.[52]

In the United States, Marshall is widely championed for his role in elevating the status of the Constitution and the Supreme Court, broadly defining the powers invested in the federal government and securing the conditions for economic integration and expansion.[53] But in the many books and articles that celebrate Marshall as the legal architect of the nation, *Johnson v. M'Intosh* is often relegated to a few scant pages, sometimes to a mere footnote.[54] Many scholars have puzzled over Marshall's opinion in the case, wondering why he devoted so much of his opinion to an epic discursion on discovery and conquest when he could have simply upheld the lower court decision.

Lindsay Robertson concludes his meticulous history of the case by suggesting that Marshall had "a lot on his plate" at the time.[55] The Court's decision was handed down within eight days; Marshall evidently drafted his opinion while listening to other arguments, riding circuit, and maintaining an active social life (for which he was also famed). Robertson suggests that perhaps Marshall invoked the discovery doctrine, even though the case hardly warranted it, because he hoped that by doing so he might put to rest the separate controversy involving the land claims of Revolutionary War veterans, which had become increasingly contentious in his home state of Virginia.[56] As such, Robertson frames his study of the case as a cautionary tale of unintended consequences "offering an instructive picture of how intelligent people can sometimes unthinkingly create catastrophic problems they find themselves power-less to fix."[57]

For Robertson and others, Marshall's genuine regret over his decision, and the disastrous impact it would have on Indian life, are evidenced by his opinion in two later Indian cases, *Cherokee Nation v. Georgia* (1831) and *Worcester v. Georgia* (1832). Marshall's assertion of federal suprem-acy over Indian matters in those cases is often championed as a heroic attempt to "protect" Indians from the relentless state encroachment dur-ing the era of President Andrew Jackson by announcing that the federal government's relation to Indians is as a "guardian" to his "ward."[58] Indig-enous scholars and activists are far less forgiving of Marshall, holding the Chief Justice responsible for laying the legal foundations for Indian removal.[59] While a growing number of legal scholars have sought to re-vive what is known as the "trust doctrine" in federal Indian law, Seth Davis reminds us that these redemptive gestures reinscribe rather than repudiate the colonial foundations of U.S.-Indian relations.[60]

Moreover, Marshall's reputation as a protector of Indians does not square easily with the legacy with which the justice is most often identi-fied: fashioning a "constitutional nationalism" that would allow the new nation to become a global empire. In an essay examining "what makes Marshall a great Justice," Jack Balkin explains that, apart from having had the opportunity to provide an "initial gloss" on the Constitution and to establish early precedent, "Marshall is honored today because he guessed correctly about the direction of the country's growth."[61] In Balkin's account, "Marshall has had the great fortune to be on the right side of most of the national disputes about which he wrote." Today, Balkin explains, most Americans look favorably upon Marshall's record of expanding national government, integrating national commerce, and asserting the power of national government over individual states. But the ways in which *Johnson v. M'Intosh* laid the groundwork for colo-nial expansion and the assertion of national sovereignty over noncitizen others are also part of Marshall's legacy as a great nation-builder and seldom acknowledged.

What really distinguishes Marshall from other great justices, in Balkin's view, is what he identifies as Marshall's "prophetic vision" of the United States. Balkin illustrates this claim by reciting a favorite passage from Marshall's "masterpiece," *McCulloch v. Maryland*, in which the Chief Justice turns from making an argument "about how the text of the Constitution supports his expansive view of federal power" to offer "a very different kind of argument for why the national government must be given the widest authority." In Marshall's words:

> Throughout this vast republic, from the St. Croix to the Gulf of Mexico, from the Atlantic to the Pacific, revenue is to be collected and expended, armies are to be marched and supported. The exigencies of the nation may require, that the treasure raised in the north should be transported to the south, that raised in the east, conveyed to the west, or that this order should be reversed. Is that construction of the constitution to be preferred, which would render these operations difficult, hazardous and expensive? Can we adopt that construction (unless the words imperiously require it), which would impute to the framers of that instrument, when granting these powers for the public good, the intention of impeding their exercise by withholding a choice of means?[62]

Balkin praises Marshall for his foresight: in 1819, when the case was decided, the boundaries of the United States did not yet extend to the St. Croix or the Pacific. "Marshall engages in prophecy. Someday, this is what the country might be: great and mighty, spanning an entire continent. Such a country needs a flexible Constitution that will allow it to fight wars, to expand its reach, to bring this enormous land under its sway." Balkin acknowledges that national expansion would mean "slaughter and displacement" for Native Americans but maintains that, "nevertheless, fate has smiled on Marshall's vision of America as a great continental power."[63]

What Balkin characterizes as Marshall's gift for prophesy sounds like tautology on the part of Balkin, who ascribes to Marshall an extraordinary, superhuman capacity to see into the future while obscuring his very human hand in creating that future. Balkin also reproduces a historical narrative that presents westward expansion and native elimination as inevitable—as the effect of a history without responsible agents. But Marshall and the Court were among the agents of that brutal history.

Plenary Power and the Stillness of Sovereignty

In 2015, soon after Donald Trump, then a candidate for president, called for a "total and complete shutdown of Muslims entering the United States," legal scholars debated whether the Supreme Court would uphold such a plainly discriminatory policy as constitutional. In an op-ed published in the *New York Times*, Peter Spiro suggested that, in the "ordinary, non-immigration world of constitutional law," a law that singled out Muslims for differential treatment would almost certainly be found to violate constitutional guarantees of equal protection and religious freedom.[64] But it was far less certain whether the Court would strike down such a plainly discriminatory policy in the extra-ordinary context of immigration law. In the immigration context, the Court routinely upholds laws that would be considered unconstitutional in the domestic context.

Spiro anticipated that the Muslim ban, however offensive, would almost certainly be upheld given the Court's century-long practice of granting Congress broad deference in its regulation of immigration. Within the immigration context, this judicial deference was first announced in the late nineteenth century, in the Chinese Exclusion cases, in which the Court held that Congress had an absolute power to exclude and deport foreigners "as it may see fit."[65] Announcing what is often referred to as the "plenary power" doctrine, the Court explained that Congress's power to exclude foreigners was neither set forth nor limited by the Constitution; the power to exclude foreigners was inherent to sovereignty itself.[66]

Adam Cox, responding to Spiro and others, suggested that law scholars exaggerate or misunderstand the plenary power doctrine. The doctrine, Cox argued, "does not stand for the proposition that blatant discrimination . . . is constitutionally permissible."[67] He acknowledged that "the canonical plenary power cases," notorious among scholars and students of immigration law, "are indeed cases that upheld policies that blatantly discriminated on the basis of race, sex, ideology or other grounds that ordinarily receive [constitutional] protection." But, Cox argued, what these immigration scholars tend to overlook is that, in each of those infamous cases, the Court's discriminatory treatment of immigrants roughly mirrored its discriminatory treatment of citizens. Cox illustrated his point by comparing the ill-treatment of immigrants in a series of infamous cases with the ill-treatment of citizens: *Chae Chan Ping* v. *United States* (1889), upholding a racial bar to immigration, was decided in the era of *Plessy v. Ferguson* (1896), when the Court routinely upheld laws of racial segregation; *Harisiades v. Shaughnessy* (1952), upholding the deportation of communists, was decided at the height of the Red Scare, when the Court routinely upheld the criminal prosecution of communists; and *Fiallo v. Bell* (1977), upholding immigration preference categories that discriminated on the basis of gender and parentage, was decided at a moment just before second-wave feminism had begun to transform the Court's sex equality jurisprudence.[68]

Cox's redemptive reading of the plenary power doctrine is a sympathetic one. Ultimately a critique of Congress's unchecked power over immigration, Cox's rereading of *Chae Chan Ping*, among other infamous immigration cases, is an attempt to render the case errant and exceptional rather than exemplary. But to read the plenary power doctrine into conventional narratives of national progress and constitutional evolution is to overlook the remarkable consistency of the doctrine, which remains largely unchanged after more than a century. Though the nativism expressed in the Chinese Exclusion Act has long been repudiated, the expansive norm announced in the Chinese Exclusion *cases*—granting Congress almost absolute authority to restrict and deport immigrants—remains cemented into the foundations of contemporary immigration law.

Moreover, by comparing the Court's treatment of citizen-insiders to its treatment of foreigner-outsiders, Cox's account of the plenary power doctrine obscures the fundamental power it preserves—that is, the sovereign prerogative to determine who is *inside* and who is *outside* the juridical order, who the Constitution protects from sovereign power and who it leaves exposed to violence.[69] It is for this reason that Kevin Johnson suggests that the plenary doctrine appears as a "dark mirror": it gives us a glimpse of how the government might treat its citizens if it were *not* constrained by the Constitution.[70] While the Constitution is understood to protect citizen-insiders from the abuse of state power, the plenary power allows the state to exercise power over other-outsiders without juridical restraint. Thus, to compare the Court's treatment of citizen-insiders and foreigner-outsiders is to overlook the extraordinary power of the doctrine, the power to *differentiate* between the two—to define who is an insider or outsider, who can become a citizen and who cannot, who is protected by rights and who is rendered rightless.[71]

In June 2018, after the Supreme Court issued its decision in *Hawaii v. Trump* upholding the Muslim ban, Cox, joined by others, doubled down on his original position, insisting that the Court's opinion—granting the president extreme deference in his dealing with foreign nationals— marked a surprising "new twist" in the historical trajectory of the plenary power doctrine.[72] But, again, to regard the Court's approach to plenary power as a "departure from the past, rather than continuity," is to overlook the many ways in which the United States continues to wield its enormous power over noncitizen others. It is to overlook that Indigenous dispossession and imperial expansion are continuous, ongoing affairs. It is to overlook that the plenary power doctrine allows Congress to deny citizenship and withhold voting rights from the four million people living in its overseas "possessions" of Puerto Rico, Guam, and American Samoa and to detain "enemy combatants" in Guantánamo for decades.

The plenary power doctrine was formalized in the late nineteenth century, a high moment of both nationalism and expansionism, marked by the closing of the frontier, the raising of borders, and the acquisition of the country's first overseas colonies.[73] Though the doctrine received its most forceful articulation in the late-nineteenth-century immigration context, it found early expression in Marshall's Indian trilogy and had been harnessed and honed over more than a century of federal dealings with Indians.[74] In 1846, two decades after *Johnson v. M'Intosh*, the Court asserted that the federal government not only possessed legal title to Indian lands but also legal authority over Indian people. The occasion for the Court's ruling, *United States v. Rogers*, was a case involving the prosecution of William S. Rogers, a white man who had married a Cherokee woman and was living in Indian territory when he murdered his brother-in-law, another white man married to a Cherokee woman. Rogers asserted that, as an adopted Cherokee living in Indian territory, the United States had no jurisdiction over him. The Supreme Court dismissed his claim, asserting that Congress had absolute authority to regulate Indian tribes. Chief Justice Roger B. Taney, writing for the Court, rooted this power not in the language of the Constitution but in the customary practices of imperial sovereigns who "divided up and parceled out" the continent at the time of discovery.[75]

Much like Marshall, Taney placed the question of federal authority over Indians beyond justiciability: if "the propriety of exercising this power [is] now open to question, . . . it is a question for the law-making and political department of the government, and not for the judicial."[76] But Taney went further than Marshall in rewriting colonial history, asserting that Indians "have *never* been acknowledged or treated as independent nations," a claim belied by hundred of treaties. Taney insisted that *"from the very moment* the general government came into existence . . . , it has exercised its power over this unfortunate race," transforming a long and varied history of contestation, negotiation, and resistance into a *fait accompli*—over before it had even begun.[77] If Marshall lamented that the Court was powerless to prevent a tragedy from unfolding, Taney insisted that things had never been otherwise. Scholars of U.S. settler colonialism observe that Indians are often represented in historical narratives as always already extinct.[78] Imagining that Indians disappeared in some distant past absolves contemporary Americans of responsibility for fairly recent and ongoing acts of displacement.

Adam Cox's redemptive reading of the plenary power doctrine tracks familiar narratives of national progress, according to which the Constitution is reinterpreted to embrace an ever-widening diversity of peoples as equals. In his account, Chinese Exclusion and Jim Crow appear as the foreign and domestic versions of a turn-of-the-century racial formation. Just as racial segregation was abolished by the civil rights acts of the 1960s, the argument goes, the racial bars to immigration were abolished from our immigration system with the Immigration and Nationality Act of 1965.[79] But what this narrative fails to account for is that both U.S. settler imperialism and the plenary power doctrine have survived the civil rights era "largely unscathed," as Matthew Lindsay has written.[80] While the crude racism of the Chinese Exclusion Act is longer tolerated by the Court, as *Hawaii v. Trump* affirms, the legal architecture announced by the Court in *Chae Chan Ping* remains settled at the foundations of immigration law. Rather than read the Chinese Exclusion Act as a plot point along a familiar trajectory of racial redemption, we might instead situate the law along the trajectory that Byrd describes as "the transit of empire," or the United States' historical movement from settler colony to imperial nation.

In 1888, Chae Chan Ping challenged the Chinese Exclusion Act, arguing in part that the United States, by denying his entry, had violated rights guaranteed to him under an existing treaty between the United States and China. The Supreme Court acknowledged as much but held that Congress was not bound by the treaty. It went on to explain that Congress could not waive—by treaty or otherwise—its "exclusive and absolute" power to exclude and deport foreigners.[81] Neither would the Court subject Congress's actions to constitutional review: "That the government of the United States . . . can exclude aliens from its territory is a proposition which we do not think open to controversy. Jurisdiction over its own territory is to that extent an incident of every independent nation. It is a part of its independence. If it could not exclude aliens it would be to that extent subject to the control over another power."[82]

With its decision, the Court changed the course of immigration law in two ways. Before Congress enacted the Chinese Exclusion Act, the regulation and restriction of migration from China had been achieved by mutual agreement—by treaty. But in the *Chinese Exclusion cases*, the Court affirmed Congress's abrogation of its own commitments and its move toward a unilateral exercise of sovereign power. At the same time, the Court shifted the source of Congress's authority to regulate immigration from the Constitution's Commerce Clause to an extra-constitutional source: powers "inherent in sovereignty."[83] The plenary power doctrine, thus articulated, would allow the political branches to regulate immigration without constitutional limit or judicial constraint. Until the late nineteenth century, the Court recognized that Congress could exercise its expansive powers "inherent in sovereignty" in limited circumstances such as declaring war, making treaties, and regulating foreign commerce.[84] The Court justified its deference to Congress by adopting its characterization of Chinese immigration as an "invasion," furnishing the emergent plenary power doctrine with what has proven to be an especially durable rationale for immigrant exclusion: "national security."[85] Mae Ngai notes that the characterization of Chinese immigration as an invasion is doubly ironic in that English settlers colonized the northeastern United States under royal authority, whereas the Chinese who left for California in the late nineteenth century often did so in violation of laws restricting *emigration*.[86] Nonetheless, according to the plenary power doctrine, the powers of sovereignty once reserved for dealings with other—generally hostile—sovereign *powers* might be wielded against any foreign *individuals*, no matter how vulnerable.

In the late nineteenth century, the Supreme Court's treatment of racialized immigrants resembled its treatment of Indians during the same period.[87] Through most of the nineteenth century, Congress regulated its affairs with Indian tribes by treaty. But in 1871, Congress abruptly ended the practice of entering into new treaties with Indians, no longer recognizing Indian tribes as independent nations. Having seized most of their land and confining them to reservations, the United States no longer recognized Indians as sovereign nations. Instead, it would deal with tribes as "local dependent communities."[88] In 1887, under the terms of the Allotment Act, Congress began to seize and distribute tribal lands (which until then had been held communally) to individual Indians as private property owners.[89] "Surplus" land was sold to white settlers; funds raised by the sale were used to establish so-called Indian schools to which Indian children were sent, often against the will of their parents, to be "civilized" and prepared for industrial work and domestic labor. Despite resistance, tribes lost nearly 60 million acres of tribal territory during allotment, roughly 60 percent of their reserved lands.[90]

In *Lone Wolf v. Hitchcock*, a 1903 decision bearing striking resemblance to *Chae Chan Ping*, the Court rejected a tribal claim that Congress had violated rights established by treaty, explaining that Congress was not bound by its earlier treaty. In an extraordinary gesture, the Court added that "[p]lenary authority over the tribal relations of Indians has been exercised *from the beginning*, and the power has *always* been deemed a political one, not subject to be controlled by the judicial department of the government."[91] Again, by declining to restrain Congress in its dealing with others—aliens and Indians—the Court placed beyond its own judgment a relationship that stands outside the time of national progress and constitutional improvement, having "always" already been settled "from the beginning."

By the time of the Spanish–American War, in 1898, when the United States acquired its first overseas possessions, there was little question that Congress had inherent power to acquire and govern new territories. Through the nineteenth century, U.S. expansion followed a general pattern: new territories were subject to federal plenary power until they were able to establish their own elected governments and finally admitted as independent states within the federal system.[92] But unlike most territories acquired during the nineteenth century, overseas territories acquired after the Spanish–American War—the Philippines and Puerto Rico, in particular—were densely populated and by peoples considered racially inferior.[93] Imperialists and anti-imperialists on the mainland disagreed over the constitutionality and desirability of ruling over subject peoples in distinct colonies, but no one seemed to support the idea of granting statehood to overseas colonies or extending citizenship to their inhabitants.[94] At the conclusion of the war, President William McKinley executed a treaty with Spain that carefully avoided defining the status of the United States' new territories and subjects, leaving to legislators and judges the task of "reshaping the constitutional law of empire," as Sam Erman put it, as the United States entered the next phase of its imperial development.[95]

The question posed by overseas expansion, as it was often phrased, was whether the Constitution followed the flag—whether the Constitution limited the federal government's authority over acquired territories. Lawmakers drew on the history of federal Indian policy to fashion a mode of imperial governance in the overseas territories, according to which constitutional provisions and protections were suspended indefinitely. Addressing Congress, Senator Henry Cabot Lodge argued that the Supreme Court had laid the legal foundations for colonial rule over the Philippines with its early-nineteenth-century decisions extending federal authority over Indians as "domestic dependent nations," invoking Justice Marshall's tortured formulation in *Cherokee Nation v. Georgia*.[96] A similar argument was advanced by Abbott Lawrence Lowell, a Harvard law professor who proposed that the United States' overseas territories might occupy the sort of "third space" to which Indians and, later, Mexicans living in annexed territories, had been consigned—neither inside nor outside the United States but "so acquired as *not* to form a part of the United States."[97] In *Downes v. Bidwell*, a controversy involving the scope of Congress's authority over Puerto Rico, the Supreme Court adopted Lowell's "third view" of the constitutional question, characterizing Puerto Rico as neither foreign nor domestic but "foreign . . . in a domestic sense."[98]

In the *Insular Cases*, a series of roughly two dozen cases decided between 1901 and 1922, the Supreme Court innovated a framework for governing the country's overseas colonies, one that (purportedly) conformed to the pattern of expansion and incorporation established through the nineteenth century, while also granting Congress considerable flexibility in its dealing with its new territories.[99] According to this new "territorial incorporation" doctrine, the Constitution did not necessarily follow the flag; its provisions would not extend by their own force, *ex proprio vigore*, over the peoples and places over which the United States asserted control.[100] Instead, constitutional protections would be extended over territories that only had been formally "incorporated" by an act of Congress. In territories that had not been incorporated or granted statehood, only "fundamental" constitutional protections would apply. Accordingly, people living in Alaska Territory were guaranteed Sixth Amendment rights to a trial by jury in criminal cases, but people living in Puerto Rico were not. Alaska Territory, with its vast resources and sparse population, had been "incorporated" by treaty and legislation. But Congress had shown no interest in granting statehood to Puerto Rico.[101]

Calls for faith in constitutional redemption are bound up with the United States' founding mythology, the idea that, through the Declaration of Independence, the United States established a definitive break with imperial Europe to establish a new kind of republic, one uniquely founded on principles of freedom, equality, and democratic self-government. But in the *Insular Cases*, decided in the early twentieth century, the Court would continue to draw on its early Indian cases to reconcile constitutional republicanism with overseas colonial expansion. Addressing the "Philippine Question," Senator Albert Beveridge, an ardent imperialist, argued that the Constitution should not limit U.S. expansion. His view, shared by others at the time, was that the Constitution was only one expression of the essential capacity to govern shared by Anglo-Saxons. Arguing that Americans rather than Filipinos should govern Filipinos, Beveridge explained that the United States' imperial policy arose "not from necessity but from an irresistible impulse, from instinct, from racial and unwritten laws inherited from our forefathers."

This inherent capacity, which he described as "our institutional law," was "not established by the Constitution. Institutional law existed before the Constitution."[102] Instead, the right and capacity to govern were a racial inheritance. Beveridge, after retiring from the Senate, would go on to author a four-volume biography of John Marshall, still widely credited with cementing the chief justice's reputation.

As in earlier Indian and immigration cases, the Court articulated an expansive view of sovereign power, one that drew vaguely on established principles of international law rather than constitutional interpretation. Scholars have shown that, within the Anglo tradition, "international" law was largely reinvented over the course of the nineteenth century to serve the interests of the expanding British Empire.[103] At the height of the late nineteenth century, as the United States entered the world stage as an imperial power, the Court invoked these principles of international law to redefine both the scope of sovereign power and the limitations imposed by the Constitution. In *De Lima v. Bidwell*, one of the first *Insular Cases*, Justice Henry Brown acknowledged that the Constitution imposed certain limits on government authority, but not in a manner that would diminish its imperial power. As Brown explained, the Constitution will "serve and assist government, not destroy it."[104] The compromise between the Constitution and colonialism struck in the *Insular Cases*, Justice Brown explained, would "enable the United States . . . to move with strength and dignity and effect among the other nations of the earth to such purpose as it may undertake or to such destiny as it may be called."[105] In *Downes v. Bidwell*, Justice Brown was even more explicit about what was at stake in the *Insular Cases*, warning his colleagues that "a false step at this time might be fatal to the development of what Chief Justice Marshall called the American Empire."[106]

Race, Redemption, and the Colonial Remains

In a law review article published in 2011, Jamal Greene observed that a handful of constitutional decisions have become so infamous that their public repudiation has become almost a requirement for judicial confirmation. These decisions are subject to ritual condemnation not because they exemplify poor reasoning but because they have come to represent, as Greene writes, a set of "ethical propositions that we have collectively renounced."[107] These cases appear in law school casebooks and professional treatises not because they offer valuable lessons on what the law is but instead what it can no longer be and perhaps what it should become. *Johnson v. M'Intosh* appears on the long list of cases included in Greene's "anticanon," based on his survey of citational practice, and it is the only case involving Indian policy to make the list.[108] Greene's short list includes just four cases: *Dred Scott v. Sandford, Plessy v. Ferguson, Lochner v. New York*, and *Korematsu v. United States*. With the exception of *Lochner*, the anticanon consists primarily of cases representing the legacy of institutionalized slavery, specifically the persistence of racial ordering. As a series, *Dred Scott, Plessy*, and *Korematsu* project an arc of continuous national progress, measured as the embrace of a growing diversity of racial outsiders as civic equals.

But this narrative, of course, leaves much out. Among its many shortcomings, as scholars of Indigenous studies have argued, the prevailing narrative further naturalizes settler colonialism as the founding and ongoing condition for constitutional republicanism, civil rights, and multicultural inclusion.[109] As racial inclusion becomes the main plot line in the national drama, settler colonialism recedes into the background. As Mark Rifkin has written, historical dramas often "treat the space of the United States as a given in which to set the unfolding of events . . . as something of an atemporal container for the occurrences, movements . . . and pulsations of history" rather than the product of ongoing historical violence and contestation.[110] Moreover, indigenous scholars and activists insist, the principles of nondiscrimination and inclusion that tend to define prevailing narratives of racial progress are inadequate to understanding the particularity of indigenous grievances—dispossession and denial of sovereignty.[111]

While this basic narrative leaves the legal and ideological foundations of settler imperialism unexamined, narratives of redemption-as-inclusion tend to affirm rather than challenge collective faith in the perfectibility of our political institutions. James Young, in his study of efforts to memorialize past wrongs, observes an irony: monuments and rituals intended to disrupt triumphant narratives about a nation's destiny have a way of becoming absorbed in those same narratives.[112] Within legal discourse, as within popular memory, the history of slavery—often truncated to the final struggle to *abolish* slavery—succumbs to this irony. Cases such as *Dred Scott* and *Plessy* serve less as reminders of the epistemic conventions that allow Americans to reconcile, for instance, slavery and its afterlife with the constitutional ideals of freedom and equality than they do as assurances of just how far we have come. Ritual condemnation of these cases tends to affirm, to borrow Young's words, "the righteousness of a nation's birth, even its divine election."[113] But as I want to suggest here, the narrative of racial progress traced by the movement from abolition to civil rights obscures the relative stasis of colonial relations.

In *Dred Scott v. Sandford*, notoriously, the Supreme Court declined to hear a lawsuit brought by a black man challenging his enslavement, holding that black Americans, whether free or enslaved, were not citizens of the United States. As Chief Justice Taney explained, the framers of the Constitution never intended for black Americans to become citizens: "[T]he line of division which the Constitution has drawn between the citizen race, who formed and held the Government, and the African race, which they held in subjection," was intended to remain a "perpetual and impassible barrier."[114] Dred Scott had argued that he and his family had become free after living in the free state of Illinois and in Wisconsin Territory. While denying Dred Scott standing to sue, the Court held that provisions of the Missouri Compromise, which banned slavery in the Northern territories, were unconstitutional because they deprived white Americans of their Fifth Amendment rights to private property.

Although Taney's reputation has sometimes been the subject of scholarly rehabilitation, his association with *Dred Scott*, which also pushed the country toward the Civil War, has rendered him a singularly villainous figure in popular memory.[115] After Taney's death in 1864, congressmen resisted the installation of the Chief Justice's bust in the Capitol building, where the busts of his predecessors were displayed. Senator Charles Sumner warned his colleagues that future Americans would look unkindly upon the author of the *Dred Scott* opinion, anticipating that Taney would be "hooted down the page of history. Judgment is beginning now; and an emancipated country will fasten upon him the stigma which he deserves. He had administered justice wickedly, had degraded the judiciary, and degraded the age."[116] Sumner's words illustrate the way collective redemption is imagined to begin with public judgment and repudiation—the fastening of "stigma." By disavowing *Dred Scott*, we put behind us the "degraded" age of institutional slavery and emerge a freer, "emancipated country." Just the repudiation of *Dred Scott* cleaves past from present; it reaffirms national unity over division. The disavowal of a case such as *Dred Scott* serves to renew a shared faith in national progress and in the essential goodness of our founding institutions.

But redemptive rituals often mask ongoing conflict and dissent. To pillory Justice Taney is to pardon the Constitution while failing to question the social, political, and legal institutions that broadly reflected his assertion that citizenship was a privilege reserved for white people. To denounce the formal institution of slavery without dismantling the material and ideological structures that supported and were supported by it is to render abolition incomplete. And to regard slavery as "the original sin in the New World garden," as one constitutional scholar put it, is to leave unexamined the crime in claiming the garden.[117] The national identity that is reaffirmed by the repudiation of *Dred Scott* remains an unreconstructed settler identity, one that would propel the nation to continue its expansion and with renewed intensity after the Civil War.

Much of *Dred Scott* was effectively overruled by the Thirteenth and Fourteenth Amendments, which abolished slavery (Thirteenth) and extended the formal rights and privileges of citizenship to black Americans (Fourteenth). But much of *Dred Scott* would also survive and gain new relevance as the United States continued to expand. As Sanford Levinson has suggested, the "meta-issue" in *Dred Scott* was "whether Congress possesses truly 'plenary,' that is, unconstrained power in regard to the territories of the United States. No issue was more relevant at the turn of the twentieth century" when the United States claimed control over what is now the continental United States and acquired its first overseas territories.[118] As Levinson demonstrates, *Dred Scott* would become infamous for its accommodation of slavery yet remain relevant for its treatment of federal authority in newly acquired territories. As the United States continued to expand westward and overseas, the case was regularly cited as significant precedent.[119]

Dred Scott's notoriety in the public imagination is perhaps rivaled only by *Plessy v. Ferguson*, the 1896 case in which the Supreme Court upheld a Louisiana law requiring train conductors to segregate black and white passengers. Decided almost three decades after the passage of the Fourteenth Amendment, the Court all but nullified the amendment's promise by finding that racial segregation did not violate its guarantee of equal protection. *Plessy* was not the only case in which the Court maintained laws of segregation during the Jim Crow era, but its special notoriety owes as much to the hollow ring of the "separate-but-equal" doctrine embraced by the majority as it does to the triumphant language of Justice Harlan's famous dissent, in which he announced that "our Constitution is colorblind."[120] Harlan's statement projected an alternative to the prevailing racial regime, one that would eventually be embraced by the Court and a critical majority of white Americans. The statement itself has become canonical, perhaps, for its temporal construction, casting colorblindness as a timeless ideal.[121] Harlan's assertion is plainly belied by histories of conquest, slavery, and segregation, but his present-tense construction places the Constitution outside of those histories, as if representing an immutable proposition that remains essentially true, if not yet fully realized. But that same present-tense construction renders colorblindness a static endpoint in the movement toward freedom and equality.

Colorblindness, as a constitutional ideal, has generated considerable critique, much of it asserting that, insofar as colorblindness misidentifies race-consciousness as the source of racial inequality, it leaves structural racism unexamined and unavailable for redress.[122] But for my purposes here, I want to bring into focus a slightly different set of exclusions constitutive of Harlan's articulation of the ideal. As scholars have observed, the constitutional colorblindness that Harlan projects does not embrace Asians or Asian Americans.[123] In his dissent, Harlan contrasts the equal treatment of Chinese passengers from the discriminatory treatment of black passengers under the Louisiana law as if to underscore its arbitrariness:

> There is a race so different from our own that we do not permit those belonging to it to become citizens of the United States. Persons belonging to it are, with few exceptions, absolutely excluded from our country. I allude to the Chinese race. But, by the statute in question, a Chinaman can ride in the same passenger coach with white citizens of the United States,

while citizens of the black race in Louisiana, many of whom, perhaps, risked their lives for the preservation of the Union . . . are yet declared to be criminals, liable to imprisonment, if they ride in a public coach occupied by citizens of the white race.[124]

As his reference to the Civil War suggests, Harlan is more concerned with eliminating the stain of slavery from American history and reaffirming national unity than he is with dismantling the ideological or material foundations of white supremacy. The colonial projects of territorial expansion and economic growth that simultaneously conditioned Asian migration and Indian removal in the wake of emancipation are, again, left unexamined.[125]

Harlan's vision is one of establishing formal equality among American *citizens*, regardless of race. But the category of citizenship, for Harlan, might be defined to exclude racialized newcomers—as it was for much of the twentieth century.[126] Neither is colorblind constitutionalism inconsistent with white supremacy. Instead, in Harlan's dissent, colorblind constitutionalism is offered as a noble reclamation of white supremacy, an affirmation of the universal quality of American legal institutions:

> The white race deems itself to be the dominant race in this country. And so it is in prestige, in achievements, in education, in wealth and in power. So, I doubt not, it will continue to be for all time if it remains true to its great heritage and holds fast to the principles of constitutional liberty. But in view of the Constitution, in the eye of the law, there is in this country no superior, dominant, ruling class of citizens. There is no caste here. Our Constitution is color-blind, and neither knows nor tolerates classes among citizens. In respect of civil rights, all citizens are equal before the law. The humblest is the peer of the most powerful.[127]

In language that resonates with Alfred Beveridge's claims about the ethno-judicial superiority of white Americans, Harlan casts white supremacy in terms of color blind constitutionalism, formal equality, and civic inclusion.

Harlan anticipated that the Court's decision in *Plessy* would "in time, prove to be quite as pernicious as the decision made by this tribunal in the Dred Scott Case."[128] He was vindicated six decades later when the

Court struck down racial segregation in public schooling in *Brown v. Board of Education*, perhaps "the most revered opinion in the Court's history," the "crown jewel" of the American legal system.[129] Greene observes that, although *Dred Scott* was controversial in its own time, it was not until the civil rights era that it became, along with *Plessy*, the historical landmark that it is now. *Dred Scott*, much like *Plessy*, was largely ignored by treatise and casebook authors; and the Court rarely cited either unfavorably. *Dred Scott* was sometimes invoked as an object lesson in constitutional avoidance, the doctrine that encourages courts to resolve legal questions in nonconstitutional terms whenever possible. But it did not come to represent the shameful failure of the judiciary to protect the rights of black citizens until the civil rights era.[130]

Similarly, before *Brown v. Board of Education*, there was no consensus that *Plessy* had been wrongly decided or was inconsistent with the intended meaning of the Fourteenth Amendment's Equal Protection Clause. To the contrary, to achieve unanimity, Chief Justice Earl Warren had to make clear in his opinion that the Court's reversal was "a new law for a new day," compelled not by the language of the Fourteenth Amendment but by a new appreciation of the harm caused by racial segregation, particularly in education.[131] As the Warren Court extended the holding in *Brown* to gradually disestablish segregation in other areas of national life, justices made routine references to both *Dred Scott* and *Plessy*, transforming public understanding of both cases, turning them into counterprecedents to reshape the Court's equality jurisprudence under the Fourteenth Amendment.[132]

Of the four cases considered most infamous in the constitutional canon, Greene notes, *Korematsu v. United States*, decided in 1944, has followed the most uneven trajectory.[133] It has been recognized time and again as authoritative precedent, notwithstanding its association with one of the ugliest episodes in twentieth-century American history— the forced removal and mass internment of more than 100,000 Japanese men, women, and children. *Korematsu* had never been formally repudiated until 2018, in *Trump v. Hawaii*, when the Court upheld an executive order denying entry to individuals traveling from certain Muslim-majority countries. President Trump and others in his administration referred to various iterations of the order as a "Muslim ban." Critics of the Muslim ban compared it to the notorious Executive Order

No. 9066 authorizing Japanese internment. Trump himself defended his order by alluding to *Korematsu*, assuring "what I'm doing is no different than FDR."[134] In her dissent from the decision in *Trump v. Hawaii*, Justice Sonia Sotomayer enumerated the many "stark parallels" between the majority's reasoning and the decision in *Korematsu*.[135] Compelled to address those comparisons, Chief Justice John Roberts concluded his opinion by insisting that "[w]hatever rhetorical advantage the dissent may see in [invoking the case,] *Korematsu* has nothing to do with this case. . . . *Korematsu* was gravely wrong the day it was decided, has been overruled in the court of history, and 'has no place in law under the Constitution.'"[136]

Fred Korematsu was arrested for violating a military order that forcibly removed "all persons of Japanese ancestry, alien and non-alien," from the western states and relocated them in internment camps.[137] The commanding general who issued the order offered no evidence of spying or subversion on the part of any Japanese American but insisted on the necessity of the order by appealing to racialized assumptions of "disloyalty," characterizing the Japanese as "subversive," as belonging to "an enemy race" whose "racial strains are undiluted."[138] The majority opened its opinion by announcing boldly that "all legal restrictions which curtail the civil rights of a single racial group are immediately suspect" and subject to "the most rigid scrutiny."[139] But after announcing this standard, the majority declined to apply it, explaining that "pressing public necessity may sometimes justify the existence of such exceptions." Acknowledging that the military order was supported by no direct evidence of necessity, the Court nonetheless deferred entirely "to the judgment of military authorities and Congress" in its defense of national security.[140]

Greene attributes the mixed treatment of *Korematsu* to an ambivalence on the part of the Warren Court justices. The same justices who unanimously overturned *Plessy*, proclaiming to inaugurate "a new law for a new day," consistently declined to invoke *Korematsu* in the way they invoked *Dred Scott* or *Plessy*, that is to say, as an intolerable form of racial discrimination. Yet they often cited the decision ("unselfconsciously," as Greene observes) for its triumphant announcement that racial classifications are subject to heightened scrutiny.[141] Greene and others suspect that the Warren Court's reluctance to denounce *Korematsu* stems from the fact that at least three of its Justices were implicated directly in the decision: Justice Hugo Black authored the majority opinion in *Korematsu*; Justice William Douglas joined the majority; and Chief Justice Earl Warren, who had been elected to the position of attorney general of California before World War II, had been an active proponent of Japanese internment.[142]

Here, I want to offer another hypothesis, one that returns us to the central theme of this essay: While the race jurisprudence of the Warren Court reflects an emerging consensus about what the federal government owes its citizen-insiders—formal equality without distinction of race—there is no such consensus about what the federal government owes noncitizen-outsiders. Leaders of the racial justice movement in the mid–twentieth century often compared the United States' treatment of racialized minorities at home to its treatment of racialized peoples abroad—sometimes using the language of "internal colonialism" to situate racial discrimination within a wider and still unfolding history of Western imperialism.[143] But the cases and legislation that have come to define the civil rights era have enshrined as a national ideal, not decolonization, but race-neutrality and nondiscrimination. The civil rights era brought an end to the most offensive expressions of racial discrimination, but it did not address the ongoing fact of settler colonialism or the intensification of U.S. imperialism. Neither did it challenge the understanding—forged in the experience of colonial conquest and imperial expansion—that the Constitution allows the federal government to exercise nearly unlimited power over noncitizen others, both abroad as well as at home.

To the contrary, only a year after *Brown*, the Warren Court would reaffirm the foundations of settler colonialism and Indian dispossession, making explicit and lengthy reference to "the great case of *Johnson v. McIntosh*."[144] In *Tee-Hit-Ton Indians v. the United States*, members of the Tlingit people sought compensation under the Fifth Amendment for timber taken from their lands by private actors granted permission by the federal government. The Tlingit argued that the trespass violated rights previously recognized by the federal government, but the Court's majority maintained that, with respect to Indians, "the power of Congress . . . is supreme."[145] Echoing language in *Chae Chan Ping* and *Lone Wolf*, the Court asserted that Congress cannot waive its plenary authority over Indians. Insofar as Americans, through their legislature, have shown "compassion for the descendants of those Indians who were deprived of their homes and hunting grounds by the drive of civilization," Americans have done so "as a matter of grace, not because of legal liability."[146] While characterizing Americans as "generous" in their efforts "to allow tribes to recover for wrongs," the Court characterized Indians as unaccountably ungrateful though they had been invited to "share the benefits of our society as citizens of this Nation"—failing to recognize, of course, that the wrong of colonial displacement cannot be righted by settler citizenship.

Korematsu's splintered trajectory reflects disagreement about *which* wrong among the multiplicity of wrongs represented in the case renders the decision irreconcilable with shared constitutional commitments. In other words, insofar as *Korematsu* is now held in infamy, it is infamous for some reasons but not others. The justices who dissented from the decision raised at least three distinct objections to Korematsu's arrest: First, the order that Korematsu violated amounted to obvious and inexcusable "racial discrimination"; second, because roughly a third of those forcibly relocated were "born on our soil," the order violated the constitutional rights of American *citizens*; and third, because the military's justifications for relocating *all* Japanese residents were so plainly false, the Court had abandoned its duty by giving complete deference to the military.[147]

In *Trump v. Hawaii*, Chief Justice Roberts, expressing the view of the Court's majority, makes very clear that *Korematsu* was wrong for the first two reasons but not the third: *Korematsu* was wrong because it sanctioned the racial profiling and imprisonment of American citizens, but not because it granted excessive deference to the military. Roberts's very careful construction of the ruling in *Korematsu* is revealing. As he writes: "[T]he forcible relocation of *U.S. citizens* to concentration camps, *solely and explicitly on the basis of race*, is objectively unlawful and outside the scope of Presidential authority."[148] Roberts contrasts Japanese internment from the Muslim ban by characterizing the latter as "a *facially neutral* policy denying certain *foreign nationals* the privilege of admission," one well within the authority of the executive branch.[149] Though the Trump administration was widely criticized for barely recasting its promised "Muslim ban" in "vague words of national security," Roberts maintained that the president was owed deference.[150] As long as the president offered any "legitimate grounding in national security, quite apart from any religious hostility, we must accept that independent justification."[151] For critics of the decision, the Court's repudiation of *Korematsu* was belied by the repetition of its essential error: declining to restrain the excesses of sovereign power as exercised against designated outsiders in the name of national security. As Hiroshi Motomura remarked: "[I]f the majority really wanted to bury *Korematsu*, they would have struck down the travel ban."[152]

Roberts's highly qualified repudiation of *Korematsu* leaves open a number of unsettling possibilities. If it was wrong to force "U.S. citizens" into "concentration camps," in Roberts's words, would it be wrong to force noncitizens into concentration camps? If it was wrong to force people into concentration camps "solely and explicitly" on the basis of race, would it be wrong to do so solely but not explicitly on the basis of race? Not quite put to rest, the ghost of *Korematsu* would return to haunt the Court as an emboldened executive branch sought to wield its tremendous authority to confine asylum-seekers to tent cities at the border, to separate immigrant children from their parents, and to detain children in what critics have called "concentration camps."

Within a year of the Court's declaring that *Korematsu* had been "overruled in the court of history," the Trump administration announced its plan to open a detention center at Fort Sill, a military base in Oklahoma where 700 Japanese Americans had been interned during World War II.[153] Seventy years before that, it had been the site of an Indian boarding school and a prisoner of war camp for Apaches resisting relocation. The fort was opened in 1869 to house U.S. soldiers fighting Indians.[154] The site represents the relative stillness of sovereign time, or a power that stands outside the time of national progress. In June 2019, a group of Japanese survivors of internment gathered at Fort Sill to protest the planned detention of 1,200 children. A seventy-five-year-old activist and scholar, Satsuki Ina, holding an enlarged photograph of herself as a child at the camp, urged the United States, simply, to "stop repeating history."[155]

* * *

What is at stake in refocusing our attention if refocusing also means turning away from the narrative of racial progress, progress measured by the historic movement from *Dred Scott* to *Brown v. Board of Education*?

The cases that constitute the anticanon provide us with moral orientation and a sense of direction, but its coordinates are limited and few.
The emphasis these few cases place on temporal development and the
longing they attach to historical transcendence obscure the material
foundations—the very ground—on which the constitutional project
stakes its claim. Writing in a different context, Sarah Ahmed asks, "[W]
hat does it mean to be oriented? How do we begin to know or to feel
where we are or where we are going, but lining ourselves up with the
features of the grounds we inhabit, the sky that surrounds, or the
imaginary lines that cut through the map?"[156] Ahmed's references to
our relationship to the grounds we inhabit and the lines on the map
invite us to reflect on the ways in which colonial histories consciously
and unconsciously affect our movement through the world. We might
also recognize that shared points of reference orient our collective
understanding of where we are heading. The constitutional canon and
anticanon point us in a particular direction—to the exclusion of others.
As Ahmed writes, "[T]he direction we take excludes things for us, before
we even get there. . . . Depending on which way one turns, different
worlds might come into view."[157]

NOTES

1 Jack Balkin, *Constitutional Redemption: Political Faith in an Unjust World* (London: Harvard University Press, 2011), 2.

2 Ibid.

3 Ibid., 5–6.

4 Ibid.; Sanford Levinson, *Constitutional Faith* (Princeton: Princeton University
Press, 1988), 4.

5 *See, e.g.,* J. M. Balkin and Sanford Levinson, "The Canons of Constitutional Law,"
Harvard Law Review 111, no. 4 (1998): 964–1022; Robert W. Gordon, "Foreword:
The Arrival of Critical Historicism," *Stanford Law Review* 49, no. 5 (1997): 1023–29;
Mark A. Graber, "Redeeming and Living With Evil," *Maryland Law Review* 71, no.
4 (2012): 1073–97; Ariela Gross, "The Constitution of History and Memory," in *Com-
panion to Law and the Humanities,* ed. Austin Sarat, Catherine Frank, and Mathew
Anderson (Cambridge, MA: Cambridge University Press, 2010), 416–52; Ariela
Gross, "When is the Time of Slavery? The History of Slavery in Contemporary Le-
gal and Political Argument," *California Law Review* 96, no. 1 (2008): 283–321; Amy
Kapczynski, "Historicism, Progress, and the Redemptive Constitution," *Cardozo
Law Review* 26, no. 3 (2005): 1041–1117; Richard Primus, "Canon, Anti-Canon, and
Judicial Dissent," *Duke University Law Journal* 48, no. 2 (1998): 243–303; Norman W.
Spaulding, "Constitution as Counter Monument: Federalism, Reconstruction, and

the Problem of Collective Memory," *Columbia Law Review* 103, no. 8 (2003): 1992–2051. Seth Davis and Aziz Rana have powerfully intervened in the redemptive discourse by focusing on the role that colonialism has played in shaping constitutional democracy in the United States. Seth Davis, "American Colonialism and Constitutional Redemption," *California Law Review* 105, no. 6 (2017): 1751–1806; Aziz Rana, "Colonialism and Constitutional Memory," *UC Irvine Law Review* 5 (2015): 263–88. Though I do not address them here, a number of feminist legal scholars have also considered the role that patriarchy and gendered exclusion have played in constituting modern liberalism. A few well-known examples include Carole Pateman, *The Sexual Contract* (Palo Alto: Stanford University Press, 1988); Martha A. Fineman, "The Vulnerable Subject: Anchoring Equality in the Human Condition," *Yale Journal of Law and Feminism* 20, no.1 (2008): 1–23, Martha C. Nussbaum, *Sex and Social Justice* (Oxford: Oxford University Press, 1999).

6 Robert Gordon, "Critical Legal Histories," *Stanford Law Review* 36 (1984): 57–125; Gross, "The Constitution of History," 445–52.

7 Kapczynski, "Historicism, Progress," 1102 (citing Walter Benjamin, "Theses on the Philosophy of History," in *Illuminations*, ed. Hannah Arendt; trans. Harry Zohn (New York: Harcourt Brace Jovanovich, 1955), 253–64, 257). Norman Spaulding advances a similar view when he recommends that we abandon traditional "monumentalist" approaches to the Constitution, given their "didactic, demagogic, and amnesiac liabilities," in favor of a more experimental "counter-memorial" approach, which would force us to foreground and confront constitutional failures. Spaulding, "Constitution as Counter Monument," 2000.

8 Ibid. For this reason, Sanford Levinson, also a leading theorist of constitutional redemptive constitutionalism, claims that he no longer teaches the "great case" of *Marbury v. Madison* in his introductory constitutional law classes, focusing instead on what he considers the more revealing history of chattel slavery. Sanford Levinson, "Why I Do Not Teach Marbury (Except to Eastern Europeans) and Why You Shouldn't Either," *Wake Forest Law Review* 38 (2003: 553.

9 The loss of faith in constitutional redemption is perhaps best reflected in the fact the black power movement gained momentum not before but after *Brown* and the passage of landmark civil rights legislation. The Black Panther Party, identifying black Americans in the United States with colonized peoples in Asia and Africa, called for a dismantling of colonial institutions and a re-founding of the nation, beginning with the adoption of a new constitution. At the Revolutionary People's Convention, Huey Newton explained that "black people and oppressed people in general have lost faith . . . in the very structure of the American Government (that is, the Constitution, its legal foundation). This loss of faith is based upon the overwhelming evidence that this government will not live according to that Constitution because the Constitution is not designed for its people." Rana, "Colonialism and Constitutional Memory," 284–85 (citing Huey Newton), at 381. In recent years, a growing number of scholars identify themselves with a tradition of "afropessimism," which, in Frank Wilderson's stark expression, recognizes modern life

to be conditioned on antiblack violence. Frank B. Wilderson III, "Afro-Pessimism and the End of Redemption," Humanitiesfutures.org (2015). A few examples of afro-pessimism in various disciplines include Saidiya Hartman, *Scenes of Subjection: Terror, Slavery, and Self-Making in Nineteenth-Century America* (Oxford: Oxford University Press, 1997); Jamal Greene, "Originalism's Race Problem," *Denver University Law Review* 88, no. 3 (2011) 517–22; Achillle Mbembe, "Necropolitics," *Public Culture* 15, no. 1 (2003): 11–40; Charles W. Mills, *The Racial Contract* (Ithaca: Cornell University Press, 1997); Jared Sexton, "Unbearable Blackness," *Cultural Critique*, 90 (2015): 159–78.

10 Balkin, *Constitutional Redemption*, 110–23.

11 Justice Marshall declared that "[w]hile the Union survived the Civil War, the Constitution did not." Slavery was ended by a civil war, not the Constitution. He and others have argued that the Reconstruction Amendments now assume greater authority, insofar as they represent the aspirations of a more inclusive "we the people" and project a more compelling vision of the United States' future. Thurgood Marshall, "Commentary: Reflections on the Bicentennial of the United States Constitution," *Harvard Law Review* 101, no. 1 (1987).

12 Laurence Tribe, "Bicentennial Blues: To Praise the Constitution or to Bury It?" *American University Law Review* 37: 3. (1987).

13 Ibid.

14 See Guyora Binder, "The Slavery of Emancipation," *Cardozo Law Review* 17, no. 6 (1996): 2063–2102.

15 Amy L. Brandzel, *Against Citizenship: The Violence of the Normative* (Urbana: University of Illinois Press, 2016), 9; Audra Simpson, *Mohawk Interruptus: Political Life Across the Borders of Settler States* (Durham: Duke University Press, 2014), 7. In the late nineteenth century, after Congress determined that it would no longer engage in treaty-making with Indians, thus withholding recognition of Indian sovereignty, assimilation and education were embraced as explicit strategies for native elimination—"kill the Indian, and save the man," in Richard Henry Pratt's famous formulation. Richard Henry Pratt, "The Advantages of Mingling Indians with Whites," in *Official Report of the Nineteenth Annual Conference of Charities and Correction* (Boston: Press of Geo. H. Ellis, 1892), 46.

16 Joanne Barker, "For Whom Sovereignty Matters," in *Sovereignty Matters: Locations of Contestation and Possibility in Indigenous Struggles for Self-Determination*, ed. Joanne Barker (Lincoln: University of Nebraska Press, 2005), 14.

17 Jodi A. Byrd, *The Transit of Empire: Indigenous Critiques of Colonialism* (Minneapolis: University of Minnesota Press, 2011), xxiii–iv.

18 Ibid. Aziz Rana uses the enormously useful phrase "settler empire" to refer to the constitutional and political structures of settler colonialism that have allowed the United States to guarantee freedom, equality, and self-government to certain groups while continuously expanding its power over others, territorially and otherwise. Aziz Rana, *The Two Faces of American Freedom* (Cambridge, MA: Harvard University Press, 2010), 3, 12–13.

19 Rana, "Colonialism and Constitutional Memory," 266, 280; Byrd, *The Transit of Empire*, xx.

20 Johnson v. M'Intosh, 21 U.S. 543, 587 (1823).

21 Ibid., 588.

22 Though perhaps few Americans are familiar with *Johnson v. M'Intosh* and its legacy, a growing number of scholars have begun to recognize the foundational role that the case—and Federal Indian law generally—has played in shaping our major legal institutions. See T. Alexander Aleinikoff, *Semblances of Sovereignty: The Constitution, the State, and American Citizenship* (Cambridge, MA: Harvard University Press, 2002); Maggie Blackhawk, "Federal Indian Law as Paradigm Within Public Law," *Harvard Law Review* 132, no. 7 (2019); Philip P. Frickey, "Marshalling Past and Present: Colonialism, Constitutionalism, and Interpretation in Federal Indian Law," *Harvard Law Review* 107, no. 2 (1993); Jedediah Purdy, "Property and Empire: The Law of Imperialism in *Johnson v. M'Intosh*," *George Washington Law Review* 75, no. 2 (2007); Ezra Rosser, "Assumptions Regarding Indians and Judicial Humility: Thoughts From a Property-Law Lens," *Court Review* 45, no. 40 (2017): 40–46; Natsu Taylor Saito, *Settler Colonialism, Race, and the Law: Why Structural Racism Persists* (New York: New York University Press, 2020); Joseph William Singer, "Well-Settled? The Increasing Weight of History in American Indian Land Claims," *Georgia Law Review* 28 (1994): 481.

23 Justin Mueller, "Temporality, Sovereignty, and Imperialism: When Is Imperialism?", *Politics* 36, no.4 (2016): 428–40.

24 Lindsay Gordon Robertson, *Conquest by Law: How the Discovery of America Dispossessed Indigenous Peoples of their Lands* (Oxford: Oxford University Press, 2007), 5.

25 William D. Wallace, "Book Review: Lindsay G. Robertson, *Conquest by Law: How the Discovery of America Dispossessed Indigenous Peoples of their Lands*," *American Indian Law Review* 29, no. 2 (2005): 447.

26 Harlow Giles Unger, *John Marshall: The Chief Justice Who Saved the Nation* (Boston: Da Capa Press, 2014), 10–13.

27 Richard Brookhiser, *John Marshall: The Man Who Made the Supreme Court* (New York: Basic Books, 2018): 144; Martin v. Hunter's Lessee, 14 U.S. 304 (1816).

28 Royal Proclamation of 1763.

29 Greg Grandin, *The End of the Myth: From the Frontier to the Border Wall in the Mind of America* (New York: Metropolitan Books, 2019), 20.

30 Ibid.

31 Ibid. Eric Kades suggests that the Marshall court perhaps recognized the economic efficiency of creating a monopsony regime within a sovereign power which exercised an exclusive right to purchase lands, limiting competition and keeping prices low. Eric Kades, "The Dark Side of Efficiency: *Johnson v. M'Intosh* and the Expropriation of American Indian Lands," 148 *University of Pennsylvania Law Review* (2000): 1065–1190.

32 Grandin, *End of the Myth*, 23.

33 Ibid.
34 Jack M. Sosin, "The Yorke-Camden Opinion and American Land Speculators," *Pennsylvania Magazine of History and Biography* 85, no. 1 (1961): 38, 38–9.
35 Robertson, *Conquest by Law*, 14–23; Eric Kades, "History and Interpretation of the Great Case of Johnson v. M'Intosh," *Law and History Review* 19, no. 1 (2001): 67, 69.
36 Robertson, *Conquest by Law*, 50–53.
37 Johnson v. M'Intosh, 572.
38 Ibid., 573.
39 Frickey, "Marshalling Past," 381, 387.
40 Johnson v. M'Intosh, 589–90.
41 Ibid., 584.
42 Ibid.
43 Ibid., 573.
44 Ibid., 589.
45 Barker, "For Whom Sovereignty Matters," 7.
46 Johnson v. M'Intosh, 591 (emphasis added).
47 Marbury v. Madison, 5 U.S. 137, 177 (1803).
48 Ibid., 588.
49 Frickey, "Marshalling the Past," 389 (emphasis added).
50 Johnson v. M'Intosh, 590 (emphasis added).
51 See, for instance, Jean M. O'Brien, *Firsting and Lasting: Writing Indians Out of Existence in New England* (Minneapolis: University of Minnesota Press, 2010); Kevin Bruyneel, *The Third Space of Sovereignty: The Postcolonial Politics of U.S.-Indigenous Relations* (Minneapolis: University of Minnesota Press, 2007); Mark Rifkin, *Beyond Settler Time: Temporal Sovereignty and Indigenous Self-Determination* (Durham: Duke University Press, 2017).
52 See Aileen Moreton-Robinson, *The White Possessive: Property, Power, and Indigenous Sovereignty* (Minneapolis: Minnesota University Press, 2015).
53 Jean Edward Smith, *John Marshall: Definer of a Nation* (New York: Henry Holt & Company, 1996).
54 See, for example, Jack Balkin, "The Use that the Future Makes of the Past: John Marshall's Greatness and Its Lessons for Today's Supreme Court Justices," *William and Mary Law Review* 43 (2002): 1321; Albert J. Beveridge, *The Life of John Marshall* (vols. 1–4) (Boston: Houghton Mifflin Co., 1919); Brookhiser, *John Marshall*; Smith, *John Marshall*. Unger, *John Marshall*.
55 Robertson, *Conquest by Law*, xiii.
56 Ibid., 77–93. In short, by transforming the sovereign *right of preemption* (exclusive right to purchase from Indians) under the Proclamation of 1783 into sovereign *title*, acquired by "discovery," *Johnson v. M'Intosh* would allow Virginia, as a successor in sovereignty, to make good on land warrants issued to revolutionary militia.
57 Ibid.

58 Cherokee Nation v. Georgia, 30 U.S. (5 Pet.) 1, 2.
59 See, for example, Blackhawk, "Federal Indian Law as Paradigm"; Peter d'Errico, "John Marshall: Indian Lover?," *Journal of the West* 39, no. 3 (2000): 19–30; Walter R. Echo-Hawk, *In the Courts of the Conqueror: The Ten Worst Indian Law Cases Ever Decided* (Golden, CO: Fulcrum Publishing, 2010); Robinson, *The White Possessive*.
60 Davis, "American Colonialism," 1757–59.
61 Balkin, "The Use that the Future Makes," 1326.
62 Ibid., 1337 (citing McCulloch v. Maryland, 17 U.S. 316, 408 (1819)).
63 Ibid.
64 Peter J. Spiro, "Trump's Anti-Muslim Plan Is Awful. And Constitutional," *New York Times*, December 8, 2015.
65 Fong Yue Ting v. United States, 149 U.S. 698, 713 (1893).
66 Chae Chan Ping v. United States, 130 U.S. 581, 603–04 (1889); Nishimura Eiku v. United States, 142 U.S. 651, 662 (1892).
67 Adam Cox, "Why a Muslim Ban is Likely to Be Held Unconstitutional: The Myth of Unconstrained Immigration Power," Justsecurity.org, January 30, 2017, www.justsecurity.org.
68 Ibid.
69 Susan Bibler Coutin, Justin Richland, and Veronique Fortin, "Routine Exceptionality: The Plenary Power Doctrine, Immigrants, and the Indigenous Under U.S. Law," *UC Irvine Law Review* 4 (2014): 97–120, 99.
70 Kevin R. Johnson, "Race, the Immigration Laws, and Domestic Race Relations: A 'Magic Mirror' into the Heart of Darkness," *Indiana Law Journal* 73, no. 4 (1998): 116.
71 Rana, "Colonialism and Constitutional Memory," 266; Giorgio Agamben, *Homo Sacer: Sovereign Power and Bare Life* (Stanford: Stanford University Press, 1995), 23–24; Hannah Arendt, *The Origins of Totalitarianism* (New York: Harcourt Brace, 1951), 267–304.
72 Adam Cox, Ryan Goodman, and Christina Rodríguez, "The Radical Supreme Court Travel Ban Opinion—But Why It Might Not Apply to Other Immigrants' Rights Cases," Justsecurity.org, June 27, 2018, www.justsecurity.org.
73 Aleinikoff, *Semblances of Sovereignty*, 11–38. Natsu Taylor Saito, "Asserting Plenary Power Over the 'Other': Indians, Immigrants, Colonial Subjects, and Why U.S. Jurisprudence Needs to Incorporate International Law," *Yale Law & Policy Review* 20 (2002): 427–80.
74 The doctrine would receive perhaps its most forceful articulation in a 1936 case involving the president's authority to become involved in foreign conflicts. In that case, *United States v. Curtiss-Wright Export Corp.*, the Court announced that the president's authority over foreign affairs, even "if they had never been mentioned in the Constitution, would have vested in the federal government as necessary concomitants of nationality." The Court located the source of the president's extra-constitutional authority in imperial Great Britain. When "the external sovereignty

of Great Britain in respect of the colonies ceased, it immediately passed to the Union. . . . The Union existed before the Constitution." That external-facing extraconstitutional power, the Court explained, had been clearly recognized by the Court "as the power to acquire territory by discovery and occupation" and "the power to expel undesirable aliens." United States v. Curtiss-Wright Export Corp., 299 U.S. 304 (1936), 316–19.

75 United States v. Rogers, 45 U.S. 567, 572 (1846); *See* Bethany Berger, "'Power Over This Unfortunate Race': Race, Politics, and Indian Law in United States v. Rogers," *William & Mary Law Review* 45, no. 5 (2004): 1957–2052.

76 United States v. Rogers, 572.

77 Ibid. (emphasis added).

78 O'Brien, *Firsting and Lasting*; Rifkin, *Beyond Settler Time*.

79 David J. Bier, "Trump's Immigration Ban is Illegal," *New York Times*, Jan. 27, 2017; Sherally Munshi, "Manners of Exclusion: From the Asiatic Barred Zone to the Muslim Ban," in *Deepening Divides: How Territorial Borders and Social Boundaries Delineate Our World*, ed. Didier Fassin (London: Pluto Press 2020): 118–43.

80 Matthew J. Lindsay, "Immigration as Invasion: Sovereignty, Security, and the Origins of Federal Immigration Power" *Harvard Civil Rights–Civil Liberties Law Review* 45, no. 1 (2010): 4.

81 Chae Chan Ping v. United States, 604 (citing The Schooner Exchange v. McFaddon, 11 U.S. 116, 136 (1812)).

82 Ibid., 603–04.

83 Fong Yue Ting, 705.

84 Sarah Cleveland, "Powers Inherent in Sovereignty: Indians, Aliens, Territories, and the Nineteenth Century Origins of the Plenary Power over Foreign Affairs," *Texas Law Review* 81, no. 1 (2002): 15.

85 Lindsay, "Immigration as Invasion," 43.

86 Mae M. Ngai, *Impossible Subjects: Illegal Aliens and the Making of Modern America* (Princeton: Princeton University Press, 2004), 11–12.

87 Daniel Kanstroom, *Deportation Nation: Outsiders in American History* (Cambridge, MA: Harvard University Press, 2007), 92–95.

88 United States v. Kagama, 118 U.S. 375, 382 (1886).

89 Act to Provide for the Allotment of Lands in Severalty to Indians on the Various Reservations, General Allotment (Dawes) Act of 1887, ch. 119, § 6, 24 Stat. 388, 390.

90 Coutin, Richland, and Fortin, "Routine Exceptionality," 102.

91 Lone Wolf v. Hitchcock, 187 U.S. 553 (1903) (emphasis added).

92 Arnold H. Liebowitz, *Defining Status: A Comprehensive Analysis of United States Territorial Relations* (Norwell: Kluwer Academic Publishers, 1989), 6.

93 Sam Erman, "Accomplices of Abbot Lawrence Lowell," *Harvard Law Review Forum* 131, no. 4 (2018): 105, 107.

94 Daniel Immerwahr, *How to Hide an Empire: A History of the Greater United States* (New York: Farrar, Straus and Giroux, 2019), 73–87.

95 Erman, "Accomplices," 107; Mark S. Weiner, "Teutonic Constitutionalism: The Role of Ethno-Juridical Discourse in the Spanish-American War," in *Foreign in a Domestic Sense: Puerto Rico, American Expansion, and the Constitution*, ed. Christina Duffy Burnett and Burke Marshall (Durham: Duke University Press, 2001), 48–81, 65.

96 Blue Clark, *Lone Wolf v. Hitchcock: Treaty Rights and Indian Law at the End of the Nineteenth Century* (Lincoln: University of Nebraska Press, 1994), 102; 33 Cong. Rec. 2618 (Mar. 7, 1900) (citing Cherokee Nation v. Georgia, 30 U.S. 1 (1831)).

97 Abbott Lawrence Lowell, "The Status of Our New Possessions—A Third View," *Harvard Law Review* 13, no. 3 (1899): 171; Laura E. Gómez, *Manifest Destinies: The Making of the Mexican American Race* (New York: New York University Press, 2007), 45.

98 Downes v. Bidwell, 182 U.S. 244, 299 (1901) (White, J., concurring).

99 Since roughly 2010, a growing number of scholars have begun to focus their attention on the challenge that the *Insular Cases*, which set forth the constitutional framework for the US government in its overseas colonies, present to constitutional faith. Growing interest in this history, which had largely been ignored by constitutional scholars, is measured by two recent anthologies: a special issue of the *Harvard Law Review*, and a number of articles on the topic. See, for instance, Burnett and Marshall, eds., *Foreign in a Domestic Sense*; Gerald L. Neuman and Tomiko Brown-Nagin, *Reconsidering the Insular Cases: The Past and Future of the American Empire* (Cambridge, MA: Harvard Human Rights Program, 2015); Editors, "U.S. Territories: Developments in the Law," *Harvard Law Review* 130 (2017): 1617–31; Efrén Rivera Ramos, *The Legal Construction of Identity: The Judicial and Social Legacy of American Colonialism in Puerto Rico* (Washington, DC: American Psychological Association, 2001); Neil Weare, "Why *The Insular Cases* Must Become the Next Plessy," *Harvard Law Review Blog* (March 28, 2010).

100 "Developments in the Law: U.S. Territories," 1617, 1619.

101 Rasmussen v. United States, 197 U.S. 516 (1905); Balzac v. Porto Rico, 258 U.S. 298 (1922).

102 Weiner, *Teutonic Constitutionalism*, 62–63 (citing Albert J. Beveridge).

103 See Antony Anghie, "Finding the Peripheries: Sovereignty and Colonialism in Nineteenth-Century International Law," *Harvard International Law Journal* 40 (1999): 1–71; Lauren Benton and Lisa Ford, *Rage for Order: The British Empire and the Origins of International Law, 1800–1850* (Cambridge, MA: Harvard University Press, 2016).

104 DeLima v. Bidwell, 182 U.S. 1, 220 (1901).

105 Ibid.

106 Downes v. Bidwell, 286.

107 Jamal Greene, "The Anticanon," *Harvard Law Review* 125, no. 2 (2011): 384.

108 Greene's "anticanon" consists of cases that have been identified by legal academics as "antiprecedential," make frequent appearances in casebooks as negative authority, and are routinely renounced by judicial nominees.

109 Byrd, *Transit of Empire*, xx–xxiii, 9–10; Dean Itsuji Saranillio, "Why Asian Settler Colonialism Matters: A Thought Piece on Critiques, Debates, and Indigenous Difference," in *The Settler Complex: Recuperating Binarism in Colonial Studies*, ed. Patrick Wolfe (Los Angeles: UCLA American Indian Studies Center, 2016), 109.

110 Rifkin, *Beyond Settler Time*, 1.

111 Byrd, *Transit of Empire*, 55; Iyko Day, "Being or Nothingness: Indigeneity, Anti-blackness, and Settler Colonial Critique," *Critical Ethnic Studies* 1, no. 2 (2015): 102–21.

112 James E. Young, *The Texture of Memory: Holocaust Memorials and Meaning* (New Haven: Yale University Press, 1993), 2.

113 Ibid.

114 Dred Scott v. Sandford, 60 U.S. 393, 409 (1857).

115 Balkin and Levinson, "The Canons of Constitutional Law," 972.

116 Paul Finkelman, "The Taney Court (1836–1864): The Jurisprudence of Slavery and the Crisis of the Union," in *The United States Supreme Court: The Pursuit of Justice*, ed. Christopher Tomlins (New York: Houghton Mifflin, 2005), 75–99, 77.

117 Akhil Reed Amar, *America's Constitution: A Biography* (New York: Random House, 2005), 20.

118 Sanford Levinson, "Installing the *Insular Cases* into the Canon of Constitutional Law," in *Foreign in a Domestic Sense: Puerto Rico, American Expansion, and the Constitution*, ed. Christina Duffy Burnett and Burke Marshall (Durham: Duke University Press, 2001), 121–39, 130.

119 *See, e.g.*, Downes v. Bidwell, 244; DeLima v. Bidwell, 1.

120 Plessy v. Ferguson, 163 U.S. 537, 552, 559 (1896) (Harlan, J., dissenting); Primus, "Canon, Anti-Canon, and Judicial Dissent," 243–303.

121 Ariela Gross, "When is the Time of Slavery," 300.

122 *See, e.g.*, Neil Gotanda, "A Critique of 'Our Constitution is Color-Blind,'" *Stanford Law Review* 44, no. 1 (1991): 1–68.

123 *See, e.g.*, Joshua Takano Chambers-Letson, *A Race So Different: Performance and Law in Asian America* (New York: New York University Press, 2013); Gary Y. Okihiro, *American History Unbound: Asians and Pacific Islanders* (Oakland: University of California Press, 2015), 203.

124 Plessy v. Ferguson (Harlan, J., dissenting), 561.

125 The building of the transcontinental railroad itself, regarded as essential to both completing the project of westward expansion and establishing the United States as a global power, was dependent on the theft of Indian land and the hyper-exploitation of Chinese workers. See Manu Karuka, *Empire's Tracks: Indigenous Nations, Chinese Workers, and the Transcontinental Railroad* (Oakland: University of California Press, 2019).

126 Ian Haney López, *White by Law: The Legal Construction of Race* (New York: New York University Press, 1996); Sherally Munshi, "'You Will See My Family Became So American': Toward a Minor Comparativism," *American Journal of Comparative Law* 63, no. 3 (2015): 655–718.

127 Plessy v. Ferguson (Harlan, J., dissenting), 559.

128 Ibid.

129 Pamela S. Karlan, "What Can Brown* Do For You?: Neutral Principles and the Struggle Over the Equal Protection Clause," *Duke Law Journal* 58, no. 6 (2009): 1049–69, 1060.

130 Greene, "Anti-Canon," 441.

131 Ibid., 493; Edwin M. Yoder, Jr. "It's Foolish to Waver on *Brown v. Board of Education*," *News and Observer*, May 22, 2019.

132 Karlan, "What Can Brown* Do For You?," 1054.

133 Greene, "Anti-Canon," 400.

134 Meghan Keneally, "Donald Trump Cites These FDR Policies to Defend Muslim Ban," ABC News, December 8, 2015, https://abcnews.go.com.

135 Trump v. Hawaii, 138 S.Ct. 2392, 2447 (2018) (Sotomayor, J., dissenting).

136 Trump v. Hawaii, 2423 (majority opinion) (citing Korematsu v. United States, 323 U.S. 214, 248 (1944) (Jackson, J., dissenting)).

137 Korematsu v. United States, 323 U.S. 214, 216 (1944).

138 Ibid., 241, 236 (1944) (Murphy, J., dissenting) (citing a report by General John DeWitt).

139 Ibid., 216.

140 Ibid., 218.

141 Greene, "Anti-canon," 457.

142 G. Edward White, "The Unacknowledged Lesson: Earl Warren and the Japanese Relocation Controversy," *Virginia Quarterly Review* (Autumn 1979), www.vqronline.org.

143 Ramón A. Gutiérrez, "Internal Colonialism: An American Theory of Race," *Du Bois Review* 1, no. 2 (2004): 281–95.

144 Tee-Hit-Ton v. United States, 348 U.S. 272, 279 (1955).

145 Ibid., 281.

146 Ibid., 282.

147 Korematsu v. United States (Murphy, J., dissenting), 234, 242.

148 Trump v. Hawaii, 38 (emphasis added).

149 Ibid. (emphasis added).

150 International Refugee Assistance Project v. Trump, 857 F.3d 554, 572 (4th Cir. 2017).

151 Trump v. Hawaii, 100.

152 Charlie Savage, "Korematsu, Notorious Supreme Court Ruling on Japanese Internment, Is Finally Tossed Out," *New York Times*, June 26, 2018 (citing Hiroshi Motomura).

153 Nina Wallace and Natasha Varner, "Fort Sill is a Site of Ongoing Trauma," densho. org, June 12, 2019, https://densho.org.

154 Gillian Brockell, "Geronimo and the Japanese Were Imprisoned There. Now Fort Sill Will Hold Migrant Children Again, Sparking Protests," *Washington Post*, June 23, 2019.

155 Ibid.

156 Sara Ahmed, *Queer Phenomenology: Orientations, Objects, Others* (Durham: Duke University Press, 2006), 15.

157 Ibid.

3

Supreme Court Precedent and the Politics of Repudiation

ROBERT L. TSAI

Every legal order that aspires to be called just is held together not only by principles of justice but also by archetypes of morally reprehensible outcomes, villains as well as heroes. Chief Justice Roger Taney, who believed himself to be a hero solving the great moral question of slavery in the *Dred Scott v. Sanford* case, is today detested for trying to impose a racist, slaveholding vision of the Constitution upon America. Likewise, the knowledge that he might wind up on the wrong side of history in part explains the anguished quality of Justice Felix Frankfurter's dissent in the coerced flag-salute case, *West Virginia State Board of Education v. Barnette*, for he had not only lost the argument over what a postwar liberal order should look like but also saw the consensus represented in his earlier opinion on the issue collapse as his colleagues abandoned him for Robert Jackson's rights-centered vision of justice.

But what exactly renders a particular legal outcome, which surely begins as a good-faith effort to do the right thing, a despised precedent over time? Some judicial rulings are infamous because they are one day cast aside with great fanfare, as *Bowers v. Hardwick* was by Justice Anthony Kennedy in *Lawrence v. Texas* or the *Dred Scott* case was through consistent denunciation by abolitionists and a dramatic defeat for the Slave Power during the Civil War. But other precedents are treated disdainfully through a more nuanced process of shunning or erosion, so that they remain formally alive but shamble about, a vestige of their former selves—*Korematsu v. United States*, *Roe v. Wade*, and *Miranda v. Arizona* might fall into this category. This is true even though there may have been Herculean efforts by judges to rescue some aspect of each of these decisions. Whether renounced openly or surreptitiously, each of these precedents has been deeply marked by public condemnation.

This chapter investigates the politics of repudiation—the sociolegal dynamics by which losers to a contest over the meaning of the U.S. Constitution seek to castigate and delegitimate a controversial outcome. It will ask what actions can spur the sense of moral outrage with a judicial ruling, as well as what components are necessary to transform a precedent into an exemplar of public regret. The politics of repudiation begins with the notion that every judicial ruling is a first draft, a sketch of legal and political values. Judges' words are only fragments, composed by a single collection of influential individuals reading a legal text for a particular moment in time. What a judicial ruling means in the social world depends on what it becomes. Along these lines, the command to obey that is intrinsic to every ruling is satisfied through compliance by those who are immediate parties to the controversy; no one else is obliged to endorse the constitutional vision sketched by judges who presided over that dispute. The republican and federalist design features of our constitutional order therefore join with the cultural processes on which every legal system depends to foster a wide range of actions to either entrench or contest a particular vision of law.

What matters more than the ideas contained in a judicial opinion, then, is what average citizens and elites do with that legal decision once it reenters the stream of democratic discourse and, if they disagree with it, what steps they take to inscribe a very different narrative about that decision in the public imagination. Much of this work of public repudiation is done through unglamorous politics: activism of civic groups and church organizations that educates citizens and the enactment of local policies, state laws, and other texts through which the people turn a legal ruling into an object of obloquy. National party dynamics can play a significant role by sharpening and broadening the politics of repudiation. For instance, by making opposition to *Roe* a central tenet of the party platform and political identity, the Republican Party helped make *Roe* reviled among a generation of conservative lawyers who now hold a majority of seats on the United States Supreme Court. These efforts have put detractors on the cusp of codifying a final victory should the Court overrule that decision.

Interventions by elites at key moments can harness institutional advantages. Along these lines, consider the efforts by government lawyers to describe the first flag salute case, *Minersville School District v. Gobitis*, as a tragic error fostering a wave of violence against Jehovah's Witnesses, or Congress's enactment of a reparations bill for Japanese Americans interned during World War II. These actions illustrate that, insofar as the politics of repudiation entail reshaping legal culture, having ideologically friendly allies in well-placed positions is critical for turning an adverse ruling into an infamous decision.

Introduction

Disputes in the courts come and go, but the rule of law is supposed to stay. Decisions in cases, which represent the rule of law in action, are to be treated by jurists as links on a chain. Once in a while, a link becomes tarnished or weakened and must be repaired or replaced.

But what makes a precedent no longer worthy of respect—infamous, even—and therefore something that must be rejected? If one simply takes at face value how judges talk among themselves about the binding nature of the cases they decide, then it is strictly a matter of jurisprudence. A decision settles a controversy through the establishment and usage of a legal rule that represents, in the words of Oliver Wendell Holmes, "what is then understood to be convenient."[1] That rule is invoked as a matter of routine in the resolution of concrete disagreements between competing claimants and later gets adjusted when new information shows the rule to be impractical in some important way. If a rule's utility has become severely compromised—say, because a philosophical or empirical assumption has been revealed to be erroneous or application of the rule actually works manifest injustice—judges might substitute a new rule entirely and scrap the old one.

This is more or less the picture painted by the Supreme Court in *Planned Parenthood of Southeastern Pennsylvania v. Casey*,[2] when the plurality of Justices O'Connor, Souter, and Kennedy struggled to explain why they have decided to stick with *Roe v. Wade* even though they might have decided the constitutional question differently as a matter of first impression. They said that the decision whether to abide by stare decisis is "customarily informed by a series of prudential and pragmatic considerations designed to test the consistency of overrule a prior decision . . . and to gauge the respective costs of reaffirming and overruling a prior case."[3] After weighing the salient factors, the plurality deemed it worthwhile to reaffirm "the essence" of *Roe* because of the intrinsic importance of the right and the reliance interests of rights-bearing citizens, while completely revamping the doctrinal rule meant to safeguard those values.

This description of precedent largely from the internal perspective was originally rendered at the height of legal realism by men like Oliver Wendell Holmes, Benjamin Cardozo, and Louis Brandeis. At that time, the striking portrayal of judicial interpretation as a creative enterprise was intended to liberate the judge from the formalistic methods of the past and awaken him to his own power to shape the law.[4] As an ideal, this vision has largely remained intact as an exemplar of the judicial function. Even so, where it misleads greatly is in conveying the impression that the jurist operates at the center of a legal and political universe that he himself can exclusively control: He dictates what methods to use; he decides when to peer out into the world to see what has happened beyond the halls of justice that might have some bearing on a case; and he alone calculates which empirical details and "felt necessities of the time" and "prevalent moral and political theories" to endorse.[5] This is a thrilling image: what judges assemble, they alone can carefully disassemble.

But to anyone who pays close attention to these kinds of things, this judge-centered account is foolishly and dangerously incomplete. It rests, first and foremost, on the untenable assumption that a national interpretive community exists. Yet this is incompatible with the mechanics of the Constitution's original design and deeply ahistorical from the vantage point of the law's political development. In truth, there is no single interpretive community, but legion. These communities overlap with one another and are loosely bound by a handful of common texts, but they are characterized by different understandings of those texts, often divergent missions, and thus disparate warrants for political action.[6]

These overlapping communities aren't coordinated, but they take cues from one another and borrow legal ideas as they see fit while rejecting others. Some of these jurisdictions and figures enjoy formal recognition and authority, such as states and judges, whereas others enjoy only the interpretive status they can exert informally, working as groups bound by mutual interest or affinity. Any gathering of Americans that expresses "love of order and of formalities," as Tocqueville observed, can make practical meaning of the Constitution for their own lives.[7]

When it comes to the role of precedent over constitutional matters, the internal perspective leaves us with the false impression that a case represents merely a static rule rather than a political lesson imbued with social meaning. The judge-centered vision of precedent reaches the limits of its explanatory power precisely at the moment it is unable to adequately explain *how* certain precedents come to be perceived as failures—especially when the time between a legal rule's creation and its demise is extremely short. Because a legal rule is closely associated with the case in which it was originally created, the discrediting of one tends to discredit the other.

It turns out that all the *Casey* plurality describes is the final step in a complex process by which a precedent becomes embraced or discarded over time. In other words, it identifies only the public reasons judges give when they are willing to acknowledge their prior art to be a failure, and nothing more. This partial view of the common law, too, is bound up with the Supreme Court's own incessant need to create and re-create the conditions of its own adjudicative power. The Court's instinct toward self-preservation treats it as dangerous to acknowledge external competitors for interpretive authority except under the conditions that will be most conducive to the preservation of its own prerogative. So, by the time that a majority of justices is willing to acknowledge that an earlier case is deeply flawed, even reviled, most of the work from the politics of repudiation has actually been done elsewhere.

Missing in this account, therefore, is any realization that legal decisions are part of broader, more unruly institutional and social dynamics that lie beyond the capacity of judges to govern. And it's those processes of exaltation and dethronement that require far more effort to uncover. We have to read between the lines to detect the things that judges refuse to admit for fear of blurring the lines between law and the rest of the social world: the structure of electoral politics, popular and sometimes deviant culture, patterns of grassroots mobilization, and alternative modes of self-organization. We also have to look elsewhere for evidence as to how elites and ordinary citizens can leverage their proximity and influence to demonstrate to judges that their view of the world is fundamentally wrong or that circumstances have changed drastically, or that the consequences of a ruling have been disastrous.

The Contours of Infamy

There is another, more holistic way of thinking about how a precedent can become "infamous"—that is to say, irrelevant to decision making and vulnerable to repudiation—beyond the simple explanation that judges suddenly come to their senses one day. It starts with the recognition of interpretive pluralism as a basic fact about our system of government, along with the necessity of social assent: every decision requires active acceptance by key actors and acquiescence from everyone else for it to be enforced. Even more helpful is when legal principles take hold of the people's imaginations. This brute fact that an act of interpretation depends on social acceptance is rooted in judicial weakness, which the Constitution's framers appreciated as a matter of original design.[8] Interpretation is the judiciary's primary power, but it remains a practice that must be constantly justified and policed. Indeed, the point can also be generalized: every judicial utterance requires social support for it to become, in a practical sense, law.

Several inferences flow from the realization that the best evidence of a legal text's survival rate can be found in others' responses: Nonlegal actors can exert a significant impact on subsequent judicial outcomes; they can also shape the legal rationales and political values that judges endorse, as well as the terminology judges employ to present the stakes of a controversy. When things go well for the work of judges, a case can be canonized through politics.[9] When things don't go so well, politics can not only deny a precedent canonical status but also lead to its designation as part of the anticanon: a collection of despised rulings and unfortunate events that serve as negative lessons for a polity.

In fact, every judicial decision is best understood as having a life cycle, one in which the legal text passes through different stages of existence and is exposed to a variety of influences from other social actors: (1) composition; (2) reaction; (3) adaptation; and (4) dissolution.[10] First, there is the initial stage of composition, which is itself a moment in time when a judge or a panel of judges creates a legal rule and amasses a set of political principles and empirical assessments. Second, after publication, a judicial ruling passes more broadly into the cultural and political realms, where partisans have the opportunity to embrace, internalize, resist, or reshape the ideas, assumptions, and rationales associated with the decision. Assuming a precedent has survived its initial encounter with postcomposition reaction, it will then enter a phase where jurists will adapt a legal rule to new information as well as political reactions. During both the period of reaction and adjustment, opponents of a precedent try to maximize judicial and political denunciations of a particular legal outcome. Negative citations to a case or discussions by judges, activists, or high-profile elected officials create the appearance of intense and broad social disagreement, as well as momentum for change. These signals are necessary to attract attention to a legal decision as well as create the impression of widespread disapproval.

To the extent that adjustments to precedent are made by judges in a manner that is culturally responsive and doctrinally sensible, these adaptations can prolong the life of a legal ruling. To the extent that incompatible values, concepts, priorities, or criticisms become closely associated with a case, desired canonization may be thwarted and the precedent may be heading down the path toward ignominy. If a consensus in favor of a decision can't be sustained, we enter the final phase, where decisionmakers openly discuss whether to dissolve the approach inaugurated by a decision, disavow the ruling, and try again.

There is no preordained length of time associated with any particular phase of meaning-making activity. Some healthy precedents survive for a long time and remain in a period of adaptation. Others, such as *Roe*, which had already weathered an onslaught of antiabortion politics in the mid-1990s through clever and timely adaptation, seems once again on the verge of dissolution today with a Supreme Court that is openly hostile to reproductive liberties.

For some precedents, it is too early to tell what might come next, but there are reasons both cultural and institutional to think that it will survive for some time. The *District of Columbia v. Heller* decision on the Second Amendment, for instance, seems to be in a crucial period of reaction and adaptation, where an initially strong assertion of the right to individual gun ownership by the Court has given way to proregulatory realities, including the density of urban populations and persistent concern about mass shootings; a steady stream of gun crimes, suicides, and accidents; and technological advancements that make gun massacres far too easy to accomplish. At the same time, outright repudiation of the Supreme Court's gun-rights decision is unlikely to occur for the foreseeable future. Given a robust culture of gun ownership and the current makeup of the Court, it would take enormous efforts to go from a regulatory regime to a confiscatory one, or from an individualistic conception of gun rights to a collective right, that might culminate in the renunciation of *Heller*.

Party Politics as Engine of Doctrinal Subversion

It is impossible to find a more stunning instance of the power of public denunciation to erode a precedent than *Dred Scott*'s demise. Well before battlefield victories destroyed the claim of the planter class to absolute dominion over the African slave, and the Reconstruction Amendments inscribed new, postwar rights of national citizenship, other fateful public actions had been taken to deny crucial social support for the Supreme Court's strident rejection of black equality. Indeed, the inability of the *Dred Scott* ruling in 1857 to settle the slavery question definitively fueled not only political anxiety on the part of slaveholders but also more aggressive efforts by abolitionists to unsettle the slaveholders' preferred conceptual connections between whiteness and ownership, with its concomitant destruction of the dignity of labor. Once martial conflict was joined, liberating the slaves overtook restoring the Union as the principal goal of the war. Eventually, a guarantee of rights to freed persons and enhanced congressional powers emerged as the Republican Party's paramount war legacy.[11]

Abraham Lincoln's own criticism of *Dred Scott* underscored that a judicial utterance represented only the first stage of a much longer process by which a case that involves a contest over fundamental values becomes "settled doctrine." He pointed to several factors that might lead a precedent to be rejected by the public:

> If this important decision had been made by the unanimous concurrence of the judges, and without any apparent partisan bias, and in accordance with legal public expectation, and with the steady practice of the departments throughout our history, and has been in no part, based on assumed historical facts which are not really true; or, if wanting in some of these, it had been before the court more than once, and had there been affirmed

and re-affirmed through a course of years, it then might be . . . factious, nay, even revolutionary, to not acquiesce to it as a precedent. But when as it is true we find it wanting in all these claims to the public confidence, it is not resistance, it is not factious, it is not even disrespectful, to treat it as not having yet quite established a settled doctrine for the country.[12]

Notice that among the reasons Lincoln gave for refusing respect to a judicial ruling are that it departs from "public expectation," or is incongruous with tradition, or is based on erroneous "historical facts," or fails to represent a institutional consensus. Some of his concern had to do with the solidity of agreement among the justices at the moment of decision, as well as whether there has been consistent enforcement of a principle over time. But far more of Lincoln's considerations entailed reasons why a legal ruling's "claims to the public confidence" might fall short once it enters the phases of popular reaction and adaptation.

Between judicial elaboration and political legitimation, then, are the many opportunities for citizens outraged by a ruling to engage the politics of repudiation. Lincoln provided a roadmap used so diligently by others. Opposition to *Dred Scott* linked militant abolitionists such as John Brown to centrists such as John Bingham, the principal author of the Fourteenth Amendment. These prominent figures warmed to the task at hand, arguing that Chief Justice Roger B. Taney's stridently pro-slavery opinion was steeped in bias, departed from natural rights theory, and made mincemeat of the careful wording of the Constitution when it came to slavery—an institution the Framers themselves refused to mention by name in the nation's charter.

And it wasn't merely Northern objections to the principles and assumptions contained in *Dred Scott* that denied that judicial exposition a strong claim to "public confidence." The fragility of the regime represented by *Dred Scott* was further confirmed by the flurry of secessionist activity on the part of slaveholding states in the Deep South at the mere election of a Northern Republican in Lincoln. The planter class may have agreed with every word of Taney's opinion, but they didn't believe for a moment the Court could enforce the ruling in the face of rising antislavery sentiment. Before Lincoln had even taken the oath of office, "fire-eaters" from the Deep South had decided to consolidate what remained of their resources and energy to embark on a new nationalist experiment founded explicitly on slavery. To save *Dred Scott*, the planter class would risk war and destruction to create an entirely new normative universe dedicated to the proposition that the African slave was forever unequal.[13]

The dramatic choice of exit over voice by the slaveholding states—with political loyalty irreparably split by December 1860—left the Republican Party with exclusive control over the fate of the federal government's objectives and, after the Confederacy's surrender, the capacity to dictate the terms of the rebel states' readmission to the Union.[14] When the time came, partisan control of the apparatus of governance increased the odds that *Dred Scott*'s vision of constitutional order could be dismantled once and for all. Not even President Andrew Johnson, seen by the defeated South after Lincoln's assassination as the last "hope of a white man's government," could derail a Republican Party that found a way to unify over the goals of emancipation and citizenship for formerly enslaved people.[15]

This party-led process eventually drove the decimation of many of the cultural premises of *Dred Scott*—particularly the assumption that African slaves were "beings of an inferior order" and "altogether unfit to associate with the white race either in social or political relations."[16] The erosion of these sentiments occurred through black soldiers' participation in efforts to preserve the Union, nascent experiments in black landownership and popular sovereignty, political realignments, and a sweeping moral judgment ultimately rendered against those who tried to re-create nearly the same conditions of black subjugation in the immediate postwar years.

To be sure, *Dred Scott* would continue to be invoked during Reconstruction by forces opposed to civil rights for freed persons. No precedent ever truly dies but, through the processes of infamy, is instead relegated to the anticanon, where unrecognized or subordinate interpretive communities can still seek to keep its precepts alive. Governor Benjamin Perry of South Carolina, for instance, invoked the decision at a citizen convention to argue against the extension of suffrage to formerly enslaved people.[17] But there was nowhere close to national support for Taney's claims that black people were incapable of citizenship or political rights. Enemies of equality would have to move to different terrain, both inside and outside of the courts, if they wished to keep black citizens in an inferior social or economic condition.

Today, *Dred Scott* is reviled by the mainstream community for articulating principles beyond the constitutional pale, and it is certainly taught in universities and law schools as a flagrant example of overweening confidence and poor historical judgment. But the precedent remains on life support in other quarters, remembered by underground worlds populated by neo-Confederates, self-described "Aryans," and "alt-right" provocateurs online. They continue to valorize the infamous ruling, adding it to others such as *Plessy v. Ferguson* or *Bowers v. Hardwick* for expressing traditionalist principles or sentiments that have become verboten.

Prevailing in a military action and codifying the war's legacy through constitutional amendment aren't the only ways to engage the politics of repudiation. In fact, most of the time, social actors can deny legitimacy to judicial decisions on a smaller scale and work through political parties to create social conditions that will be congenial to dissolution of a legal regime. American politics has largely been dominated by two major parties at any given moment, and within such a bipolar system, a single political party can effectively harness anger at a Supreme Court decision. Grassroots activists work hand-in-glove with party elites to codify rejection of a ruling in the party's platform, back candidates who run on the issue by denouncing core features of a case, enact laws to codify opposing values, and then secure the election or appointment of judges with compatible views who will chip away at despised rulings. This strategy takes time, an enormous investment of resources, and years of planning and execution.

In recent years, the GOP's party platform has called for constitutional amendments to protect the right to life and to allow states to define marriage—reactions to *Roe v. Wade* and *Obergefell v. Hodges*. The Democratic Party, by contrast, has endorsed constitutional amendments that would wipe out *Buckley v. Valeo* and *Citizens United v. FEC*—decisions that treat campaign donations and expenditures as speech and protect corporate spending in campaigns.[18] Gains from such activity go beyond judicial renunciation of precedent; short-term partisan and mobilization effects are valuable even if overruling a case seems out of reach.

When electorally focused efforts to discredit a ruling are successful, the precedent can become notorious in the public imagination, improving the odds that judges will adapt to an intense political reaction by creating formal exceptions that insert opposition ideas within the original juridic framework, heightening ideological tension within the law and leading to inconsistent outcomes. If polarizing the issue has increased the numbers of civic leaders committed to the cause, with sufficient party discipline, it will then lead to the restocking of the judiciary, which will be receptive to these more negative entreaties.[19]

A stunning example of this phenomenon is the number of appointees to the federal judiciary during President Donald Trump's first three years who have refused to say that *Brown* was properly decided.[20] This is powerful evidence that the case has come to represent a conception of equality or type of judicial activism disfavored among some grassroots conservatives.

Something similar happened in the aftermath of *Roe v. Wade*. Harnessing the righteous fury of evangelicals and then hoping to broaden disgust for what they believed to be the destruction of vulnerable human lives, members of the modern Republican Party caused major jurisprudential disruptions that led to the dramatic weakening of *Roe*'s intended framework. For a period of time, this see-saw quality of the Court's decision-making led to confusion over legal principles and methods. That sense of doctrinal haphazardness created new political possibilities and emboldened opponents by giving them fresh lines of attack.

One day, mention of a state's belief that life begins at conception was evidence supporting an inference of legislative intent to interfere with a woman's reproductive rights. The next day, such language, even contained in a preamble of a bill, was brushed off as innocuous sentiment.[21] Increasingly, majoritarian rhetoric from the political ecosystem such as "fetal life," "unborn child," "informed consent," and "maternal regret" entered judicial discourse and began to vanquish pro-rights rhetoric focused on "potential life," "privacy," "personal autonomy and bodily integrity," and "medical decision."[22]

Since *Casey*'s rejection of the trimester framework in favor of the elastic "undue burden" test in 1992—the most visible manifestation of the judiciary's accommodation of political outrage—the Court's abortion case law has settled into a general toleration of a wide range of state and local restrictions under the federal Constitution, except for the occasional extreme law that endangers the life or health of a woman. This hasn't satisfied those who have tried so very hard to give *Roe* a bad name, but the jurisprudential changes have largely accommodated negative political reaction to *Roe*—to the point that 89 percent of U.S. counties have no clinics that provide abortions.[23]

This raises the possibility that a precedent can become simultaneously valorized in the abstract but effectively marginalized through public sentiment such that it can lead to a separation of principle from practice. *Roe* remains important as a symbol, signifying the importance of individual rights to the modern political order and marking the advancement of women's role in public life. But in reality, the right to terminate one's pregnancy safely simply cannot be meaningfully exercised for large swaths of the community, particularly women who are less wealthy and those who happen to be born in restrictionist parts of the country. Linda Greenhouse and Reva Siegel put the point this way: "[I]t is now *Casey* more than *Roe* that defines the reach of the abortion right. Yet *Roe* continues to exert a powerful pull on the nation's politics . . . conveying wildly different meanings to different audiences."[24]

For true believers, *Roe* has not yet been made immortalized in infamy, for the project feels incomplete without a formal public renunciation. Nothing less than the reunification of symbol and practice can guarantee the right to life. The Court's management of competing legal interests, which has already redirected most abortion politics back to the states, doesn't satiate the politics of repudiation conducted by prolife forces but merely reminds *Roe*'s opponents of what is tantalizingly within reach.

The Politics of Repudiation: Elite or Popular?

A persistent question is this: Just how popular must the politics of repudiation be for it to succeed? One way to answer is by identifying and addressing obstacles to efforts to erode legal precedent from the outside. First, although a judge's authority to interpret the law rests largely on the power to persuade others, a culture of judicial independence nevertheless stands between the doctrinal target of citizens' ire and those who would see that case undone. Thus, the politics of repudiation carry a risk that tactics seen by Americans as too overtly antagonistic can be construed as attacks on the judiciary itself. If that happens, the reaction may trigger a broad defense of judicial review that causes institutionalists to ally themselves with those invested in preserving substantive outcomes—including outcomes perceived to be unjust.

This suggests that, while it can be useful to secure grassroots rejection of a troubling ruling, there may be a limit to any approach that depends exclusively on rallying majoritarian sentiment. Conversely, it also means that more sophisticated strategies—i.e., investing more resources to convert or replace influential elites, or that rely on a mix of elite and popular methods—are more likely to yield dividends.

In fact, it may be less critical to reach any particular numerical threshold of converts than it is to destabilize the social conditions surrounding a constitutional matter. For a freshly inked decision, the goal is to keep conditions in such a tremulous state that a new ruling simply cannot take hold of the public's imagination cleanly—to hold off the day that a decision acquires durable support for as long as possible. For a disfavored ruling that has been on the books for some time, the task is that much harder: to create the impression that a long-settled question is once again contestable. The destabilization of a judicial outcome, in turn, paves the way for others to exert influence over the political precepts and cultural beliefs at stake. Elites dedicated to overthrowing a legal regime are then able to operate in this space.

A second factor that can limit the effectiveness of repudiation is that it must overcome acceptance of precedent by key elites and stasis within bureaucracies. Such acceptance can come from unthinking obedience to those with power, out of substantive agreement with an outcome or method, or path dependence for other reasons such as efficiency. Cases and legal rules are associated with the communities and bureaucracies that come to depend upon them. In that sense, judicial rulings can even create constituencies that didn't exist before. This means that the race to deny legitimacy to a decision commences at the moment of publication and must be a multiprong effort to prevent the codification of associated principles and the entrenchment of power associated with a ruling. When the goal is to overturn an established case, enormous energy must be expended to unsettle existing expectations and provoke elites to rethink their reliance interests.

But then we encounter a third obstacle to the politics of repudiation—popular culture—which establishes at any historical moment the outer boundaries of possibility for the processes of infamy. Popular culture serves other functions, too, such as providing raw material for legal and political arguments. But in its demarcating function, popular culture can—if support for a practice is widely shared and deemed important enough—constrain politics. It does so by raising the costs for opposing or suppressing that culture. At some point, resistance may become cost prohibitive and take other, narrower forms.

This helps us to understand why opponents of same-sex marriage on cultural grounds switched gears so quickly to take up arguments about religious exemptions for dissidents. Yes, they could rally like-minded opponents of *Obergefell* to demand a constitutional amendment, but successfully navigating the arduous process is fanciful in the short run. Beyond the high formal hurdles, the fact is that a majority of Americans today supports same-sex marriage—far more than support for interracial marriage. When *Loving v. Virginia* was decided in 1967, only 20 percent of Americans accepted interracial marriage; plurality support for marrying across the racial line did not emerge until twenty-five years later.[25] By contrast, *Obergefell* can be considered a truly majoritarian outcome in that, by 2015, when the case was decided, most polls put support for gay marriage at between 55–60 percent—with majority support remaining stable since 2010. After *Obergefell*, support climbed to about 67 percent. In 2021, GOP support for same-sex marriage exceeded the 50 percent mark for the first time.[26] The numbers are even more stunning and demoralizing for traditionalists when the preference of the younger generation are examined: In 2017, 79 percent of Americans aged 18–29 endorsed the right of gay people to marry.

Given such a stunning collapse of general sentiment against same-sex marriage (in the neighborhood of 28–36 percent in opposition), being singularly committed to undermining that ruling would be costly and yield few results—and quite possibly dissipate political resources needed for other initiatives. Instead, by moving to friendlier terrain such as the First Amendment, conservatives can harness popular support for individual rights to maintain, and even broaden, the spaces in public life where traditionalists can create disruptions in what seems to them to be a relentless egalitarian project. That would allow incremental, but important, conservative victories to be won and set up constant clashes between equality and liberty that are so crucial to maintaining momentum for political outrage.

Cultural dissidents can take heart in the fact that legal change isn't always unidirectional or permanent. What's more, for the first time in several generations, the Supreme Court is significantly more conservative compared to the rest of the country. When such a disjunction exists between a governing institution and the citizenry, the risk of rearguard rulings (where an institution renders an unpopular decision in the name of tradition or to protect an institution under siege) increases. But to convince the justices to repudiate *Obergefell* one day, traditionalists would have to convince large numbers of Americans that the experiment of same-sex marriage isn't working. The clarity of the legal rule in this context—immediate access to a valuable social good previously denied on the basis of sexual orientation—takes an alternative strategy off the table: introducing tensions and inconsistencies in a legal approach that leads to a fundamental rethinking of the original precedent.

Insofar as it is easier to harness popular belief in the values of dissent and pluralism, using the First Amendment to create alternative precedents can certainly aid the traditionalist cause. But if the objective is to introduce potent contradictions into gay-friendly jurisprudence, *Masterpiece Cakeshop, Ltd. v. Colorado Civil Rights Commission* did not quite fit the bill beyond reinforcing the principle against religious animus. That decision failed to articulate a clear right on the part of traditionalists who engage in commerce to resist the demands of equality or otherwise not be associated with same-sex marriages.[27] There remains, too, general risks with the approach, as some jurists' commitment to federalism will limit how motivated they might be to create large exceptions to local public accommodations laws. Rulings that wind up expanding a state's ability to enforce equality over objecting individuals will force traditionalists to make even more difficult choices about whether to continue participating robustly in the public sphere or else live in greater "nomian insularity"—without necessarily casting same-sex marriage into doubt.[28]

All of this acutely suggests that a motivated set of factions in society need not secure decisive, or even majority, support to undermine a legal precedent. Instead, the necessary ingredients for success seem to be: (1) fomenting cultural dispute over fundamental values, with an eye toward fostering ideological cohesion among jurists; (2) augmenting an existing voting bloc by installing sympathetic partisans or converting skeptical figures to the cause; (3) inscribing alternative understandings of a contested constitutional provision or law into ordinances, statutes, or state constitutional law; and (4) inviting sympathetic jurists to revisit a reviled precedent and codify new understandings in doctrine, washing away the old case.[29]

It should be emphasized that the overarching project is to alter the cultural connotations of a precedent so that it is no longer believed to be compatible with the polity's collective sense of justice. Thus, the project of repudiation is not primarily a technocratic or jurisprudential enterprise but instead one of political morality. As a strategy, it succeeds to the extent that legality and authority can be stripped from past juridic statements and recharacterized in broader moral terms.

Perhaps the best evidence that a nationwide movement is unnecessary to render a case infamous can be found in the cautious dismantling of *Plessy v. Ferguson* and the tentative emergence of *Brown v. Board of Education* in the mid-1950s. There, a motivated group in the form of the NAACP pursued a strategy of targeted local activism and lawsuits that introduced ideological and empirical contradictions into the jurisprudence that links judges to one another.

One win was built upon another, as newer decisions undercut older precedents and cried out for fresh synthesis. Public expectations of fair and equitable treatment in the domains of employment, voting, housing, and higher education then became inscribed in the law books. By securing the aid of patrons and supporters at critical junctures, they were able to incrementally destabilize the system of racial segregation judicially authorized by *Plessy* in the decades before the civil rights movement became a truly national phenomenon. These lawyers and activists were able to demonstrate that, contrary to the *Plessy* Court's incredulous statements that racial segregation didn't harm black citizens, in fact such measures interfered with access to critical social goods and opportunities.[30]

But it must be remembered that, despite careful work, the prospect of racially integrated schools remained extremely controversial in 1954. Even after *Brown* was decided, only a bare majority of Americans supported that outcome. The fragility of the consensus is obscured by the unanimity of *Brown* but hinted at by the justices' decision not to overrule *Plessy* explicitly but instead extend *Brown*'s logic into other social domains through a series of subsequent summary orders; ultimately the Court was forced to respond to local defiance by permitting a wide flexibility to lower court judges to craft the substantive remedies and time for defendants to comply with desegregation decrees.

Incisive observers of the Supreme Court have noticed two salient features of its work that can be exploited by those who wish to assail a judicial outcome. First, some individuals' opinions matter more than others during the adjudicative process. For instance, when a federal constitutional provision or statute is under review, the justices will often ask for the views of the U.S. solicitor general, a repeat player who has colloquially been referred to as "the 10th Justice."[31] Securing the backing of elites within an administration on a key point of law, especially if the goal is to greatly narrow or demolish existing precedent, leads to intense behind-the-scenes lobbying by stakeholders. Since the solicitor general's office will consult other agencies affected by a matter in the federal courts before staking out a position, taking advantage of these other opportunities to sway well-placed figures can increase the odds of favorable position-taking by the federal government.

Second, while it's too crude to say that judges simply follow the election returns, it is certainly true that particular justices—including, lately, whoever occupies the role of chief justice—have been acutely sensitive to popular opinion. Justices Anthony Kennedy and Sandra Day O'Connor often cared about external reactions to an older decision. As the Supreme Court became more predictably conservative, John Roberts has occasionally exhibited such a trait, such as changing his mind on Obamacare and in the dispute over the 2020 Census. The positions he staked out in these controversies demonstrated his concern about the reputation of the Court—something that is threatened by a precedent that appears overly partisan or works manifest injustice.[32] Being on the right side of history, and appearing to stand in solidarity with the president or Congress rather than appearing institutionally isolated, are tendencies that can be exploited by advocates.

Appeals to these sentiments are accomplished through lobbying, the legal briefs filed by parties in the cases as well as from "friends of the court," and the articles and interviews that might penetrate the news cycle and become part of the coverage of the Court's work. To the extent one's objective is to convince the Court to declare a precedent infamous, the goals during the period of adaptation are twofold: first, to shift the window of jurisprudential reasonableness away from the consensus once represented by an older decision; and second, to deliver a public rebuke that a precedent is now too tarnished to follow (i.e., its philosophical or empirical assumptions have been revealed to be false or that the case has caused unjustified suffering). When advocates are successful in this endeavor, they are in fact nudging a legal regime through the phase of adaptation and toward dissolution.

In *Brown*, the U.S. Department of Justice (DOJ) filed a brief in December 1952 signaling that the federal government had decided to back the forces of racial equality. DOJ lawyers made clear the administration's commitment to "equal treatment before the law," as well as its view that segregated public schools "undermine[d] the foundations of a society dedicated to freedom, justice, and equality." Importantly, they described racial equality as a Cold War imperative—"the present world struggle between freedom and tyranny." Dwight Eisenhower's administration fleshed out this argument even further, telling the justices that racial discrimination impeded presidential policies in two ways: by serving as "a source of constant embarrassment to this Government in the day-to-day conduct of its foreign relations," and by "jeopardiz[ing] the effective maintenance of our moral leadership of . . . free and democratic nations of the world."

The Department of Justice offered more than one option to the justices in grappling with problematic case law. It was not essential to overrule *Plessy* in order to conclude that the Fourteenth Amendment barred racially separate public schools because "the *Plessy* case plainly does not preclude a district court from finding . . . that segregation can, and in the particular instance does, produce unequal and inferior treatment." In other words, that ruling "did not purport to lay down an inexorable rule of law . . . that segregation could *never* create inequality." Creating some daylight between the older precedent and the specific facts in the current controversies opened the door to the possibility of different alliances within the Court itself to reach pro-equality outcomes—a crucial move given that public opinion on the matter was so equivocal.

Government lawyers then confirmed the department's preferred position that "racial segregation imposed or supported by laws is per se unconstitutional." Because "'separate but equal' is a contradiction in terms," they welcomed the possibility of the justices overruling *Plessy* should they wish to do so. "This judicial contraction of the constitutional rights secured by the [Fourteenth] Amendment is irreconcilable with the body of decisions which preceded and followed *Plessy v. Ferguson*," the DOJ insisted, "and is not justified by the considerations adduced to support it." In other words, the logic and facts of intervening cases like *Sweatt v. Painter* and *McLaurin v. Oklahoma State Regents* had already cast doubt on the continuing vitality of *Plessy*.[33] Finally, they appealed to changed circumstances as a reason to repudiate the Court's prior case law: "Whatever the merits in 1896 of a judgment as to the wisdom or reasonableness of the rule of 'separate but equal,' it should now be discarded as a negation of rights secured by the Constitution."[34]

Such an intervention by DOJ, with its implicit promise of institutional cooperation and its roadmap of public reasons for repudiation, proved critical to accelerating *Plessy*'s passage through the phase of adaptation straight into dissolution. Government lawyers signaled that the executive branch had many sound reasons for wanting to broadly enforce the principle of racial equality, that they would expend resources to do so, and that going out on a limb to take down *Plessy* would not undermine the Court's own agenda. This welcome message not only eased justices' concerns about the scope of the anticipated backlash among certain states and localities but also responded to their understandable desire for allies before undertaking a major reform project.

But the episode also tells us something else that is important about the processes of infamy: It is not enough for those who disagree with a legal ruling to convince a bunch of prominent people to denounce it; those in power must be able to imagine an alternative world in which a different legal regime can do a better job of ensuring justice. Judges aren't likely to knock down even a rotting building unless they are assured people are willing to dwell in a new structure.

Although calling attention to social ills is an important function of all social movements, activism becomes most valuable to the project of dislodging older precedents when mobilization produces legislation. In many areas of constitutional rights, judges have either explicitly formulated doctrines that take into account relevant extrajudicial developments or have taken it upon themselves to do so without binding themselves to such a practice in the long term. Even in the latter scenario, the meaning of constitutional terms such as "liberty," "equal protection of the laws," "due process," and "cruel and unusual punishment" have been shaped by favorable developments that occur outside a judge's direct sphere of influence. The fact that jurists have looked far and wide for evidence of fundamental values, even sporadically, creates incentives for political actors to attempt to influence federal judges by inscribing new values and methods into state laws, ordinances, and even agency policies and rules.[35]

Social movements—whether regional or national in character—have the best shot at convincing multiple jurisdictions to safeguard individual rights through legislative reform and spreading the news about fundamental principles. Members do so by creating pressure for change, electing friendly politicians, and presenting templates of ready-made bills that can expand rights in the desired fashion.

Take, for instance, *Lawrence v. Texas*, in which the Supreme Court finally rid itself of the 1986 precedent *Bowers v. Hardwick*. The *Bowers* Court had upheld a Georgia law that criminalized consensual sodomy against a privacy-based challenge. Justice Byron White's opinion had characterized Harwick's claim as an effort to vindicate a right to engage in same-sex sodomy. Scouring history, White found no "fundamental right [for] homosexuals to engage in acts of consensual sodomy." Chief Justice Warren Burger, concurring in the result, would have gone even further to say that "condemnation of those practices is firmly rooted in Judeo-Christian moral and ethical standards."[36]

Justice Anthony Kennedy's opinion in *Lawrence* nearly two decades later reveals the political spaces where activism can later affect judicial interpretation. Much of his analysis covered why the original case had misconstrued the constitutional inquiry as well as the historical record. Yet a surprising amount of the opinion was also dedicated to sorting through changed social and political circumstances. As evidence of how "the deficiencies in *Bowers* became even more apparent in the years following its announcement," he pointed to the decriminalization of homosexual conduct on the part of the states, as well as a trend of not enforcing those laws that remained on the books. He also cited *Casey* and *Romer v. Evans* as evidence of "serious erosion" of *Bowers* in addition to scholarly criticism of that decision and its rejection by many state courts and international tribunals as additional proof of its weak social foundations. These rulings would not have been possible without large-scale political activism and targeted interest-group litigation.

Kennedy's comments toward the end of his opinion indicated something else: a conviction that a judge's own attitudes ought to shift as public sentiment changes and new social facts emerge. He tried to put the point in historical terms even though many self-described originalists reject his form of socially adaptive jurisprudence. Invoking the Constitution's Framers, Kennedy said, "They knew times can blind us to certain truths and later generations can see that laws once thought necessary and proper in fact serve only to oppress. As the Constitution endures, persons in every generation can invoke its principles in their own search for greater freedom." In both method and analysis, this approach simultaneously represents a plea for raw materials and a license to engage in extrajudicial efforts to reshape constitutional meaning.

Political Elites: Shaping a New Narrative of Power and Justice

Before his untimely death, Yale law professor Robert Cover famously explained in the pages of the *Harvard Law Review* that "[n]o set of legal institutions or prescriptions exists apart from the narratives that locate it and give it meaning." Cover located the process of interpretation within nationalist traditions and the more varied imagined communities that are affected by that drive to create coherent legal meaning. In this "normative world" fashioned by lawgivers and law enforcers, every prescription is "supplied with history and destiny, beginning and end, explanation and purpose." Cover detected two competing tendencies in the law that he labeled "jurisgenerative"—the imperative to create authoritative legal meaning—and "jurispathic"—the desire to kill off alternative story lines and legal worlds in the name of clarity and hierarchy.[37]

Seen in this light, canonical precedents teach a society's denizens what is right and good about the world, whereas infamous decisions sow doubt about the political community's true nature and encourage evil. Such pollutants must be dealt with eventually—destroyed in whole or in part—to restore a sense of order and reassure people about society's commitment to justice.

But Cover diagnosed only part of this dynamic, and he offered only a vague sense of the dynamics in play. Because the law can't exist apart from the human beings and institutions that interpret and apply the law, it's those finer motivations to secure power or prerogative, enhance one's reputation, gain bureaucratic advantage, or accomplish some agenda that feed the law's tendencies to simultaneously create and destroy legal meaning. Thus, the finer aspects of the politics of repudiation lay beyond Cover's grasp.

An exquisite illustration of these more nuanced motivations can be found in the sudden jurisprudential abandonment of the democratic nomos created by the first Pledge of Allegiance case involving school-age Jehovah's Witnesses. In that episode can be found the elements of institutional self-interest and world-making that drive legal narratives. In 1940, Justice Felix Frankfurter authored *Minersville School District v. Gobitis*, an 8–1 ruling that rejected the children's religious objection to a compulsory flag salute (with only then–Associate Justice Harlan Stone dissenting). A mere three years later, in 1943, Justice Robert Jackson's opinion in *West Virginia School Board v. Barnette* overruled *Gobitis* and held that the children's refusal to salute the flag was constitutionally protected as a form of symbolic dissent.[38]

Cover's writings are instructive, for the two men's visions of democratic life were utterly incompatible. It's almost as if one was the Bizarro World version of the other, and the admiration you felt for one ruling would be matched by contempt for the other. One vision had to die so that the other might live. But which would triumph?

Justice Frankfurter, who had first crack at sketching what a postwar order might look like, insisted that individual rights had to be submerged to the needs of a nation at war. "National cohesion" as a "great common end" was in his view "an interest inferior to none in the hierarchy of legal values." Throughout, Justice Frankfurter pounded the themes of collective security and individual sacrifice. By contrast, Jackson's victorious vision insisted that individual rights need not be sacrificed at the altar of national unity—even in a time of war. "Authority here is to be controlled by public opinion," he said, "not public opinion by authority." Far from undermining national cohesion, Jackson argued, "[a]ssurance that rights are secure tends to diminish fear and jealousy of strong government, and, by making us feel safe to live under it, makes for its better support."

This turnabout was shocking not only for its swiftness but also for its completeness. But how to explain it? The historical record shows that the switch cannot be attributed solely to judges changing their mind. External developments played a significant part in the dissolution of the consensus backing *Gobitis*. But unlike legal advances won by gay-rights activists in later years, the Jehovah's Witnesses had no dependable social movement they could rely on. Instead, their own persistent suffering gained the attention of elites who helped convince the justices that no sane, freedom-loving American would want to live in the normative world the justices had devised in 1940.[39]

For one thing, two new additions to the Court in the intervening years—Jackson and Wiley Rutledge—were both outspoken in their disgust for the portrait of democracy articulated in *Gobitis* before their appointment to the Court. Jackson expressed "astonishment and chagrin" at Frankfurter's efforts to wrap the coercion of religious dissidents in patriotic themes, while Rutledge in a graduation speech contended "that it is [in] the regimentation of children in the Fascist and Communist salutes that the very freedom for which Jehovah's Witnesses strive has been destroyed."[40] For another, Harlan Fiske Stone, who was the lone holdout in *Gobitis*, was elevated to chief justice by President Franklin Roosevelt. All three men shared the conviction that respect for individual rights, particularly in a time of ascending fascism, must be an essential component of any democratic vision.

Perhaps most crucially, DOJ lawyers powerfully reshaped the public narrative surrounding the meaning of *Gobitis* and the coerced flag salute. They characterized the salute as oppressive and divisive and denounced the Court's precedent as unwise, counterproductive, and incompatible with the Roosevelt administration's support for religious liberty, "one of the four great freedoms for which this nation is now fighting!" In this way, government lawyers harnessed the justices' own vital desire for consensus within their own institution and an alliance with other branches of government to convince them to renounce an earlier decision.

During that era, rules limited the department's participation to cases in which the United States was a party. But although DOJ did not enter a formal appearance in *Barnette*, two lawyers from the civil rights division, Victor Rotnem and F. G. Folsom, published an article that laid the blame for a spate of atrocities visited upon Jehovah's Witnesses squarely at the feet of the Supreme Court. They first described a wave of terror against this religious minority as "intense animosity in every state of the Union," which called out for a national response. "This ugly picture of the two years following the *Gobitis* decision is an eloquent argument in support of the minority" view expressed by Stone, they wrote. Meanwhile, Attorney General Francis Biddle took to the airwaves and denounced the "swiftly increasing cases of mob violence in connection with Jehovah's Witnesses." He vowed that "we shall not tolerate such Nazi methods."[41]

High officials within the administration didn't just argue that *Gobitis* was counterproductive; they also insisted that the justices should reverse it immediately to present a united front with the Roosevelt administration. In their essay published in a political science journal, Rotnem and Folsom argued that taking this step would help restore public order and also predicted that an about-face would "profoundly enhance respect for the flag." Jackson agreed, and he said as much in *Barnette* after eviscerating *Gobitis*: "To believe that patriotism will not flourish if patriotic ceremonies are voluntary and spontaneous, instead of a compulsory routine, is to make an unflattering estimate of the appeal of our institutions to free minds."

Jackson's original draft of *Barnette* cited both the DOJ essay and the administration's timely labors to stem vigilante violence, but during the writing process those references were edited out. While the collaborative adjudicative process prompted the justices to obscure the evidence of out-of-court influences on the law's development, there can be little doubt that political appointees and civil servants had a large hand in casting *Gobitis* in dark terms as the source of manifest injustice and pressuring the Court to realign itself with an administration publicly committed to helping religious minorities around the world.

The Fall of *Korematsu* as Feigned Dissolution

We come, finally, to a most troubling possibility: that precedent can be overruled to aggrandize interpretive authority and obscure democratic pathologies. If the Stone Court's realignment with FDR's "Four

Freedoms" initiative underscored a genuine desire on the part of judges to be surrounded by allies, then the rise and fall of *Korematsu v. United States*—which ratified America's wartime internment policies—in the public imagination revealed the always-present risk that judges may present themselves as heroes when their actual decisions neither encourage sound decision-making nor ameliorate unequal suffering.

What the Roberts Court did by overruling *Korematsu* during its consideration of the Trump administration's Muslim travel ban is the mirror image of what the Rehnquist Court accomplished in *Casey*, where the justices upheld *Roe* but then hollowed out its doctrinal potency. In *Trump v. Hawaii*, Chief Justice Roberts overruled *Korematsu* with a flourish, but upon closer inspection, this formality didn't much alter the status quo. The move thus raised a problem we might call "feigned dissolution," where decision makers overrule a precedent because of the negative connotations it has acquired, without disassembling its component philosophies or methods. Yet this sets a trap for the unwary, who might get tripped up by hidden legal rules not mentioned; or, as in this case, allow government actors to continue treating political minorities more harshly than those who belong to the majority, despite the impression that such activity would not be permitted in the future.

The life span of *Korematsu*, the 1944 Supreme Court ruling that approved the wartime exclusion and internment of some 110,000 Japanese Americans, thus involved several intriguing patterns. Almost out of a sense of regret, justices subsequently began citing that decision for the proposition that race-based laws are subject to strict scrutiny, even though the *Korematsu* Court originally failed to rigorously enforce that formula in the internment cases.[42]

But the bulk of the heavy lifting to discredit *Korematsu* and convert it into an anticanonical work came from outside the courts. These legal liberals, outraged by the decision, pursued a two-prong strategy of litigation and legislation to undermine its factual and legal underpinnings within a broader narrative about America's enduring political values.

Nearly four decades after that legal opinion had become final and internees had scattered throughout the United States, lawyers pursued a *coram nobis* action that led a federal district court judge to gut the factual predicate for the Roosevelt administration's original claim that Japanese Americans represented a national security threat. Ruling in favor of the internees, Judge Marilyn Hall Patel could only correct the record in the older case; as a mere trial judge she had no formal authority to overrule *Korematsu*. But the findings she made absolutely destroyed the factual basis for the government's earlier assertion that internment of all people of Japanese ancestry on the West Coast was justified by military necessity. Although General John DeWitt insisted that Japanese people were signaling to ships from the shore, the Department of Justice suppressed naval intelligence showing that this national security claim was false. All that was left after this inflammatory allegation was stricken, Judge Patel concluded, were "unsubstantiated facts, distortions, and . . . views [that] were seriously infected by racism."[43]

These yeoman efforts to relitigate the issues and facts related to internment accompanied a round of political activism directed at the president and Congress. In 1980, President Jimmy Carter established a presidential commission to investigate the policies of exclusion and detention. The commission's report in December 1982 found "not a single documented act of espionage, sabotage, or fifth column activity committed by an American citizen of Japanese ancestry or by a resident Japanese alien on the West Coast."[44] The commission concluded that people of Japanese ancestry were rounded up along the West Coast (but not Hawaii) and detained in camps because of "race prejudice, war hysteria and a failure of political leadership" rather than military necessity. In 1988, relying on the commission's report, Congress enacted a reparations bill, which was signed by President Ronald Reagan. Beyond the $ 1.6 billion disbursed to surviving internees, the reparations bill acknowledged "the fundamental injustice of the evacuation," apologized for causing "significant human suffering" for interning them "without adequate security reasons" and for "fundamental violations of the basic civil liberties and constitutional rights of these individuals." Taken together, these sentences represent a powerful congressional disavowal of *Korematsu*.[45]

Activism throughout the 1980s didn't immediately cause the Supreme Court to renounce *Korematsu*, but it did have a tremendous impact on elite legal culture, eroding the social foundations of that precedent. Lawyers became loathe to cite the case given its negative connotations, beyond doing so for the simple proposition that a race-based law is supposed to trigger stringent review from judges. This reticence has been compounded by withering criticism from academics, who from the start had called the case bad law—even "very bad law."[46]

Particularly noteworthy was the "confession of error" published by Neal Katyal in 2011 as acting solicitor general, expressing regret for the office's role in suppressing the so-called Ringle Report. That memo had indicated that "only a small percentage of Japanese Americans posed a potential security threat, and that the most dangerous were already known or in custody," but this document was never turned over to the internee's lawyers or revealed to the courts. Katyal also apologized for the past solicitor general's decision to tell the justices that "it was impossible to segregate loyal Japanese Americans from disloyal ones" and to rely on "gross generalizations about Japanese Americans, such as that they were disloyal and motivated by 'racial solidarity.'"[47] The import of his apology was unmistakable: the *Korematsu* decision was corrupted by elites who violated ethical standards when they hid unfavorable evidence and misled the courts and the American people. Lawyers helped perpetuate injustice by repeating unfounded racial stereotypes, which judges then repeated as their own justifications for treating a vulnerable population harshly.

Katyal's statements confirmed the crucial role that institutions can play within the politics of repudiation. They reflected the historical judgment of elites as to who they want Americans to be as a people and what rules they think we should all live by. Such judgments are always forward-looking, and this one was no different. The internment-era ruling now seemed jarringly out of place in a modern democracy characterized by pluralism and respect for equality and dignity. There are downstream institutional effects as well that can lock in the whiff of infamy surrounding a case: once such a confession of bad behavior is made, it becomes harder for successors to withdraw such a statement or for others to cite an infamous precedent without incurring denunciations.

Ironically, even before this burst of activism in the 1980s, *Korematsu* had already become doctrinally irrelevant to most disputes involving war making or racial equality. The world had already changed from one where wars were declared to one with a nearly constant state of emergencies often based purely on unilateral presidential action. Other precedents had overtaken *Korematsu*, so one could rely on any number of emergency-based decisions and safely ignore the wartime precedent. In another sense, the civil rights movement of the 1960s had also somewhat undercut the need to repudiate *Korematsu*, by underwriting the principle of racial equality robustly in a democratic fashion. This development made it less urgent to renounce the racially stereotypical forms of analysis that ran throughout Justice Hugo Black's opinion.

In that light, the Supreme Court actually confronted both fewer opportunities to revisit the internment decision and less of a need to do so—that is to say, until a president came along who was willing to invoke (and perhaps manufacture) an emergency to rationalize the unequal treatment of some travelers on the basis of religion or country of origin. President Trump's executive order fulfilling his long-promised Muslim travel ban finally raised many of the analogous concerns at stake in the internment dispute.[48] Yet the law's development in the aftermath of internment allowed advocates on both sides of the travel ban dispute to talk past one another. On the one hand, lawyers for the challengers to the ban took every opportunity to tar the president's travel ban with the negative connotations of *Korematsu*. So did several organizations and individuals who filed briefs in the Court. Some of the children of people detained in the wartime camps filed briefs contending that the president's policy "repeated" all of the mistakes of Roosevelt's internment policies: weak on national security justifications, harmful to political minorities, and infected by racial bias.

On the other hand, while Trump publicly cited the internment of Japanese Americans as precedent for a Muslim ban during the 2016 campaign, the government attorneys wisely shied away from *Korematsu* during litigation. Instead, lawyers preferred to rely on other cases that gave a president broad latitude to exclude individuals for national security reasons.[49]

In the end, the resolution in *Trump v. Hawaii* warns us that the politics of repudiation has its limits. In that decision, which approved Trump's ban by a 5–4 margin, the moral judgment mounting against *Korematsu* was finally acknowledged by Chief Justice Roberts. As he put it, *Korematsu* was "gravely wrong the day it was decided, [and] has been overruled in the court of history." For emphasis, Roberts added: "[T]o be clear [*Korematsu*] has no place in law under the Constitution." This is a welcome statement that should make it more difficult for others to claim that race-based roundups are compatible with civil liberties. The majority had taken umbrage at the comparison to *Korematsu*, and lawyers henceforth would be disarmed from citing that case for such nefarious programs.

And yet, the legal landscape is a little more complicated than that. There is an earlier wartime decision that approved a race-based curfew against people of Japanese ancestry captioned *Hirabayashi v. United States*, and Chief Justice Roberts made no move against that precedent; in fact, he didn't even mention it. His unwillingness to criticize or uproot that case left unclear what the government can do to its own citizens in a time of crisis, short of race-based detention. It's possible that less coercive race-based methods would be constitutional, especially in an emergency.[50]

Moreover, the exceedingly deferential review afforded the president's assertion that visitors from certain Muslim-majority countries represented a real threat, coupled with a refusal to parse the ample evidence of anti-Muslim bigotry on the part of the president and his close aides, suggest that an infamous wartime decision has simply been replaced by another dangerous precedent. Indeed, there is evidence that, afterward, President Trump saw the ruling not merely as a victory on one particular point of policy but rather as an invitation to act expansively and unilaterally in the nation's interest across multiple fronts.

Time will tell whether *Trump v. Hawaii* is perceived by the people as a legitimate ruling or instead one that, as Justice Sonia Sotomayor contends in her scathing dissent, "def[ies] our most sacred legal commitments" and employs "the same dangerous logic underlying *Korematsu*" to "sanction a discriminatory policy."[51] For that judgment of moral disapproval to take hold, however, sizeable numbers of Americans would have to reject the ruling as a thinly veiled ratification of religious animus and therefore as a major departure from our tradition; see it as partisan or biased or otherwise unjust; and discover ways of codifying a sense of outrage with what the Court has done. If such sentiments spread far enough, elites can capitalize on the outcry to take down President Trump's legacy and relegate it to the dustbin of history just like so many other infamous precedents.[52]

Whatever happens, the historical pattern of precedents that have unraveled over time teaches us that interpretation isn't merely an act of reading legal text; it's also a matter of synthesizing political and moral judgments. Constitutional meaning is intelligibly made only by reference to existing bodies of knowledge, and its claim to wisdom and justice ultimately depends on social acceptance by the many interpretive communities affected. And when the gap between judicial reading and communal understanding grows too wide, something will have to give.

NOTES

1 Oliver Wendell Holmes, *The Common Law*, ed. Mark DeWolfe Howe (Cambridge, MA: Belknap Press, 1963), 6.
2 Planned Parenthood of Southeastern Pennsylvania v. Casey, 505 U.S. 833 (1992).
3 Relevant questions include "whether the rule has proved to be intolerable simply in defying practical workability; whether the rule is subject to a kind of reliance that would lend a special hardship to the consequences of overruling and add inequity to the costs of repudiation; whether related principles of law have so far develop as to have left the old rule no more than a remnant of abandoned doctrine; or whether facts have so changed or come to be seen so differently, as to have robbed the old rule of significant application or justification." *Ibid.*
4 Whether there really was ever a crowning era of formalism or antiformalism is merely a recurring trope in political discourse and is a different question. See Brian Z. Tamanaha, *Beyond the Formalist-Realist Divide: The Role of Politics in Judging* (Princeton: Princeton University Press, 2009); Brian Leiter, "Legal Formalism and Legal Realism: What Is the Issue?," *Legal Theory* 16, no. 2: 111–33.
5 Holmes. See also Benjamin N. Cardozo, *The Nature of the Judicial Process* (New Haven: Yale University Press, 1929).
6 *See generally* Nan Goodman and Simon Stern, eds., *Law and the Humanities in Nineteenth-Century America* (Milton Park, UK: Routledge, 2017); Robert L. Tsai, *America's Forgotten Constitutions: Defiant Visions of Power and Community* (Cambridge, MA: Harvard University Press, 2014); Stephen Skowronek, *The Politics Presidents Make: Leadership from John Adams to Bill Clinton* (Cambridge, MA: Harvard University Press, 1997); Kathryn Abrams, "Law's Republicanism," *Yale Law Journal* 97 (1988): 1591–1608.
7 Alexis de Tocqueville, *Democracy in America*, trans. Henry Reeve (1835; New York: Gryphon, 1992), Book I, ch. 16, 254–25.
8 Alexander Hamilton famously expressed the view in *Federalist No. 78* that the judiciary "has no influence over either the sword or the purse; no direction either of the strength or of the wealth of society . . . and must ultimately depend upon the aid of the executive arm even for the efficacy of its judgments."
9 Jamal Greene, "The Anticanon," *Harvard Law Review* 125 (2011): 379–475; J. M. Balkin and Sanford Levinson, "The Canons of Constitutional Law," *Harvard Law Review* 111 (1998): 964–1022; Richard A. Primus, "Canon, Anti-Canon, and Judicial Dissent," *Duke Law Journal* 48 (1998): 243–303.

10 *See generally* Robert L. Tsai, *Eloquence and Reason: Creating a First Amendment Culture* (New Haven: Yale University Press, 2008), 80–82.

11 Dred Scott v. Sandford, 60 U.S. 393 (1857).

12 Roy P. Basler et al., eds., *The Collected Works of Abraham Lincoln (1953–55)*, 401, quoted in Don E. Fehrenbacher, *The* Dred Scott *Case: Its Significance in American Law & Politics* (New York: Oxford University Press, 1978), 442–43. See also Mark A. Graber, Dred Scott *and the Problem of Democratic Evil* (New York: Cambridge University Press, 2008).

13 For an account of regime theory that emphasizes inputs and outcomes rather than discourse and beliefs, see Mark J. Richards and Herbert M. Kritzer, "Jurisprudential Regimes in Supreme Court Decision Making," *American Political Science Review* 96 (2002): 305–20.

14 See Albert O. Hirschman, *Exit, Voice, Loyalty: Responses to Decline in Firms, Organizations, and States* (Cambridge, MA: Harvard University Press, 1970).

15 Eric Foner, *Reconstruction: America's Unfinished Revolution, 1863–1877* (New York, NY: Harper Perennial, 2014), 192; Bruce Ackerman, *We the People: Transformations*, vol. 2 (Cambridge, MA: Belknap Press, 1991).

16 Dred Scott v. Sanford, 60 U.S. 393, 407 (1857).

17 Foner, 195.

18 Roe v. Wade, 410 U.S. 113 (1973); Obergefell v. Hodges, 576 U.S. 644 (2015); Buckley v. Valeo, 424 U.S. 1 (1976); Citizens United v. FEC, 558 U.S. 310 (2010).

19 Jack Balkin and Sandy Levinson call this process "partisan entrenchment." Jack M. Balkin and Sanford Levinson, "The Processes of Constitutional Change: From Partisan Entrenchment to the National Security State," *Fordham Law Review* 75 (2006): 489–535. While redirecting party politics is probably the most efficient way to destabilize a judicial ruling, it's not the only way to do so. Moreover, while the party-centric model has significant explanatory power, anything that can claim to represent constitutional principle must satisfy other conditions that measure the breadth and depth of support for legal change beyond partisan interest.

20 "Trump Judicial Nominees and 'Brown v. Board of Education,'" NPR, May 19, 2019 ("more than 20 Trump judicial nominees have declined to affirm a Supreme Court decision desegregating public schools"). This shift is noticeable given that past conservative judicial nominees, including John Roberts, Samuel Alito, and Brett Kavanaugh, have had no trouble expressing support for *Brown*.

21 Cf. City of Akron v. Akron Center for Reproductive Health, 462 U.S. 416 (1983), with Webster v. Reproductive Health Servs., 492 U.S. 490 (1989).

22 Griswold v. Connecticut, 381 U.S. 479 (1965); Roe v. Wade, 410 U.S. 113, 166 (1973); Planned Parenthood of Southeastern Pennsylvania v. Casey, 505 U.S. 833, 857, 885 (1992) (O'Connor, Kennedy, and Souter, J.J.); Gonzalez v. Carhart, 550 U.S. 124, 134, 159–60 (2007). For more on this transformation of justifications in favor of abortion regulation, see Reva B. Siegel, "Dignity and the Politics of Protection: Abortion Restrictions Under *Casey/Carhart*," *Yale Law Journal* 117 (2008): 1694–

1800; Courtney Megan Cahill, "Abortion and Disgust," *Harvard Civil Rights–Civil Liberties Law Review* 48 (2013): 409–56.

23 State Facts About Abortion: Louisiana, www.guttmacher.org. For useful accounts of abortion politics, see Mary Ziegler, *After* Roe: *The Lost History of the Abortion Debate* (Cambridge, MA: Harvard University Press, 2015); Robert Post and Reva B. Siegel, "Roe *Rage: Democratic Constitutionalism and Backlash,*" *Harvard Civil Rights–Civil Liberties Law Review* 42 (2007): 373–433; Austin Sarat, "Abortion in the Courts: Uncertain Boundaries of Law and Politics," in Allan Sindler, *American Politics and Public Policy* (Washington, D.C.: CQ Press, 1982).

24 Linda Greenhouse and Reva B. Siegel, "The Unfinished Story of *Roe v. Wade,*" *Reproductive Rights and Justice Stories,* ed. Melissa Murry et al. (Eagan, MN: Foundation Press, 2019).

25 Joseph Carroll, "Most Americans Approve of Interracial Marriages," *Gallup,* Aug. 16, 2007.

26 Sarah Polus, "Poll: Majority of Republicans Support Same-Sex Marriage for the First Time," *The Hill,* Mar. 23, 2021.

27 Masterpiece Cakeshop v. Colorado Civil Rights Commission, 138 S. Ct. 1719 (2017).

28 Robert Cover coined this phrase to delineate the forces that act upon a social group's view of the legal world when an authoritative decision is rendered that casts doubt upon its members' sense of what is right and good. See infra note 28.

29 Neal Devins, "Ideological Cohesion and Precedent (Or Why the Court Only Cares About Precedent When Most Justices Agree with Each Other)," *North Carolina Law Review* 86 (2008): 1399–1442.

30 Mark Tushnet, *The NAACP's Legal Strategy Against Segregated Education, 1925–1950* (Chapel Hill: University of North Carolina Press, 1987); Richard Kluger, *Simple Justice: The History of* Brown v. Board *of Education and Black America's Struggle for Equality* (New York: Knopf, 1975).

31 Philip Elman and Norman Silber, "The Solicitor General's Office, Justice Frankfurter, and Civil Rights Litigation, 1946–1960: An Oral History," *Harvard Law Review* 100 (1987): 817–52; Mark Tushnet and Katya Lezin, "What Really Happened in *Brown v. Board of Education,*" *Columbia Law Review* 91 (1991): 1867–1930.

32 See generally Lawrence Baum and Neal Devins, "Why the Supreme Court Cares about Elites, Not the American People," *Georgetown Law Journal* 98 (2010): 1515–81.

33 Sweatt v. Painter, 339 U.S. 629 (1950); McLaurin v. Oklahoma State Regents, 339 U.S. 637 (1950).

34 Brief for the United States as Amicus Curiae, Brown v. Board of Education, 1952 WL 82045, Dec. 2, 1952. *See generally* Mary M. Dudziak, *Cold War Civil Rights: Race and the Image of American Democracy* (Princeton: Princeton University Press, 2000); Rogers M. Smith and Philip A. Klinkner, *The Unsteady March: The Rise and Decline of Racial Equality in America* (Chicago: University of Chicago Press, 1999).

35 Eighth Amendment jurisprudence explicitly contemplates consideration of a broad consideration of legal trends and statutory developments to ascertain "evolving standards of decency." Trop v. Dulles, 356 U.S. 86 (1958).

36 Lawrence v. Texas, 539 U.S. 558 (2003); Bowers v. Hardwick, 478 U.S. 186 (1986); *see generally* Dale Carpenter, *Flagrant Conduct: The Story of* Lawrence v. Texas (New York: W.W. Norton, 2012).

37 Robert M. Cover, "Foreword: Nomos and Narrative," *Harvard Law Review* 97 (1983): 4–68. See also James Boyd White, *Heracles' Bow: Essays on the Rhetoric and Poetics of the Law* (Madison: University of Wisconsin Press, 1985); Austin Sarat, *Law, Violence, and the Possibility of Justice* (Princeton: Princeton University Press, 2002); Kathryn Abrams, "Contentious Citizenship: Undocumented Activism in the Not1More Deportation Campaign," *Berkeley La Raza Law Journal* 26 (2016): 46–69; Robert A. Ferguson, "The Judicial Opinion as Literary Genre," *Yale Journal of Law and the Humanities* 2 (1990): 201–19.

38 Minersville School District v. Gobitis, 310 U.S. 586 (1940); West Virginia School Board v. Barnette, 319 U.S. 624 (1943).

39 Robert L. Tsai, "Reconsidering *Gobitis*: An Exercise of Presidential Leadership," *Washington University Law Review* 86 (2008): 363–443; Mark Graber, "Counter-Stories: Maintaining and Expanding Civil Liberties in Wartime," in *The Constitution in Wartime: Beyond Alarmism and Complacency*, ed. Mark Tushnet (Durham: Duke Univerity Press, 2005); Austin Sarat, *Speech and Silence in American Law* (New York: Cambridge University Press, 2010); *see generally* Kevin J. MacMahon, *Reconsidering Roosevelt on Race: How the Presidency Paved the Road to* Brown (Chicago: University of Chicago Press, 2004).

40 Harold L. Ickes, *The Secret Diary of Harold L. Ickes, The Lowering Clouds, 1939–1941* (New York, NY: Simon & Schuster, 1954), 199; "Judge Rutledge Raps Flag-Salute Rule in Schools," *Evening Star* (Washington, DC), June 10, 1940, 19, in John M. Ferren, *Salt of the Earth, Conscience of the Court: The Story of Justice Wiley Rutledge* (Chapel Hill: University of North Carolina, 2004), 188.

41 Victor W. Rotnem and F.G. Folsom, "Recent Restrictions Upon Religious Liberty," *American Political Science Review* 36 (1942): 1053–68.

42 *See, e.g.*, Adarand Constructors, Inc. v. Peña, 515 U.S. 200, 214 (1995); Loving v. Virginia, 388 U.S. 1, 11 (1967).

43 Korematsu v. United States, 584 F. Supp. 1406 (N.D. Cal. 1984).

44 Personal Justice Denied, Report of the Commission on Wartime Relocation and Internment of Civilians, Dec. 1982, 3, 18.

45 An Act to Implement Recommendations of the Commission on Wartime Relocation and Internment of Civilians, Public Law No. 100–383, 100th Cong., Aug. 10, 1988.

46 *See, e.g.*, Bruce Ackerman, "The Emergency Constitution," *Yale Law Journal* 113 (2004): 1029–91, 1043; David Cole, "Judging the Next Emergency: Judicial Review and Individual Rights in Times of Crisis," *Michigan Law Review* 101 (2003): 2565–95, 2575; Eric L. Muller, "12/7 and 9/11: War, Liberties, and the Lessons of History,"

West Virginia Law Review 104 (2002): 571–92, 586; Eugene Rostow, "The Japanese American Cases—A Disaster," *Yale Law Journal* 54 (1945): 489–533, 532.

47 Neal Katyal, Acting Solicitor General, Confession of Error: The Solicitor General's Mistakes During the Japanese-American Internment Cases, May 20, 2011.

48 For a rising concern about presidents who, in a time of corroding democratic norms, lie about the nature or severity of an emergency, see Robert L. Tsai, "Manufactured Emergencies," *Yale Law Journal Forum* 129 (2020): 590–609.

49 Adam Liptak, "Travel Ban Case is Shadowed By One of Supreme Court's Darkest Moments," *New York Times*, Apr. 16, 2018; Brief of Karen Korematsu et al. as Amici Curiae, Trump v. Hawaii, No. 17–965, Mar. 30, 2018.

50 Hirabayashi v. United States, 320 U.S. 81 (1942).

51 Trump v. Hawaii, 138 S. Ct. 2392 (2018), 138 S. Ct. at 2433 (Sotomayor and Ginsburg, J.J., dissenting). Americans were divided over the travel ban before the Court ruled, with some polls showing that a plurality opposed the ban. At the same time, a majority of Americans see it as an attempted Muslim ban despite the Court's characterization of it in religiously neutral terms; 59% backed lower court rulings that had enjoined earlier versions of the policy. Grace Sparks, "Americans Have Been Split on Trump's Travel Ban for a While," *CNN Politics*, June 26, 2018.

52 Charlie Savage, "Korematsu, Notorious Supreme Court Ruling on Japanese Internment, Is Finally Tossed Out," *New York Times*, June 26, 2018 (highlighting Sotomayor's prediction that "Trump v. Hawaii may go down in Supreme Court history as a second coming of *Korematsu*").

4

Law's Infamy in the U.S. "War on Terror"

RICHARD L. ABEL

"Infamy" is a capacious concept with multiple definitions converging on the idea of extreme evil. Because the most fundamental ideals of justice are embodied in the concept of the rule of law, its violation epitomizes law's infamy. The nearly two decades of the U.S. "war on terror" have been tragically replete with such violations: torture, detention without trial, electronic surveillance, extraordinary rendition, war crimes against civilians, and denials of due process and freedom of speech and religion. I documented these numerous transgressions in two recent books.[1] Here I want to focus on efforts to *defend* the rule of law against those whose actions rendered law infamous.

The rule of law embodies basic notions of fairness.[2] Those due process guarantees enable lawyers to redress other injustices and have the potential to enlist support across the political spectrum.[3] As a new law graduate, I saw firsthand what civil rights lawyers were able to achieve in Mississippi.[4] A quarter-century later, I was privileged to witness the courage, commitment, competence, and surprising victories of lawyers in the struggle against apartheid in South Africa.[5] When the Abu Ghraib atrocities were exposed in 2004, I felt impelled to investigate how the American legal system responded to this latest threat to the rule of law. I expected American lawyers to be at least as successful as their South African counterparts. After all, the United States has a written constitution with a bill of rights, an independent judiciary that has reviewed the constitutionality of executive and legislative decisions for more than two centuries, an independent media free from government control, a large and diverse legal profession, and sophisticated and well-resourced NGOs.

Yet like many others, I have been deeply discouraged by how little human rights lawyers were able to achieve during the war on terror. This was not for want of trying. Organizations such as the ACLU, Human

Rights First, Human Rights Watch, Amnesty International, the Center for Constitutional Rights (CCR), and Reprieve fought vigorously. Hundreds of lawyers from firms of all sizes, as well as legal aid and public defender offices, brought habeas corpus petitions on behalf Guantánamo detainees.[6] Military lawyers, ranging from the general counsels of the four armed services to the Judge Advocates General and Staff Judge Advocates, challenged the legal framework of the "war on terror" and aggressively represented accused persons before military commissions.[7] Lawyers courageously performed their roles in difficult situations. In the Department of Justice (DOJ) Office of Professional Responsibility, Jesselyn Radack criticized the FBI, first for interrogating John Walker Lindh after his parents had retained counsel for him, and then for failing to inform the federal judge hearing Lindh's case that she (Radack) had opposed interrogation. After leaving the DOJ, she was criminally investigated, fired by her law firm, and referred for investigation by the Maryland and the District of Columbia bars.[8] Acting Attorney General James Comey raced to Attorney General John Ashcroft's hospital bedside to stop White House counsel Alberto Gonzales from obtaining Ashcroft's signature on an authorization for illegal wiretapping. Comey was rewarded by being named FBI director by President Barack Obama, only to be dismissed and excoriated by President Donald Trump.[9]

Here, however, I will not discuss such heroes—although they cannot be honored too greatly.[10] Instead I want to analyze the two extremes on the spectrum of responses to law's infamy in the war on terror. The first is the legal system's abject failure to punish lawyers who rendered the law infamous (with one revealing exception). The second are those rare lawyers whose personal encounters with infamy *impelled* their advocacy for the rule of law. Because we lack adequate theories to explain such complex behaviors, I will present thick descriptions before offering my own interpretations.[11]

The Impunity of the Legal Architects of the "War on Terror"

Lawyers in the DOJ Office of Legal Counsel (OLC) under President George W. Bush constructed the legal framework for what the administration called its global "war on terror" by writing memos authorizing indefinite detention at Guantánamo Bay (which they pronounced was outside the jurisdiction of American courts); trial by military commission (unconstrained by the Constitution); harsh interrogation techniques including torture; extraordinary rendition to countries known to torture; secret CIA prisons; warrantless surveillance; and assassination by drones. These OLC opinions—which carry the force of law for the executive branch—were widely condemned and sometimes withdrawn.[12] But the authors suffered no consequences. John Yoo returned to his tenured position at UC–Berkeley, escaping professional discipline and civil liability, and the Justice Department's Office of Professional Responsibility exonerated him.[13] Despite numerous student protests, he was named to the Emanuel S. Heller chair. He remains brazenly unapologetic about his memos but may be seeking to redeem himself by criticizing Trump.[14] Jay Bybee was appointed to the United States Court of Appeals for the Ninth Circuit before the memos surfaced. Alberto Gonzales was forced to resign as United States Attorney General for appointing "loyal Bushies" as United States Attorneys, not for his involvement in the war on terror. He joined the law faculty at Belmont University and became dean. Robert Delahunty was hired by the University of St. Thomas Law School. Steven Bradbury became a partner in the global law firm Dechert and was named general counsel of the U.S. Department of Transportation by Trump. William Haynes stepped down as Department of Defense general counsel to become general counsel of Chevron when his judicial nomination foundered. After serving as Dick Cheney's counsel for eight years, David Addington joined the conservative Heritage Foundation.

Given the impunity of high legal officials complicit in the infamy of law in the U.S. war on terror, the saga of Charles "Cully" Stimson is instructive. In July 2004, Bush appointed this former prosecutor to the newly created position of deputy assistant secretary of defense for detainee affairs. A July 2006 interview revealed him to be an apologist for *indefinite detention*, not an advocate for *detainees*:[15]

We're proud of the care and treatment we provide detainees at Guantánamo. They get three square meals a day, culturally sensitive meals, blessed by an imam. They have a menu . . . that they get to order from. . . . They practice call to prayer five times a day. There are arrows pointing towards Mecca. . . . They get first class medical care, dental care. . . .

[D]uring some interrogations, which are no different than you or I sitting across from each other today, some of them ask for McDonald's, and sure, I've watched some interrogations where they're chowing down on a Big Mac. . . . This country is entitled to detain enemies against it. We don't have any obligation to give them a quarter so they can call a lawyer. We don't have any obligation when we had 400,000 Nazis here in this country at the beginning of World War II, to give them a trial.

(Of course, the U.S. never held 400,000 Nazis, though it did deny a trial to detained German Americans.)

Six months later, Stimson assailed corporate law firms for providing pro bono representation to Guantánamo detainees petitioning for habeas corpus:[16]

I think the news story that you're really going to start seeing in the next couple of weeks is this. As a result of a FOIA [Freedom of Information Act] request through a major news organization, somebody asked, "Who are the lawyers around this country representing detainees down there?" And you know what, it's shocking.

He named more than a dozen "major law firms," hoping to shame their corporate clients into firing them:

I think, quite honestly, when corporate C.E.O.'s see that those firms are representing the very terrorists who hit their bottom line back in 2001, those C.E.O.'s are going to make those law firms choose between representing terrorists or representing reputable firms, and I think that is going to have major play in the next few weeks. And we want to watch that play out.

Asked who was paying, Stimson replied:

It's not clear, is it? Some will maintain that they are doing it out of the goodness of their heart, that they're doing it pro bono, and I suspect they are; others are receiving moneys from who knows where, and I'd be curious to have them explain that.

The next day, a *Wall Street Journal* op-ed stated that a "senior official"—presumably Stimson—

> speculates that this information might cause something of a scandal, since so much of the pro bono work being done to tilt the playing field in favor of al Qaeda appears to be subsidized by legal fees from the Fortune 500. "Corporate CEOs seeing this should ask firms to choose between lucrative retainers and representing terrorists" who deliberately target the U.S. economy.[17]

As Stimson had boasted, the story got "major play"—but not exactly what he had sought. Instead of shaming corporate clients into pressuring their law firms to jettison Guantánamo detainees, it provoked a tsunami of criticism. Declaring that "most Americans understand that legal representation for the accused is one of the core principles of the American way," the *Washington Post* denounced Stimson's "repellant" and "shocking" interview.[18] Although unsurprised that "a member of [Bush's] team scorns American notions of justice," the *New York Times* wrote that "even by that low standard . . . the administration's new attack on lawyers" was "contemptible."[19] It also published letters from lawyers condemning Stimson.[20] Calling it "an axiom of the American justice system that the accused is entitled to a vigorous defense," the *Chicago Tribune* demanded that Stimson offer "an explanation, and an apology."[21] Likening Stimson's "crankish comments" to McCarthyism, the *Los Angeles Times* said they "reflect a more pervasive reluctance by the Bush administration to acknowledge that injustices have occurred at Guantánamo."[22] "Advocacy on behalf of due process is a form of patriotism and public service." Even the generally apolitical *USA Today* said the 500 lawyers representing detainees pro bono "show . . . the American system at its best."[23]

Senator Patrick Leahy urged Bush to "disavow" these "reprehensible comments [which] go against some of the basic tenets of our society."[24] The president of the American Bar Association said that "lawyers represent people in criminal cases to fulfill a core American value. To impugn those who are doing this critical work . . . is deeply offensive to members of the legal profession."[25] The president of the

American Judicature Society called the "shameful and irresponsible" comments a "blatant attempt to intimidate lawyers and their firms who are rendering important public service in upholding the rule of law and our democratic ideals."[26] The Society of American Law Teachers denounced Stimson for having "violated the highest standards of our profession."[27] Describing it as "one of the most severe blows the Bush administration has dealt to our constitutional democracy," the National Lawyers Guild demanded that Bush "renounce Stimson's threats and relieve him of his duties."[28] A letter from fifty-seven law school deans noted that "we teach our students that lawyers have a professional obligation to ensure that even the most despised and unpopular individuals and groups receive zealous and effective legal representation."[29]

The White House had no comment. A Defense Department spokesman denied that Stimson spoke for the administration.[30] Attorney General Gonzales distanced the Justice Department: "[G]ood lawyers representing the detainees is the best way to ensure that justice is done in these cases."

Stimson wrote to the *Washington Post*:[31]

Regrettably, my comments left the impression that I question the integrity of those engaged in the zealous defense of detainees in Guantánamo. I do not. I believe firmly that a foundational principle of our legal system is that the system works best when both sides are represented by competent counsel.

As a Navy JAG "I zealously represented unpopular clients." "I hope that my record of public service makes clear that those comments do not reflect my core beliefs."

But the *New York Times* responded that "it is hard to render a convincing apology when you are not really apologizing."[32] It was not "just an impression" that Stimson had attacked lawyers' integrity, "it was exactly what he did." "President Bush and Defense Secretary Robert Gates should have fired him." Attorney General Gonzales "actually expanded the attack . . . claiming that it has taken as long as five years to bring detainees to trial because of delays caused by their lawyers."

Mr. Stimson's appalling behavior should not be overlooked by the relevant bar disciplinary committee. Existing rules for lawyers deem it professional misconduct to do things that are prejudicial to the administration of justice. Even if the administration does not, the legal profession imposes a higher duty on those holding public office to obey proper standards of behavior.

Although the San Francisco Bar Association asked the California State Bar to investigate Stimson, legal ethicists doubted he had violated professional rules, and he was never charged.[33] Yet just three weeks after making his statements, Stimson quit to join the conservative Heritage Foundation.[34] The American Bar Association expressed satisfaction that, by reacting to his comments, "the American public reaffirmed its commitment to a core principle of our justice system: that every accused person deserves adequate legal representation." Trump twice unsuccessfully nominated him to become general counsel of the United States Navy.

The contrast between the treatments of Yoo and Stimson could not be greater. Yoo's violations of the rule of law were far more infamous. He and other OLC lawyers deliberately concocted the dubious legal rationales enabling the indefinite detention of hundreds of detainees, the egregious abuse of many, the secret surveillance of hundreds of millions, and the deaths of dozens of drone attack victims, many of them innocent civilians. Stimson's offensive but offhand comment only *strengthened* the commitment of pro bono lawyers representing Guantánamo detainees. Yet he felt compelled to resign, whereas the OLC opinion writers went unpunished. How should we understand those divergent responses? Was Stimson simply a disposable low-level official, much like the "bad apples" who took the rap for Abu Ghraib?[35] Was it the uncomfortable parallel with Joseph McCarthy?[36] Was it because zealous advocacy—especially on behalf of those detained without trial—is such a fundamental, unambiguous tenet of the American legal profession?[37] Or because Stimson naively targeted the professional elite? What makes it so difficult to specify how Yoo behaved unethically? Is it possible to demarcate the limits of lawyer fidelity to client interests? Does that vary with the client's identity? Who was Yoo's client: the executive branch, which sought the opinions? The people of the United States whom he served? The Constitution to which he had sworn allegiance? If the hired-gun theory justifies zealous advocacy on behalf of a criminal accused, does it do so when the federal government seeks to wield its awesome power? When does a lawyer have a moral obligation to refuse a client's request? When does a legal argument become too flimsy to be asserted? Given that Yoo was writing legal opinions that bound the executive branch, was he functioning as an advocate or in a quasijudicial capacity? If all law is indeterminate, as legal realists and critical legal theorists maintained, are there no limits on interpretation? Many Justice Department lawyers declined assignments to oppose habeas corpus petitions by Guantánamo detainees. And during apartheid, South Africans debated whether judges should resign.[38] Should the OLC lawyers have done so? I frame this analysis as a series of rhetorical questions because I do not have the answers.

Lawyers on the Road to Damascus

If the legal system generally failed to provide any counterweight to infamous administration lawyers violating the rule of law in the name of waging a "war on terror," a few individual lawyers experienced dramatic conversions in the course of performing their legal duties. I offer five inspiring examples.

Matthew Diaz

Matthew Diaz is a Horatio Alger story with a tragic ending.[39] After his parents went through a bitter divorce when he was six, custody battles sent Matthew and three siblings back and forth between their mother and father, so often that he had attended nine schools by seventh grade. In ninth grade, he lived with his father, Robert, a nurse, in a Southern California dream house with a swimming pool and a pair of horses. Two years later, however, his father was charged with euthanizing twelve elderly patients. Diaz dropped out of school at 16, moved into a motel room with his 28-year-old girlfriend, and washed dishes for a living. Having enlisted in the army at 17 (with his mother's permission), he was in Germany when he learned that his father had been convicted of the twelve murders and sentenced to death. Convinced of his father's innocence, he completed an AA degree in law enforcement and then a BA in criminology while in the military. Although he planned to leave it for the police, seeing the Jimmy Smits character on *L.A. Law* and hearing an Army lawyer speak in class persuaded him to leave the military and go to law school. He graduated a semester early, while driving a mail truck on weekends, and then enlisted in the Navy, completing an LLM after seven years in the JAG Corps. Toward the end of his ten years as a Staff Judge Advocate, he was recommended for early promotion to commander as a "consummate naval officer" and "a stellar leader of unquestionable integrity." He patriotically volunteered for a six-month tour in Guantánamo, arriving in July 2004.

At the time, his daughter was 15, close to the age he had been when his father was charged with murder—falsely, in Diaz's view. At Guantánamo, he was quickly outraged by government lies. He felt pity, not fear, for detainees unfairly maligned as "the worst of the worst." In the wake of Abu Ghraib, the administration kept protesting that "we do not torture." But assigned to investigate detainee abuse allegations, Diaz soon filled two large binders with evidence, including a senior FBI agent's assertion that the military had ignored valid complaints. Diaz felt "a good case could be made for allegations of war crimes."

He was liaison for the DOJ and the Navy Office of the General Counsel in a U.S. district court case in which the government argued that the military should be able to eavesdrop on detainee conversations with their civilian lawyers (even though military intelligence at Guantánamo thought this unnecessary). The DOJ prepared an affidavit for the base commander, asserting that some detainees had been trained to pass "coded messages in furtherance of terrorist operations." Diaz was asked to show how twelve Kuwaiti detainees could do this; but he could find only three who were even plausibly dangerous and felt the argument was "a reach. We were just throwing up these obstacles in the way of implementing the *Rasul* decision," in which the United States Supreme Court had decided (the week before he arrived in Guantánamo) that detainees were entitled to petition for habeas corpus.[40] (That essential right had personal significance for Diaz because it had saved his father from execution.) He was copied on a letter from the Navy secretary refusing to disclose detainees' names to Barbara Olshansky, a lawyer at the Center for Constitutional Rights, which was arranging pro bono representation for habeas petitions (the very lawyers Stimson later attacked). These names were indispensable for those petitions. Diaz was convinced that "no matter what the courts said, [the military] would just keep stonewalling." Charged with managing civilian lawyers, he met—and was charmed by—Gitanjali Gutierrez, a CCR lawyer to whom he wished a happy birthday in an email message scheduling one of her visits to the island.

Working late on January 2, 2005, he found a list of the names and nationalities of all 551 detainees, with "Source ID" codes indicating their interrogators and the value of the information elicited. (Although a prosecutor called these codes "gobbledygook," the government claimed that they put intelligence "sources and methods" at risk.) The list was not marked as secret. "I knew that if I didn't do anything, nobody else was going to." He printed the list, cut it into thirty-nine sheets to fit inside a Valentine's Day card, and mailed it to Olshansky in an unmarked envelope on January 15—his last day in Guantánamo. After receiving it and agonizing for weeks, she called the chambers of the federal judge hearing her habeas petitions and was told by the clerk to give it to the FBI. Diaz was quickly identified through fingerprints and his computer hard drive.

By the time he was court-martialed, an Associated Press FOIA lawsuit had compelled the government to release all the names. Diaz said "my oath as a commissioned officer is to the Constitution of the United States. I'm not a criminal." "I made a stupid decision, I know, but I felt it was the right decision, the moral decision, the decision that was required by international law." He knew he should have raised the issue through the chain of command, "but nothing I said would have ever left the island." Following a weeklong trial, he was acquitted of disclosing national defense information with intent or reason to believe it would be used against the United States but convicted of knowingly communicating information "to a person not entitled to receive it." Although he faced up to fourteen years, he was sentenced to just six months and discharged. After his release, he visited his father on death row and explained what had happened. Robert said proudly that his son had done the right thing. But the Kansas Supreme Court disbarred him, against the recommendation of its disciplinary committee, ending his legal career. He was awarded the Ridenhour Prize for Truth Telling. After moving to New York, he passed the bar exam in 2011 but waited until just before the three-year deadline to apply for admission. At his initial character and fitness examination, the interviewer indicated he was inclined to recommend denial but instead recommended a panel hearing. Morris Davis (whose case is described below) testified during the two-day hearing, and the panel's two members split; the full committee denied the application. On appeal, the Second Department Appellate Division upheld the denial but granted leave to reapply in a year, which Diaz did, gaining admission in May 2018. He is now an intake coordinator at Bronx Defenders.

Stephen Abraham

Stephen Abraham was a conservative Republican who cried when President Richard Nixon resigned.[41] As the son of a Holocaust survivor who emigrated to the United States after World War II, Abraham felt an obligation to repay his country for the opportunities it had given his family. He spent twenty-six years as an Army Reserve intelligence officer, rising to lieutenant colonel and being decorated twice: in the 1980s for heading a counterespionage operation that led to the detention of three Soviet agents; and after 9/11 for exceptionally meritorious services as "lead counterterrorism analyst." In September 2004, he jumped at the "fantastic opportunity" of a six-month tour of duty at Guantánamo in the Office for the Administrative Review of the Detention of Enemy Combatants (OARDEC), helping to build the evidentiary database for the Combatant Status Review Tribunals (CSRTs), which determined whether detainees could be held, and sitting on a CSRT for Abdel Hamid al-Ghazzawi. He quickly became skeptical of the government claim that all detainees were jihadists:

> As an intellagent, I would have written "junk statement" across that. . . . Anything that resulted in a "not enemy combatant" would just send ripples through the entire process. The interpretation is, "you got the wrong result. Do it again." . . . [T]he hearings amounted to a superficial summary of information, the quality of which would not have withstood scrutiny in any serious law-enforcement or intelligence investigation.

As a lawyer, he began to feel he should not be involved. "There were too many assumptions. Too many presumptions." On December 10, he wrote OARDEC director Rear Admiral James M. McGarrah, asking to be relieved because his participation "may be in conflict with my obligations as an attorney"; but he got no reply. After his tour ended, he returned to his two-person commercial practice in Newport Beach, California. But during visits to Washington, he stayed with his sister, a lawyer whose colleagues began representing Guantánamo detainees in 2006. In June 2007, after she shared her brother's concerns with those colleagues, Matthew J. MacLean, who was seeking habeas on behalf of al-Ghazzawi, asked Abraham to look at McGarrah's affidavit in opposition to the petition. Outraged by what he saw as its distortions, Abraham wrote his own declaration on June 18:[42]

> I communicated to Rear Admiral McGarrah . . . the fundamental limitations imposed upon my review of the organization's files and my inability to state conclusively that no exculpatory information existed relating to CSRT subjects. . . . It was well known by the officers in OARDEC that any time a CSRT panel determined that a detainee was not properly classified as an enemy combatant, the panel members would have to explain their finding to the OARDEC Deputy Director. There would be intensive scrutiny of the finding by Rear Admiral McGarrah who would, in turn, have to explain the finding to his superiors, including the Under Secretary of the Navy.

In the CSRT on which he had served, "all of us found the information presented to lack substance."

> [W]e determined that there was no factual basis for concluding that the individual should be classified as an enemy combatant. Rear Admiral McGarrah and the Deputy Director immediately questioned the validity of our findings. They directed us to write out the specific questions that we had raised concerning the evidence to allow the Recorder an opportunity to provide further responses. We were then ordered to reopen the hearing to allow the Recorder to present further argument. . . . Ultimately, in the absence of any substantive response to the questions and no basis for concluding that additional information would be forthcoming, we did not change our determination. . . . In each of the meetings that I attended with OARDEC leadership following a finding of NEC [not enemy com-

batant], the focus of inquiry on the part of the leadership was "what went wrong." I was not assigned to another CSRT panel.

Al-Ghazzawi had hepatitis B and tuberculosis. He had not seen or talked to his family for almost six years and was "rapidly losing his mind as he sits in total isolation. He's about my age. He's got a daughter," as did Abraham. "He hasn't seen her in a long time. He's close to death."

Two weeks after MacLean filed Abraham's declaration, the Supreme Court agreed to hear the appeal in *Boumediene v. Bush*, ultimately reaffirming the right to habeas.[43] The habeas lawyers subsequently learned that, two months after Abraham's CSRT unanimously found that al-Ghazzawi was "not properly classified as an enemy combatant," the Defense Department rejected the finding and resubmitted the case to another CSRT, which unanimously found the opposite. Abraham said that "conducting new CSRTs—even discussing the possibility—repudiates every prior assertion that the original CSRTs were valid acts. . . . [T]hey are, in essence, both a hypocritical act as well as an act of moral cowardice." The CSRTs "were specifically designed to reach a result and, in the few instances where a contrary result was reached, pressure was exerted to change the decision, a new tribunal was selected," or the decision was disregarded. An Army major who had sat on forty-nine tribunals also submitted an affidavit criticizing them. After Abraham testified before the House Armed Services Committee that the evidence before the CSRTs was "garbage," McGarrah told the committee that Abraham saw only "a very narrow piece of the process." President Obama eventually replaced the CSRTs with Periodic Review Boards offering more due process. Al-Ghazzawi was transferred from Guantánamo to the nation of Georgia in 2010. Abraham continued practicing in Newport Beach.

Morris "Moe" Davis

Air Force Colonel Morris "Moe" Davis was the fiercely aggressive chief prosecutor of the military commissions.[44] Before being appointed, he had spent twenty-two years in the military, thirteen as a Staff Judge Advocate. During pretrial hearings, he denounced sympathetic portrayals of Omar Khadr by his civilian lawyer as "nauseating" and pronounced Khadr a "guilty" "terrorist":[45]

Remember if you dragged Dracula out into the sunlight he melted? Well that's kind of the way it is trying to drag a detainee into the courtroom. The facts are like sunlight to Dracula. The last thing they want is to face the facts in the courtroom. But their day is coming.[46]

He declared "there is no evidence we are going to offer that I have seen that I would call tantamount to being derived from torture."[47] He resisted applying the laws of war, misrepresenting Justice Stephen Breyer as having said "this is not a war, at least not an ordinary war."[48] When a defense attorney "desperately" asked "what I . . . want to know here is: What are the rules?" Davis was casually dismissive: "[A]ll processes have a start. At the start, there's nothing you can turn to."[49] He expected to charge "about two dozen" detainees, some of whom had been "specifically training to build bombs to kill coalition forces."[50] Davis was unsympathetic to a military defense attorney who expressed ethical qualms about representing a client who wanted to act for himself: "[R]ight now they're military officers and they're ordered to" represent even unwilling clients.[51] When President Bush transferred the fourteen high-value detainees from secret CIA prisons to Guantánamo for trial, Davis said that "even though we'll be starting over, we won't be starting over from scratch."[52] Khalid Sheikh Mohammed could be charged with murdering more than 2,700 people: "[H]e is liable for the actions he set in motion." Davis now expected to prosecute seventy detainees.[53] He repeated his prejudgment of Omar Khadr: "We have a crime scene, we have facts, we have witnesses."

Davis attacked defense attorney Major Michael Mori, who had visited Australia seven times on behalf of David Hicks (an Australian), warning Mori that such "politicking" could prompt charges under the Uniform Code of Military Justice:[54]

I don't know what Major Mori's plans are right now, but if he wants to come back home and represent his client, that would be helpful. Certainly in the U.S. it would not be tolerated having a U.S. Marine in uniform actively inserting himself into the political process. . . . [I]f that was any of my prosecutors, they would be held accountable. . . . Go back and look at some of the things he has said. He's on the [defense] side and he doesn't seem to be held to the same standards as his brother officers.

A military law expert speculated that Davis could be charged with unlawful command influence. Mori asked: "[A]re they trying to intimidate me?" Davis's threat raised the question: "[A]m I doing what I'm doing because it is in the best interests of my client, or to avoid being charged?" The *Washington Post* warned that Stimson's spirit "lives on."[55] Davis's "unsubtle effort to quiet Maj. Mori may be even more disturbing . . . it's the prosecution that really needs reining in."

Davis summarily rejected criticism of the commissions: "[T]he idea that we've created this Frankenstein, cobbled-together system is not accurate."[56] When Mori moved to replace him because of the threatening remarks, Davis insisted he had done "nothing wrong."[57] But Hicks's trial was aborted when he pleaded guilty to a single charge of material support.[58] Blindsided by the negotiations, in which he had not participated, Davis did not claim this as a "victory" but said he was "satisfied where we stand at this moment." "There's a notion that this is a rigged system. I think this shows that's not true." Hicks was "very fortunate. He's getting a second chance." While conceding that the young adventurer had not been "at the top of the pyramid," Davis expressed shock at learning that the deal was for just nine months: "I wasn't considering anything that didn't have two digits." He still planned seventy-four prosecutions.

Davis renewed his public vituperation of Omar Khadr.[59] In response to defense claims that Omar had been a juvenile and strongly influenced by his father at the time of the alleged crime, Davis declared "there is a difference between a 15-year-old who makes a spur-of-the-moment decision and someone who made a long-term choice." "If the United Nations has signed on to [the] principle that people who are 15 can be prosecuted for war crimes, the notion that we're blazing a new trail with Mr. Khadr is a false assumption."

> You'll see the evidence when we get into the courtroom of the smiling face of Omar Khadr as he builds bombs to kill Americans. I don't think it's a great leap to figure out why we're holding him accountable. They weren't making s'mores and learning how to tie knots.

In a *New York Times* op-ed, Davis echoed Stimson's defense of[60] the daily professionalism of [Guantánamo Bay's] staff, the humanity of its detention centers and the fair and transparent nature of the military commissions . . . most of the detainees are housed in new buildings modeled after civilian prisons . . . detainees receive three culturally appropriate meals a day. Each has a copy of the Koran. Guards maintain respectful silence during Islam's five daily prayer periods, and medical care is provided by the same practitioners who treat American service members. Detainees are offered at least two hours of outdoor recreation each day. . . . Standards at Guantánamo rival or exceed those at similar institutions in the United States or abroad.

Military commissions provided the "fundamental guarantees" of the Third Geneva Convention. Although "any statement by a person whose freedom is restrained . . . can be viewed as the product of some degree of coercion," Davis made "the final decision on the evidence the prosecution will introduce," thereby ensuring "robust safeguards." His claims provoked vehement rebuttal letters to the *Times* from lawyers at Human Rights Watch, Human Rights First, and the Center for Constitutional Rights.[61]

When the Court of Military Commission Review reinstated the case against Khadr (after the trial judge held that the CSRT had never determined he was an unlawful enemy combatant), Davis declared he was looking forward "to getting back into court soon."[62] He was "hopeful we can resolve" some "internal" issues "quickly and start some new cases."

But on October 4, less than two weeks later, he abruptly resigned as chief prosecutor.[63] He had clashed with Brigadier General Thomas W. Hartmann, a former corporate lawyer appointed the previous summer as legal adviser to Susan J. Crawford, the Convening Authority (executive in charge of military commissions). In August, Hartmann challenged Davis's authority, urging prosecutors to accelerate charging and to prioritize dramatic cases that could attract public attention. Davis formally complained that Hartmann had exceeded his authority and created a conflict of interest. It was improper for Hartmann to be involved in the filing of cases whose adequacy he would later have to assess. On September 21, Crawford sided with Hartmann. In a public statement, Davis now said "for the greater good, Brig. Gen. Hartmann and I should both resign and walk away or higher authority should relieve us of our duties."

The Defense Department found that Hartmann had not tried to coerce the prosecution team, but it advised him to "diligently avoid aligning himself with the prosecutorial function so that he can objectively and independently provide cogent legal advice" to the Convening Authority. Davis asked to be reassigned and was appointed head of the Air Force judiciary. He said: "I'm under direct orders not to comment with the media about the reasons for my resignation or military commissions."

But he did so two weeks later.[64] A year earlier, senior defense officials had discussed the "strategic political value" of prosecuting particular detainees, urging Davis to pursue "sexy" cases rather than those that were strongest or closest to trial. Recently, newly appointed senior officials had pressed him to use classified evidence in closed sessions. And the entire operation was subordinated to William Haynes, the Defense Department's general counsel. "There was a big concern that the election of 2008 is coming up. People wanted to get the cases going. There was a rush to get high-interest cases into court at the expense of openness." "The guy who said waterboarding is A-okay I was not going to take orders from." Hartmann had inappropriately requested detailed information on pending cases, defined their sequencing, and conducted pretrial negotiations with defense counsel. He engaged in "nano-management," insisting on overseeing specific cases. Although Davis wanted to focus on cases with declassified evidence so the public could observe the entire trial, two officials said he was wasting time declassifying evidence since Hartmann wanted cases that would require closed sessions. Reading from notes of a September 10 phone conversation, Davis said Hartmann had expressed irritation at the slow pace of prosecutions, asking rhetorically: "Who ever said we had to have open trials?" Hartmann twice cited the legal rule allowing proceedings to be closed, declaring "we've got to use it." "He said, the way we were going to validate the system was by getting convictions and good sentences. I felt I was being pressured to do something less than full, fair and open." "No matter how perfect the trial is, if it's behind closed doors, it's going to be viewed as a sham." "This whole process is under a cloud." Criticism of the commissions could be rebutted only "by keeping it as open and transparent as possible."

Two months later, Davis was scheduled to testify before a Senate Judiciary Committee subcommittee that military commissions were subject to improper political influence, including pressure to use information obtained through waterboarding.[65] But the Defense Department ordered him not to do so, declaring that Hartmann was "the best informed and most capable witness." The next day, Davis wrote in a *Los Angeles Times* op-ed that he had resigned as chief prosecutor "because I felt that the system had become deeply politicized."[66] The Convening Authority was not meeting its obligations of "honesty and impartiality." Crawford had directed her staff to assess evidence before charges were filed, oversee pretrial preparation while Davis was on medical leave, draft charges, and assign prosecutors. "Intermingling convening authority and prosecutor roles perpetuates the perception of a rigged process stacked against the accused." "[E]ven the most perfect trial in history will be viewed with skepticism if it is conducted behind closed doors." "Getting evidence through the classification review process . . . is time-consuming. . . . Crawford, however, thought it unnecessary to wait because the rules permit closed proceedings." The last straw for Davis was being subordinated to William Haynes, who had played a "role in authorizing the use of the aggressive interrogation techniques some call torture." Davis resigned a few hours after this subordination occurred. "The first step, if these truly are military commissions and not merely a political smoke screen, is to take control out of the hands of political appointees like Haynes and Crawford and give it back to the military."

Hartmann responded in his own op-ed that "Davis knows that" "Crawford has not directed or influenced the way any military commission case will be tried."[67] Davis had resigned "just hours after he learned the results of an independent military panel . . . that concluded I had not improperly asserted my authority." Months earlier Haynes had "signed a performance evaluation on Davis, suggesting that Davis was already in the chain of command." Davis had to acknowledge that the military commission "process offers unprecedented rights to alleged war criminals." "Davis knows that national security demands that certain evidence remain classified." "But there will be no 'secret' trials." "Critics will see the uniformed service members . . . conduct trials with the dignity, fairness and respect for law that defines American military justice—a system that remains the envy of the world."

Two months later Davis wrote a *New York Times* op-ed condemning harsh interrogation.[68] "Once we condemn and stop all waterboarding, what do we do in cases where it was conducted? An obvious step is to prohibit the use of evidence derived by waterboarding in criminal proceedings against detainees." "My policy as the chief prosecutor for the military commissions at Guantánamo was that evidence derived through waterboarding was off limits. . . . Unfortunately, I was overruled on the question, and I resigned my position to call attention to the issue." "We must restore our reputation as good guys who refuse to stoop to the level of our adversaries."

Davis was eager to testify for Salim Hamdan, whose military commission offered "an opportunity to tell the truth."[69] In August 2005 Haynes had boasted that "these trials will be the Nuremberg of our time":

> I said to him that if we come up short and there are some acquittals in our cases it will at least validate the process. At which point, [Haynes's] eyes got wide and he said, "Wait a minute, we can't have acquittals. If we've been holding these guys for so long, how can we explain letting them get off? We can't have acquittals, we've got to have convictions."

As early as 2003, three prosecutors—Major Robert Preston, Captain John Carr, and Captain Carrie Wolf—had complained to superiors. When Carr expressed concern about understaffing, the then–chief prosecutor Colonel Fred Borch told him not to worry because "the military panel will be handpicked and will not acquit these detainees." Carr also said FBI agents had reported detainee abuse in Afghanistan. Preston wrote that the commissions were "wrongly managed, wrongly focused and a blight on the reputation of the armed forces." Although a Defense Department investigation found no misconduct, the military transferred them to other assignments in 2005, attributing this to "miscommunication" and "personality conflicts."

Davis offered new evidence of political interference in military commissions.[70] Haynes had called on January 9, 2007 to ask how soon Hicks could be charged. At the time there was no manual, regulations, or even a Convening Authority. "You had [Australian Prime Minister] John Howard in the press, making it clear to Americans that Hicks had to be charged by February," when Vice President Cheney was due to visit. Hicks was charged five days after that visit, during which Cheney told reporters Hicks was "near the head of the queue." Davis said: "Look at the whole chronology. Certainly there appeared to be some impetus to try to help Howard out. . . . the problem went away in March." "I was getting leaned on." At the time he felt insulated by not being in Haynes's chain of command. Soon after Haynes's phone call, Davis was called by Daniel dell'Orto (DoD Deputy General Counsel), who had overheard the conversation and told Davis: "I went in and took a wire brush to it and told [Haynes] you can't be having those conversations, 'it's [Davis's] decision on when to charge Hicks.'" Davis complained that the plea bargain "was done behind our backs and it was significantly less than anything we would have negotiated."

In April Davis testified in Hamdan's military commission that he had been directed to pursue a detainee with "blood on his hands" in order to boost public support for the commissions.[71] Deputy Defense Secretary England made it clear that charging the high value detainees could have "strategic political value."

> [T]here was that consistent theme that if we didn't get this thing rolling before the election, it was going to implode. Once you got the victim families energized and the cases rolling, whoever won the White House would have difficulty stopping the proceeding.

Davis reiterated that Haynes had told him "we can't have acquittals. We've been holding these guys for years. How can we explain acquittals? We have to have convictions." Davis had refused to introduce evidence extracted by waterboarding. "To allow or direct a prosecutor to come into the courtroom and offer evidence they felt was torture, it puts a prosecutor in an ethical bind." But Hartmann had retorted that "everything was fair game—let the judge sort it out." Still, Davis conceded, "I never had any doubts about Mr. Hamdan's guilt." The next day, Lieutenant Colonel William Britt, another prosecutor, submitted a written statement that Hartmann wanted to prioritize cases that would "seize the imagination of the American public" and make a splash. Colonel Lawrence Morris (who had replaced Davis) denied that Hartmann had interfered with pending cases, dismissing Davis's complaints as "bitterness" toward Hartmann, an aggressive and tactless general.

Two weeks later, Navy Captain Keith J. Allred, the judge, suspended Hamdan's military commission and directed Crawford to replace Hartmann:[72]

Telling the chief prosecutor (and other prosecutors) that certain types of cases would be tried and that others would not be tried, because of political factors such as whether they would capture the imagination of the American people, be sexy, or involve blood on the hands of the accused, suggests that factors other than those pertaining to the merits of the case were at play. . . . [The use of] evidence that the chief prosecutor [sic—he means Hartmann] considered tainted and unreliable, or perhaps obtained as a result of torture or coercion, was clearly an effort to influence the professional judgment of the chief prosecutor.

He agreed with Davis that Hartmann had engaged in "nanomanagement of the prosecutor's office." Allred's ruling led lawyers for the five high-value detainees to make the same argument against Hartmann in their cases.[73]

Two weeks after that, Davis was denied a medal that had been recommended for his efforts in building the military commissions. The Defense Department now said he did "not serve honorably."[74] Davis commented: "I tell the truth, and I get labeled as having served dishonorably." But he still thought the military commissions were fair and the defendants guilty.[75] The Uniform Code of Military Justice offered "the most ethical process in the world." He was baffled by Hartmann's refusal to step down in the other cases after he had "been found in a judicial process to have acted unlawfully." "I'm not done yet. I'm going to keep pushing until the last commission is done or somebody's fixed this."

In June Davis responded to Haynes's testimony before the Senate Armed Services Committee:[76]

My concern as chief prosecutor was not so much whether the harsh techniques [sic] produces good intelligence (perhaps it did), it was whether the same information was also reliable evidence we should use to establish someone's guilt and perhaps sentence him to death. In my view, that is a much higher threshold. If there's genuine doubt about the reliability of the information we extracted in the intelligence context there should be no doubt the same information has no place in a judicial proceeding conducted in the name of the United States.

Davis testified in Mohammed Jawad's military commission that Hartmann had fast-tracked the case before it was adequately prepared, hoping the bloodshed would "capture . . . the imagination of the American people."[77] He told Jawad's lawyer: "[Y]our client went from the freezer to the front burner after Gen. Hartmann arrived."

After deliberating eight hours over three days, the military commission convicted Hamdan of material support but acquitted him of the other charges.[78] Davis gave the trial a "mixed scorecard" and hoped the deliberation time and partial acquittal would "dispel some of the perceptions that a military jury will just be a rubber stamp."

The next month, Hartmann was reassigned to direct operations, planning, and development for the military commissions and replaced by his deputy—an arrangement Davis cynically compared to "the Vladimir Putin-Dmitry Medvedev relationship where there's some real doubt over who pulls the strings."[79] The Defense Department insisted it was a promotion, praising Hartmann for having "driven the commissions process forward. . . . In no small part because of his efforts and his dedication, the commissions are an active operational legal system."

But a month later, the Defense Department launched an investigation of Hartmann after a preliminary inquiry found evidence he had bullied prosecutors, logistical officials, and others to bring cases prematurely and prosecute unwarranted charges, overruled prosecutorial objections to coerced evidence, and made intentionally misleading statements to minimize his role in overseeing all prosecutions.[80] The Defense Department's inspector general was conducting a separate inquiry into two complaints about Hartmann's abusive and retaliatory behavior. Davis told the investigation that Hartmann "grossly exceeded his role as a neutral and independent and impartial legal advisor." Another prosecutor who had quit said Hartmann "was hammering on other prosecutors to move faster on cases, in one instance demanding that three or more cases a month be initiated" even if they were not ready.

After Obama's election, Davis wrote in a *Toronto Star* op-ed that the new administration[81]

> should create a process that enables each detainee to confront the allegations and the evidence against him in a forum that meets the due process standards reflected in the Geneva Convention Relative to the Treatment of Prisoners of War. That means whatever evidence the tribunal considers must be provided to the detainee; no more secret evidence that leaves

a detainee wondering why he is detained. . . . Whatever forum the new administration selects must, at a minimum, afford "all the judicial guarantees which are recognized as indispensable by civilized peoples" as required by Common Article 3 of the Geneva Conventions, and it must be as transparent as possible. . . . President-elect Obama should suspend the military commissions as soon as he takes office . . . for the sake of America's beleaguered reputation.

A year later, as Attorney General Eric Holder was deciding where to try the five high-value detainees, Davis warned that using commissions for weaker cases would mean[82]

that the standard of justice for each detainee will depend in large part upon the government's assessment of how high the prosecution's evidence can jump. . . . The evidence likely to clear the high bar gets gold medal justice. . . . The evidence unable to clear the federal court standard is forced to settle for a military commission trial, a specially created forum that has faltered repeatedly for more than seven years. That is a double standard I suspect we would condemn if it was applied to us.

The same day, he wrote to the *Washington Post* affirming the ability of federal courts to try terrorism suspects. The Congressional Research Service (where he had worked since retiring from the Army) fired him for these statements.[83] Denouncing this violation of his First Amendment rights, Davis sued, represented by the ACLU and backed by the *New York Times*. In June 2012, the DC Circuit Court of Appeals dismissed his lawsuit.[84] He became executive director of the Crimes of War Education Project, served as an administrative law judge at the Labor Department, and in 2020 was the (unsuccessful) Democratic candidate for the 11th Congressional District in North Carolina.

William C. Kuebler

Two other military lawyers were deeply affected by participating in military commissions. William C. Kuebler married the first girl he dated in high school, always voted Republican, and practiced business law in San Diego. In his late twenties, however, his mother's death prompted him to become a born-again Christian and join the Navy, rising to lieuten-ant commander.[85] His sister said he realized "there's more to life than driving a BMW and having your initials on your cuff." In 2007, he was appointed to represent Omar Khadr, a Canadian accused of killing Ser-geant First Class Christopher J. Speer with a grenade when Khadr had been a juvenile. Dennis Edney, the Khadr family's Canadian lawyer, complained (accurately) that "Kuebler has no trial experience, no crimi-nal or terrorism law experience. He was a tax lawyer."

But Kuebler enthusiastically embraced his new role. He criticized the DC Circuit's refusal to stay the proceedings "despite significant doubts as to the commission's legality." At the first hearing, he accused the pros-ecution of concealing for five years an eyewitness it had identified soon after the July 2002 firefight. "They weren't going to tell us who he was or how to get in touch with him or where he was." "This is a process that's not designed to be fair, it's designed to produce convictions." Affidavits by Pakistani bounty hunters were classified secret. The prosecution was exerting "enormous political pressure . . . to get these trials moving . . . practically pounding the table." He challenged the judge, Army Colonel Peter Brownback, who had barred the defense from contesting the con-stitutionality of the military commission at this stage. In a closed-door meeting, Brownback said he had "taken a lot of heat" for ruling earlier that the commissions were illegitimate, over objections by the Defense Department and White House. Brownback was angry with Kuebler for reporting that conversation. When it was revealed that Brownback had secretly ordered the defense not to disclose the names of any prosecu-tion witnesses, Kuebler objected: "[I]nstead of a presumption of inno-cence and a public trial, we start with a presumption of guilt and of a secret trial." He had earlier told the judge and prosecution that "the manner in which this is being dealt with [i.e., off the record, via e-mail], creates an added level of difficulty by making it appear that the govern-ment is trying to keep the secrecy of the proceedings a secret itself."

In February 2008, Kuebler revealed that the military knew that an-other enemy fighter was still alive when Speer died and might have thrown the grenade. The next month, Kuebler added that an American commander reported that Speer's assailant had been killed. Canadian newspapers headlined stories about these revelations: "U.S. Doctored Evidence to Implicate Khadr, Lawyer Says" (*Toronto Star*); "Khadr Was

Likely Tortured" (*Edmonton Journal*). In April, Kuebler urged Canadians to pressure their government to ask that Khadr be returned for trial: "I don't believe anyone can get an acquittal at Guantánamo Bay." Some eyewitnesses said Speer might have been killed by friendly fire. The prosecution originally claimed that Khadr was the only fighter alive when Speer's unit stormed the compound and that there had been just one grenade blast. But a report made available to defense counsel in February disclosed that forces continued to throw grenades during the chaotic final confrontation. Denouncing these "inconsistent and contradictory" accounts, Kuebler accused the prosecution of trying to rush the case to trial because its "mythical assessment" of events was rapidly collapsing. He had just learned from a Canadian diplomat about another report, which the prosecution previously claimed had "gone missing," and asked Brownback to order its production. In April, Kuebler testified to a Canadian House of Commons subcommittee on international human rights that "lies have been told about Omar." "Justice will not result from a military commission that cannot try U.S. citizens and treats a Canadian as worth less than an American. Bring this young man home to face due process under a legitimate system." The prosecution retorted that "the time the defense has spent lobbying the Canadian Parliament would be better spent interviewing the witnesses."

At the end of May, the Convening Authority abruptly substituted Colonel Patrick Parrish for Brownback, whose return to retirement was a "mutual decision." Defense lawyers attributed the action to Brownback's anger at the prosecution's failure to produce exculpatory evidence and his threat to halt the proceedings if this was not done promptly. Brownback complained of being "badgered and beaten and bruised" by the chief military prosecutor, who wanted to accelerate the trial. Kuebler found the replacement "very odd." "The judge who was frustrating the government's forward progress in the Khadr case is suddenly gone." The prosecution denied having "anything to do with a new judge being assigned to this case."

In June, Kuebler denounced military commissions as "designed to get criminal convictions" with "no real evidence." Prosecutors "launder evidence derived from torture." "You put the whole package together and it stinks." Guantánamo's Standard Operating Procedures (SOP) manual advised that, because "the mission has legal and political issues that may lead to interrogators being called to testify, keeping the number of documents with interrogation information to a minimum can minimize certain legal issues." Kuebler feared that "if handwritten notes were destroyed in accordance with the SOP, the government intentionally deprived Omar's lawyers of key evidence with which to challenge the reliability of his statements." Colonel Morris (who had replaced Davis as chief prosecutor) accused Kuebler of having "habitually flouted the rules" and "greatly distorting" and "fabricating information." A Navy spokesman said lawyers had an obligation to defend, but "it is disappointing when counsel do not live up to these [professional] standards." Kuebler replied that serving as defense counsel was "a powerful way to be a witness for Christ by demonstrating your capacity to not judge the way everybody else is judging and to serve unconditionally."

In July, Kuebler obtained a secret Canadian intelligence report on a Canadian government visit to Khadr in 2004, which Canadian lawyers had persuaded a Canadian court to order the Department of Foreign Affairs to release. It described Guantánamo's notorious "frequent flyer program": in order to make Khadr "more amenable and willing to talk," for three weeks he was moved to a new cell every three hours (including nighttime), "denying him uninterrupted sleep." Other abusive treatment reduced him to tears. The prosecution tried to recover the report, prompting Kuebler to seek a judicial investigation into its behavior. Colonel Parrish reprimanded the prosecution for the time it had taken to decide whether another report could be given to the defense and imposed a deadline. The prosecution objected to Kuebler's request that two independent psychiatrists examine Khadr and testify about his alleged "confession."

In early September, Colonel Parrish disqualified Hartmann from further involvement in the case. Kuebler derided this as "token relief" because Hartmann had already refused to pay for the psychiatric examination. "The practical effect is to let an officer whom even the judge recognizes as biased continue to be involved in the case until the government gets its coveted conviction. No American could be tried in such a system." (As noted above, Hartmann was reassigned two weeks later.) During argument over postponing the trial for the psychiatric examination, it emerged that the prosecution had given the defense incomplete medical records for Khadr. Parrish demanded an explanation, warning the prosecution that when someone decides to violate a court order "those decisions have consequences."

On April 3, 2009, chief defense counsel Colonel Peter Masciola fired Kuebler for unnamed ethical violations. Four days later Parrish reinstated him, declaring that *he* had to approve any firing, which could occur only for cause. Kuebler said Masciola had a conflict of interest because he wanted to ensure that his office would continue to represent detainees tried in civilian courts. Kuebler sought to argue to the Obama administration's review team that Khadr should be repatriated to Canada. But in October, Khadr fired *all* his military lawyers, including Kuebler. A year later, he pleaded in exchange for an eight-year sentence; two years after that he was transferred to Canada and released in less than three years. The Canadian government paid him $10.5 million Canadian for his mistreatment. Kuebler died of cancer in 2015.

Darrel Vandeveld

My last example is Darrel Vandeveld, a devout Catholic, father of four, and senior deputy state attorney general in Erie, Pennsylvania, in charge of consumer protection.[86] Any acquaintance, he said, "will probably tell you that I've been a conformist my entire life." As an Army Reservist, he was called to active duty after 9/11, serving as a military lawyer for seven years in Bosnia, the Horn of Africa, Afghanistan, and Iraq and rising to lieutenant colonel. In June 2006, his commanding officer praised the

> absolutely outstanding, first-class performance by an extraordinarily gifted, intelligent, knowledgeable and experienced judge advocate, whose potential is utterly unlimited. One of the [JAG] Corps' best and brightest. Save the very toughest jobs in the Corps for him.

In May 2007, he was sent to Guantánamo and assigned to prosecute seven detainees, including Mohammed Jawad, who had been a juvenile in December 2002 when he allegedly threw a grenade in an Afghan bazaar, wounding two American soldiers and their Afghan interpreter. Vandeveld initially disparaged all allegations of prisoner abuse as "embellishment" and "exaggeration." He dismissed a defendant's "idiotic" challenge to the legitimacy of the military commissions. He was convinced that Jawad was a war criminal taught by an al-Qaeda affiliate to kill Americans and to claim falsely, if caught, that he was a juvenile and had been tortured. But when Davis resigned, Vandeveld began developing doubts. He kept finding sources of information and documents confirming that Jawad had been underage and drugged before the attack and had been abused during interrogation. But he encountered obstacles in releasing them. Major David Frakt, the defense lawyer, gave him records showing that in mid-2003 Jawad had been removed from the prison wing for Pashto-speakers (his language), isolated, and deprived of books and mail. In September 2003, interrogators observed him talking to posters on the wall. That Christmas, he tried to commit suicide by banging his head against metal bars and hanging himself. Like Khadr, he was moved 112 times over the course of two weeks, more than once every three hours and even more frequently between midnight and 2 AM. Vandeveld responded by seeking to negotiate a minimal sentence and rehabilitation before Jawad returned to Afghanistan. On May 22, he wrote Frakt that "if I ever thought this job required me to do anything I considered unethical, I'd be out the door." Frakt answered:

> I appreciate that and I believe you. You may have to take back your comments about Jawad's complaints being embellished and exaggerated. It looks like he was telling the truth. Did you notice that he tried to commit suicide in 2003?

Vandeveld replied, "I did notice that saddening episode . . . which is one of the reasons I am pushing for a plea in this case, and why I wanted to get this information in your hands asap." Later that day he wrote: "BTW, I will correct my misstatements on the record the next time we're in session. I know I am obliged to do so." Soon thereafter, Frakt moved to dismiss the charges on the ground of "outrageous government misconduct," citing Jawad's torture. Vandeveld responded that Jawad's abuse should just mitigate punishment. Infuriated by this admission, superiors reprimanded Vandeveld, making him withdraw it and resubmit a motion declaring that Jawad "suffered no ill-effects from his alleged sleep deprivation." But the following summer, Vandeveld's doubts increased. Photos of Jawad's arrest showed a naked, terrified boy being strip-searched. In July, Vandeveld happened to see a report on a colleague's desk about the death of another Afghan detainee. Investigators of that death had taken a statement from Jawad, who said that at Bagram he had been shackled, forced to stand, beaten if he tried to sit, and made to wear a black bag over his head. Vandeveld later said this transformed him from a "true believer" into someone who had been "truly deceived." He told Frakt he was disturbed about the abuse and the absence of any system to disclose evidence of it to the defense.

On August 5, Vandeveld emailed Father John Dear, a well-known Jesuit peace activist, that

> I am beginning to have grave misgivings about what I am doing, and what we are doing as a country. . . . I no longer want to participate in the system, but I lack the courage to quit. I am married, with children, and not only will they suffer, I'll lose a lot of friends.

Father Dear replied: "God does not want you to participate in any injustice, and GITMO is so bad, I hope and pray you will quietly, peacefully, prayerfully, just resign and start your life over." This might "save lives and change the direction of the entire policy." Two days later, Vandeveld asked Frakt "how do I get myself out of this office?" He was seeking "a practical way of extricating myself from this mess." By late August, he told Frakt he had discovered other "disquieting" things about Guantánamo, but his superiors would not let him address them or quietly transfer out. Frakt replied: "Now might be a good time to take a courageous stand and expose some of the 'disquieting' things that you alluded to." Because Frakt expected a change in government after the November 2008 election, he advised Vandeveld: "It wouldn't be a bad idea to distance yourself from a process that has become largely discredited, or at least distinguish yourself as one of the good guys, an ethical prosecutor trying to do the right thing." Frakt suggested that Vandeveld tell the Convening Authority about Vandeveld's efforts to reach a plea agreement. Vandeveld replied: "[L]et me think about that some more; I have to consider the impact on my family."

In mid-September, Vandeveld resigned as prosecutor, asking to serve the rest of his Reserve duty in Iraq or Afghanistan:

> I didn't express my concerns to Brig. Gen. Hartmann or Col. Morris before asking to be reassigned, largely because I knew both are highly-indoctrinated ideologues whose likely response would have been to have

my security clearance revoked as a punitive and preventative measure. (This concern is not happenstance; I could give examples were I not bound by my clearance itself.) The hostile, dismissive way I'd seen [another concerned officer treated by superiors] was enough for me to conclude my reservations would not be well-met.

He expected retribution for cooperating with the defense, noting that another officer who had done so received a mediocre Officer Evaluation Report.

In a four-page declaration filed with the military commission Vandeveld complained that "potentially exculpatory evidence has not been provided."[87] He continued:

I have been "accused" of forming an attorney-client relationship with [Frakt]. . . . Major Frakt and I have developed a cordial relationship of mutual respect, nothing more. I have divulged to Major Frakt those items of discovery that in my professional judgment the Rules for [sic] Professional Conduct, the Military Commissions Act, and the Manual for Military Commissions . . . have required me to relinquish, consistent with my ethical obligations as a prosecutor. . . . I have observed that a number of defense requests which I considered to be reasonable and in some cases indicated support for were nevertheless rejected by the Convening Authority, presumably on the advice of the Legal Advisor [Hartmann]. . . .

My ethical qualms about continuing to serve as a prosecutor relate primarily to the procedures for affording defense counsel discovery. I am highly concerned, to the point that I believe I can no longer serve as a prosecutor at the commissions, about the slipshod, uncertain "procedure" for affording defense counsel discovery. One would have thought that after six years since the commissions had their fitful start, that [sic] a functioning law office would have been set up and procedures and policies not only put into effect, but refined. . . . In my view, evidence we have an obligation as prosecutors and officers of the court [to disclose] has not been made available to the defense. . . . I have decided to come forward at this point and share some of my reasons for offering my resignation because I believe I have an obligation to provide truthful information to the court regardless of which side calls me as a witness.

Jawad might have been duped into joining Hezb-e Islami Gulbuddin (a group previously allied with the United States). "It seems plausible to me that Jawad may have been drugged before the alleged attack." The Afghan Interior Ministry said two other men confessed to the crime. Vandeveld also was troubled by Jawad's treatment in custody and had given the Defense Department documents demonstrating sleep deprivation. "As a juvenile at the time of his capture, Jawad should have been segregated from the adult detainees, and some serious attempt made to rehabilitate him. I am bothered by the fact that this was not done." "I am a resolute Catholic and take as an article of faith that justice is defined as reparative and restorative and that Christ's most radical pronouncement—command, if you will—is to love one's enemies."

Chief prosecutor Morris countered that Vandeveld said he was quitting for personal reasons. He was just a disgruntled prosecutor "disappointed that his superiors did not agree with his recommendations in the case." "There are no grounds for his ethical qualms. We are the most scrupulous organization you can imagine in terms of disclosure to the defense." "When in doubt we disclose every scrap of paper and piece of evidence." He refused to say whether his office had rejected a plea deal. A Defense Department official said Vandeveld had defended Hartmann against allegations of undue influence in the Jawad case; but when those allegations were upheld, Hartmann retaliated, causing Vandeveld emotional distress and prompting him to resign in protest. Hartmann then ordered Vandeveld to get a psychiatric examination, but it cleared him to remain on active duty. Vandeveld emailed Father Dear: "The reaction was the expected outrage and condemnation. I have and will maintain my equanimity and, while scared for me and for my family, know that Christ will watch over me."

Called as a witness for Jawad, Vandeveld dropped his initial request for immunity. When the prosecutor's office prevented him from traveling to Guantánamo, he testified by video that military commissions "are not served by having someone who may be innocent be convicted of the crime." "My views changed. I am a father, and it's not an exercise in self-pity to ask oneself how you would feel if your own son was treated in this fashion." "I think it is impossible for anyone in good conscience to stand up and say he or she is [sic] provided all the discovery in a case." Morris retorted that Vandeveld "never once" raised substantive concerns. These unfair allegations were "a broad blast at some very ethical and hardworking people whose performances are being smudged groundlessly." The prosecution complied "beyond what the rules [of disclosure] require." "The idea of holding out the specter of a wrongful conviction is outrageous." "It is because of the nature of this war and that there are so many elements fighting in it, information doesn't come in a tidy package." But Vandeveld named Defense Department reports withheld from defense lawyers, some suggesting that another suspect had confessed to the alleged crime. The judge, Colonel Steven Henley, ordered the prosecution to deliver these by October 3. Frakt again moved to dismiss, alleging "gross government misconduct."

Before being "reminded" that he could not talk to the press until he was released from active duty, Vandeveld vowed in an email message to do so then:

> I don't know how else the creeping rot of the commissions and the politics that fostered and continued to surround them could be exposed to the curative powers of the sunlight. I care not for myself; our enemies deserve nothing less than what we would expect from them were the situations reversed. More than anything, I hope we can rediscover some of our American values.

The prosecution dismissed without prejudice the charges against five detainees Vandeveld had prosecuted.[88] Morris denied that this had anything to do with Vandeveld, claiming that new evidence required a "re-analysis" of the cases to draft the "best possible charges." But Clive Stafford Smith, who represented a detainee whose case had been dismissed, said "Vandeveld was willing to testify for us if subpoenaed. They want new prosecutors to review the case before refiling charges so they can argue that Vandeveld is irrelevant."[89]

At the end of October, Colonel Henley excluded Jawad's initial confession.[90] Because the prosecution had not timely disclosed evidence, Henley accepted the claim that Jawad had been drugged before the attack and he and his family threatened with death if he did not confess. Vandeveld said this "eviscerated" the government's case. Jawad's other incriminating statements were "clearly tainted by mistreatment." Vandeveld expected to be called by the defense in other cases. "The commissions are in such disarray and continue to be in such chaos." A month later, Colonel Henley excluded Jawad's second confession because "the effect of the death threats which produced the accused's first confession to the Afghan police had not dissipated by the second confession to the [United States]." Vandeveld declared that "it's not the death knell of the case—it buries the case."

He said in an interview soon thereafter:[91]

> I know so many fighting men and women who are stained by the taint of Guantánamo, so I'm here to tell the truth about Guantánamo and how a few people have sullied the American military and the Constitution. I went down there on a mission . . . to convict as many of those detainees as possible and put them in prison for as long as I possibly could. I had zero doubts. I was a true believer.

He had "lived in dread" that Father Dear would urge him to resign. "I never suffered such anguish in my life about anything. It took me too long to recognize that we had abandoned our American values and defiled our Constitution." But three months later, he had no regrets: "No justice will be obtained at Guantánamo."

In January 2009, he filed a declaration in support of Jawad's habeas petition.[92] "It is my opinion, based on my extensive knowledge of the case, that there is no credible evidence or legal basis to justify Mr. Jawad's detention." Afghan police had made the functionally illiterate Jawad place his thumbprint on a statement in Farsi, a language he did not know. Although American interrogators had videotaped a statement by Jawad, Vandeveld was never able to get it. The "complete lack of organization" in the prosecutor's office affected nearly every case. "It was like a stash of documents found in a village in a raid and just put on a plane to the [United States]." Evidence was scattered throughout databases, crammed in desk drawers and vaguely labeled containers, or "simply piled on tops of desks." "Most physical evidence that had been collected had either disappeared" or been lost. As recently as June 2008, Jawad had been "beaten, kicked and pepper-sprayed while he was on the ground with his feet and hands in shackles, for allegedly not complying with guards' instructions." The government was still using the confessions that Colonel Henley had excluded as coerced.

Morris said he would be "happy to respond under oath to any of the allegations." He claimed that Vandeveld

> was disappointed when I did not choose him to become a team leader, and he asked to resign shortly thereafter, never having raised an ethical concern during the nine months I supervised him. I relied on his reports to me about Jawad and other cases I entrusted to him (which included his advocacy of a 40-year sentence for Mr. Jawad the week before he departed).

Vandeveld retorted: "I wouldn't believe a word [Morris] says."

A few days later, Vandeveld published a *Washington Post* op-ed.[93] He stated that in November 2001

> I was going off to avenge the attacks of Sept. 11, 2001, with a sense of pride and moral purpose. . . . All of us fought because we believed that we were protecting America and its ideals. But my final tour of duty made me question everything we had done. . . . Warning signs appeared early on, but I ignored them. . . . But with Father John's help, and with the unlikely support of Jawad's relentless defense counsel—a scorned adversary whose integrity and intelligence transformed him into a trusted friend—I finally resigned. . . . Now that I'm home in Erie . . . I have regained my sense of self. . . . We did not sacrifice so that an administration of partisan civilians, abetted by military officers who seemed to have lost their moral compass, could defile our Constitution and misuse the rule of law. . . . I just hope no one will see that kind of abuse—and look the other way—again.

On July 8, 2009, Vandeveld testified before the Senate Armed Services Committee:[94]

> We do not need military commissions. They are broken and beyond repair. We do not need indefinite detention, and we do not need a new system of "national security courts." Instead, we should try those whose guilt we can prove while observing "the judicial guarantees which are recognized as indispensable by civilized peoples"—in other words, using those long-standing rules of due process required by Article III courts and military courts-martial—and resettle or repatriate those whom we

cannot. That is the only solution that is consistent with American values and American law.

District of Columbia District Judge Ellen Huvelle ruled in Jawad's habeas petition on July 17 that his confessions were coerced and inadmissible and allowed the government one week to produce another justification for detaining him.[95] At the end of that period, the Justice Department acknowledged it had no other evidence but claimed—disingenuously—that it was thinking of prosecuting him in civilian court. Judge Huvelle gave the DOJ twenty-four hours to conduct an "expedited criminal investigation." When it failed to produce any evidence, she granted Jawad's habeas petition. On August 24, he was repatriated to Afghanistan and freed. Vandeveld returned to Erie County to become a public defender: "I find hope every time I stand up in court and urge the judge to see the human behind the shackled, prison-clothed person in front of him or her and to seek to do justice."[96]

In March 2010, Vandeveld coauthored an op-ed for *Salon*.[97] The military commission was "untested, likely unconstitutional, and has yet to demonstrate a single, credible result." The Defense Department "has yet to even devise rules for these proceedings." There was a "constitutional cloud lingering over critical legal issues."

> Using our federal courts is being tough on terror. There is plenty of risk but no discernible benefit to trying the 9/11 defendants in an untested system. This trial should not be a "learning experience." Too much is at stake for our national security, our values, and our future.

Stories of Resistance

Susan Sontag declared that "at the center of our moral life and our moral imagination are the great models of resistance: the great stories of those who have said 'No.'"[98] But the lesser stories are equally important: people asked to violate their ethical ideals who respond with Melville's Bartleby—"I would prefer not to."[99] The small band of human rights lawyers who nobly devote their lives to defending the rule of law deserve our profound gratitude and respect. But law's infamy can be defeated only if *ordinary* lawyers do the right thing. The five described above sought to preserve the integrity of the legal process in CSRTs that purported to identify "enemy combatants," military commissions that tried them for alleged war crimes, and habeas corpus petitions seeking their release from Guantánamo.

Little in their biographies predicted that behavior. All were proud patriots. Abraham felt a special debt to the United States, which had defeated Nazi Germany and welcomed Holocaust survivors such as one of his parents. All were career military officers—active duty or Reserve—who consistently received superb performance reviews, earning promotions and medals. The military had offered Diaz an extraordinary ladder for upward mobility. None was a rebel; this was the first disobedient act in a lifetime of conformity for both Abraham and Vandeveld. All believed deeply in the military justice system in which they practiced. Davis was an outspoken booster for the Guantánamo Bay prison and military commissions. Both he and Vandeveld were certain that those detained and tried were dangerous terrorists. But some of the five may have been predisposed to resist. Kuebler and Vandeveld were deeply religious. His father's murder conviction imbued Diaz with a strong sense of injustice.[100] Abraham had been raised with memories of the Holocaust.

What seems to have motivated them was the contrast between the due process they routinely experienced in their civilian and military legal practices and the egregious violations they encountered at Guantánamo: failure to disclose exculpatory evidence; pressure to try cases prematurely; selection of cases for political reasons (e.g., to stoke outrage at those charged with killing American soldiers and perhaps influence an election); unjustified secrecy; abuse of detainees (especially vulnerable juveniles); coercive interrogation; disregard for constitutional rights; and contempt for international law. (As noted above, general counsels and JAGs of the four armed services expressed similar feelings.) Some governmental acts were difficult or impossible to justify: concealing the identities of detainees so lawyers could not petition for habeas on their behalf and even intercepting detainees' confidential communications with their lawyers. Some political interference was brazen: assuring prosecutors there would be no acquittals; packing CSRTs with compliant members and redoing those few that found detainees not to be enemy combatants; replacing military commission judges midtrial for being too deliberative; or requiring prosecutors to fulfill their obligation to disclose exculpatory evidence. Such actions raised the question of whether the government was entitled to engage in the kind of scorched-earth litigation tactics made notorious by private litigants (just as Yoo's behavior raised the question of whether he owed obligations not only to the executive but also to the Constitution and the American people). Abraham was troubled by the military commissions' sloppiness and casual disregard for evidence and procedure. These lawyers' outrage intensified when the military blatantly lied—claiming that their clients were committed jihadists, the worst of the worst, and insisting the United States did not torture—or when it sought to cover up misconduct. Lawyers live a unique dilemma: as hired guns they must assert truths (factual, legal, and moral) that they do not believe.[101] At some point these lawyers balked, unable to speak falsely (as Galileo felt compelled to declare *eppur si muove*). They resented superiors (such as Hartmann) who violated their professional autonomy through intrusive micromanagement (including the negotiation of Hicks's guilty plea behind Davis's back). Some prosecutors developed strong sympathy for the accused—especially the juveniles Khadr and Jawad, who had been tortured and exhibited psychotic symptoms—as well as respect for opposing defense counsel. Vandeveld wondered how he would feel if his son had been treated like Jawad; Abraham was moved by the fact that al-Ghazzawi had a daughter the same age as his.

All found resistance difficult. It took most of them a long time to form the necessary resolve and then act on it. They had to reject firmly held beliefs and relinquish long, rewarding military careers. Vandeveld described his conversion from a "true believer" to one who had been "truly deceived." Although some reported up the chain of command, all soon realized that such a course would be fruitless. It took more than a year for Davis to act; even then, he continued to maintain that the military commissions were fair and those convicted were guilty. Vandeveld was prepared to make a personal sacrifice but feared the consequences for his family. Davis's resignation strengthened Vandeveld's determination to act. But though he must have known what Father Dear would counsel, Vandeveld put off resigning even after receiving that advice. He persisted in arguing that Jawad's abuse should affect only punishment, not conviction. In retrospect, Diaz felt his behavior had been stupid.

Much like Jesselyn Radack, Chelsea Manning, Edward Snowden, and others, these whistleblowers had every reason to be apprehensive. No good deed goes unpunished. Instead of honoring their fidelity to the rule of law, the military first sought to crush their resistance and then, when that failed, cynically impugned the motives of lawyers it had honored for decades. Morris claimed Davis was angry that superiors had sided with Hartmann against him. The military insisted Vandeveld's reasons were personal, even subjecting him to a psychiatric examination (a distressing echo of Soviet "justice"). The military never admitted error: Morris continued to maintain that the prosecution disclosed all evidence when this claim was patently false; Attorney General Eric Holder even contemplated a civilian prosecution of Jawad after his military commission trial collapsed (but wisely backed off). When threats failed to deter these lawyers, the military retaliated. Diaz saw his military career ended, served time in the brig, lost his license to practice law in Kansas, and faced obstacles before successfully gaining admission in New York. Davis and Vandeveld were temporarily muzzled. Davis was forced out of the military and fired by the Congressional Research Service for speaking out. As Reservists, Abraham and Vandeveld suffered less materially, but they were forced to leave an institution they deeply valued and had loyally served for years.

Once these lawyers defied their superiors, the rupture tended to be absolute—partly because of retaliation. Davis turned against the military the same zealous advocacy he had wielded on its behalf, testifying for Hamdan and Jawad. Although he had vigorously pursued David Hicks, he now claimed the prosecution had been driven by Australian and American politics. He publicly assailed the CSRTs and military commissions, sometimes seeming to maintain he had always been a critic (much like the myriad French who claimed they had been in the Resistance or the majority of white South Africans who conveniently remembered opposing apartheid). Vandeveld submitted declarations for other detainees, testified before Congress, and penned pieces for the media. Kuebler emulated Mori's advocacy for Hicks in Australia by successfully campaigning in Canada for Khadr's repatriation.

Much like ripples from a rock thrown into a pond, whistleblowing had wider ramifications—some of them surprising. Other prosecutors who had raised internal objections to procedural irregularities were quietly transferred. But these public challenges encouraged additional prosecutors to file formal complaints against Hartmann. Those, in turn, led a judge to suspend Hamdan's military commission and direct the Convening Authority to remove Hartmann from it, echoing Davis's criticism of Hartmann for prioritizing Hamdan's case, using coerced testimony, and engaging in nanomanagement. In the subsequent trial, Hamdan was acquitted of some charges and repatriated after serving a short additional sentence. Lawyers for the five high-value detainees then made similar arguments against Hartmann, who was reassigned to other tasks. A Defense Department inquiry confirmed many of Davis's complaints against Hartmann. Vandeveld's complaints convinced both judges—Brownback and Parrish—that the prosecution was withholding exculpatory evidence. Parrish reinstated Kuebler after the chief defense counsel fired him. Vandeveld succeeded in excluding both of Jawad's confessions, not only before the military commission but also in the district court, which consequently granted the habeas petition, leading to his repatriation and release. And Vandeveld's resignation forced the prosecution temporarily to withdraw charges against all the detainees he had prosecuted. Khadr's plea deal allowed him to be transferred to Canada, which soon released and compensated him.

Edmund Burke famously wrote that "the only thing necessary for the triumph of evil is for good men to do nothing."[102] Such passivity often reflects a fear of retaliation. But just as the rare judges who resisted Nazism in Germany suffered few consequences,[103] so these five men remade their lives with a sense of greater moral integrity. I hope their stories will inspire other lawyers to oppose law's infamy—not just at moments of heroic resistance but in their daily practices.

NOTES

I presented an earlier version of this chapter as the Hal Wooten Lecture at University of New South Wales Law School on March 13, 2014. I am grateful to Darrel Vandeveld for reading a draft and to Matthew Diaz for suggesting invaluable corrections and expansions.

1 Richard L. Abel, *Law's Wars: The Fate of the Rule of Law in the U.S. "War on Terror"* (New York: Cambridge University Press, 2018); Richard L. Abel, *Law's Trials: The Performance of Legal Institutions in the U.S. "War on Terror"* (New York: Cambridge University Press, 2018).

2 I presented my definition of the rule of law in Abel, *Law's Wars*, chapter 1.

3 Richard L. Abel, "Speaking Law to Power: Occasions for Cause Lawyering," in *Cause Lawyering: Political Commitments and Professional Responsibilities*, ed. Austin Sarat and Stuart Scheingold, chapter 3 (New York: Oxford University Press, 1998).

4 I worked for the Lawyers Committee for Civil Rights Under Law in Jackson in the summer of 1965.

5 Richard L. Abel, *Politics by Other Means: Law in the Struggle Against Apartheid, 1980–1994* (New York: Routledge, 1995).

6 Mark P. Denbeaux and Jonathan Hafetz, eds., *The Guantánamo Lawyers: Inside a Prison, Outside the Law* (New York: New York University Press, 2009); Jonathan Hafetz, *Habeas Corpus After 9/11: Confronting America's New Global Detention System* (New York: New York University Press, 2011); Clive Stafford Smith, *Eight O'Clock Ferry to the Windward Side: Seeking Justice in Guantánamo Bay* (New York: Basic Books, 2008).

7 Jonathan Mahler, *The Challenge* (New York: Picador, 2009); Jess Bravin, *The Terror Courts: Rough Justice at Guantanamo Bay* (New Haven: Yale University Press, 2013).

8 Abraham, "Anatomy of a Whistleblower," *Mother Jones* (Jan./Feb. 2004); "Whistleblower Charges Justice Dept. with Misconduct in Chertoff's Prosecution of John Walker Lindh," *Democracy Now!* (Jan. 13, 2005). She has continued to advocate for whistleblowers.

9 Barton Gellman, *Angler: The Cheney Vice-Presidency*, 302–21 (New York: Penguin, 2008).

10 For an interpretation of the motives of such lawyers, see Carrie Menkel-Meadow, "The Causes of Cause Lawyering: Toward an Understanding of the Motivation and Commitment of Social Justice Lawyers," in *Cause Lawyering: Political Commitments and Professional Responsibilities*, ed. A. Sarat and S. Scheingold, chapter 2 (New York: Oxford University Press, 1998).

11 Clifford Geertz, *The Interpretation of Cultures* (New York: Basic Books, 1973). I employed a similar method in two books seeking to understand lawyers' unethical behavior: *Lawyers in the Dock: Learning from Attorney Disciplinary Proceedings* (New York: Oxford University Press, 2008); *Lawyers on Trial: Understanding Ethical Misconduct* (New York: Oxford University Press, 2011).

12 David Cole, ed., *The Torture Memos: Rationalizing the Unthinkable*, 11–13 (New York: New Press, 2009).

13 Department of Justice, Office of Professional Responsibility, *Report: Investigation into the Office of Legal Counsel's Memoranda Concerning Issues Relating to the Central Intelligence Agency's Use of "Enhanced Interrogation Techniques" on Suspected Terrorists*, July 29, 2009; Abel, *Law's Trials*, 443–44.

14 *See, e.g.*, Savage, "Trump's Claim of Total Authority in Crisis Is Rejected Across Ideological Lines," *New York Times*, Apr. 15, 2020.

15 Interview with Norah O'Donnell, *Hardball* (MSNBC), June 23, 2006.

16 Lewis, "Official Attacks Top Law Firms over Detainees," *New York Times*, Jan. 13, 2007.

17 Robert L. Pollock in *Wall Street Journal*, Jan. 12, 2007.

18 "Unveiled Threats," *Washington Post*, Jan. 12, 2007.

19 "Round up the Usual Lawyers," *New York Times*, Jan. 13, 2007.

20 Letters to the Editor, *New York Times*, Jan. 17, 2007.

21 "Attorneys for the Damned," *Chicago Tribune*, Jan. 16, 2007.

22 "Too Quick to Judge," *Los Angeles Times*, Jan. 16, 2007.

23 "An Appalling Threat," *USA Today*, Jan. 15, 2007.

24 Letter from Leahy to Bush, Defense Secretary Gates and Attorney General Gonzales, Jan. 12, 2007.

25 Statement by ABA President Karen J. Mathis, Jan. 12, 2007.

26 Statement by AJS President Neal Sonnett, Jan. 13, 2007.

27 Statement by SALT Co-Presidents Eileen Kaufman and Tayyab Mahmud, Jan. 14, 2007.

28 Statement by NLG President Marjorie Cohn, Jan. 14, 2007.

29 Letter from 57 *Law School Deans*, Jan. 14, 2007 (more signed later).

30 Lewis, supra; "Pentagon Disavows Call for Boycott," *Los Angeles Times*, Jan. 14, 2007.

31 Letter to the Editor, *Washington Post*, Jan. 17, 2007.

32 "Apology Not Accepted," *New York Times*, Jan. 19, 2007.

33 Egelko, "Law Firm Boycott Call Raises Ethical Issues," *San Francisco Chronicle*, Jan. 19, 2007; Alan Dershowitz, Letter to the Editor, *New York Times*, Jan. 22, 2007; San Francisco Bar Association Press Release, Jan. 25, 2007.

34 Abruzzese, "Official Quits after Remark on Lawyers," *New York Times*, Feb. 3, 2007.

35 Abel, *Law's Wars*, chapter 2.

36 In a speech on February 9, 1950, McCarthy said: "I have here in my hand a list of 205 [State Department employees] that were known to the Secretary of State as being members of the communist party."

37 David Luban, "The Adversary System Excuse," in *The Good Lawyer*, ed. David Luban (Totowa, NJ: Rowman & Allanheld, 1984).

38 Raymond Wacks, "Judges and Injustice," 101 *South African Law Journal* 266 (1984); Raymond Wacks, "Judging Judges: A Brief Rejoinder to Professor Dugard," 101 *South African Law Journal* 295 (1984); John Dugard, "Should Judges Resign?—A Reply to Professor Wacks," 101 *South African Law Journal* 286 (1984); John Dugard, "*Omar*: Support for Wacks's Ideas on the Judicial Process," 3 *South African Journal on Human Rights* 295 (1987); Michael Robertson, "The Participation of Judges in the Present Legal System: Should Judges Resign?" in *Democracy and the Judiciary*, ed. Hugh Corder (Cape Town: Juta, 1987).

39 Wiltrout, "Navy Lawyer Once Posted at Cuba Base Is Charged," *Virginian-Pilot*, Aug. 29, 2006; "Prosecutor: A Valentine Held Names of detainees," *Los Angeles Times*, May 15, 2007; Egerton, "'Moral Decision' Jeopardizes Navy Lawyer's Career," *Dallas Morning News*, May 17, 2007; Rosenberg, "Lawyer: U.S. Policy Shield List of Captives," *Miami Herald*, May 17, 2007; "Virginia: Navy Lawyer Is Guilty of Communicating Secret Information," *New York Times*, May 18, 2007; Golden, "Naming Names at Gitmo," *New York Times*, Oct. 21, 2007.

40 Rasul v. Bush, 542 U.S. 466 (2004).

41 Glaberson, "Reserve Officer Criticizes Process of Identifying 'Enemy Combatants' at Guantánamo," *New York Times*, June 23, 2007; Goldwert, "Gitmo Panelist Slams Hearing Process," CBS News, June 23, 2007; Leonnig and White, "An Ex-member Calls Detainee Panels Unfair," *Washington Post*, June 23, 2007; Stockman, "Officer Criticizes Military Tribunals," *Boston Globe*, June 23, 2007; Glaberson, "Military Insider Becomes Critic of Hearings at Guantánamo," *New York Times*, July 23, 2007; Glaberson, "Critic and Ex-Boss Testify on Guantánamo Hearings," *New York Times*, July 27, 2007; Selsky, "Files Raise Questions on Gitmo Decisions," *Washington Post*, Oct. 3, 2007; "U.S. Military Reviews Guantánamo Enemy Combatant Hearings That Kept Hundreds Behind Bars," Associated Press, Oct. 11, 2007; Levin, "Making a Case Against Tribunals," *Los Angeles Times*, Jan. 5, 2008; Worthington, "An Interview with Guantánamo Whistleblower Stephen Abraham," www.andyworthington.co.uk, Dec. 22, 2008; Talking Dog, "Interview with Stephen Abraham," *The Moderate Voice*, Sep. 28, 2009.

42 Reply to Opposition to Petition for Rehearing, Al Odah v. U.S., USSC No. 06–1196, June 22, 2007.

43 553 U.S. 723 (2008).

44 On the military commissions, see J. Bravin, *Terror Courts: Rough Justice at Guantánamo Bay* (New Haven: Yale University Press 2013); Abel, *Law's Trials*, chapter 4.

45 Cover, "Military Commission Trial Observation," www.humanrightsfirst.org.

46 Sutton, "Prosecutor Likens Guantánamo Defendants to Vampires," Reuters, Feb. 28, 2006.

47 Kropko, "Gitmo Prosecutor Denies Detainees Tortured," *Washington Post*, Mar. 7, 2006.

48 Bravin, "U.S. Resumes Military Trials at Guantánamo," *Wall Street Journal*, Apr. 4, 2006 (Breyer had been quoting defense arguments).

49 Williams, "Defender Says Detainees Should Be Able to Represent Themselves," *Los Angeles Times*, Apr. 8, 2006.

50 Williams, "U.S. to Free 141 Terror Suspects," *Los Angeles Times*, Apr. 25, 2006.

51 Williams, "A Dilemma for Defenders," *Los Angeles Times*, Apr. 30, 2006.

52 Lewis, "Officials See Qaeda Trials Using New Law in 2007," *New York Times*, Nov. 3, 2006.

53 Bravin, "At Guantánamo, Even 'Easy' Cases Have Lingered," *Wall Street Journal*, Dec. 18, 2006.

54 Nason, "Mori Charges Could Be Laid after Trial," *The Australian*, Mar. 3, 2007; Bonner, "Terror Case Prosecutor Assails Defense Lawyer," *New York Times*, Mar. 5, 2007.

55 "Guantánamo Intimidation," *Washington Post*, Mar. 6, 2007.

56 Williams, "Guantánamo Bay Tribunals to Begin Again," *Los Angeles Times*, Mar. 26, 2007.

57 Glaberson, "Detainee's Lawyers Seek Removal of Chief Prosecutor," *New York Times*, Mar. 26, 2007.

58 Glaberson, "Plea of Guilty from a Detainee in Guantánamo," *New York Times*, Mar. 27, 2007; White, "Australian's Guilty Plea Is First at Guantánamo," *Washington Post*, Mar. 27, 2007; White, "Alleged Sept. 11 Financier Tells Tribunal He Knew Little of Plot," *Washington Post*, Mar. 30, 2007; Glaberson, "Some Bumps at the Start of War Tribunals at Guantánamo," *New York Times*, Apr. 1, 2007; Williams, "Hicks' Plea Deal Strikes Some Experts as a Sham," *Los Angeles Times*, Apr. 1, 2007; Rosenberg, "Full Scope of Tribunals Takes Shape," *Miami Herald*, Apr. 1, 2007; White, "Australian's Plea Deal Was Negotiated without Prosecutors," *Washington Post*, Apr. 1, 2007.

59 Glaberson, "A Legal Debate in Guantánamo on Boy Fighters," *New York Times*, June 3, 2007; Farley, "Guantánamo Inmate Stirs Debate in Canada," *Los Angeles Times*, June 24, 2007.

60 Davis, "The Guantánamo I Know," *New York Times*, June 26, 2007.

61 Letters to the Editor, *New York Times*, June 27, 2007.

62 White, "Court Reverses Ruling on Detainees," *Washington Post*, Sep. 25, 2007; Glaberson, "Court Advances Military Trials for Detainees," *New York Times*, Sep. 25, 2007.

63 Glaberson, "War-Crimes Prosecutor Quits in Pentagon Clash," *New York Times*, Oct. 6, 2007.

64 White, "Ex-Prosecutor Alleges Pentagon Plays Politics," *Washington Post*, Oct. 20, 2007; Glaberson, "Ex-Prosecutor Says He Was Pushed toward Closed Trials at Guantánamo," *New York Times*, Oct. 20, 2007; Melia, "Ex-Gitmo prosecutor charges Pentagon interference," *Toronto Star*, Apr. 29, 2008.

65 Bravin, "Guantánamo Testimony Is Blocked," *Wall Street Journal*, Dec. 9, 2007.

66 Davis, "AWOL Military Justice," *Los Angeles Times*, Dec. 10, 2007.

67 Hartmann, "There Will Be No Secret Trials," *Los Angeles Times*, Dec. 19, 2007.

68 Davis, "Unforgivable Behavior, Inadmissible Evidence," *New York Times*, Feb. 17, 2008.

69 Tuttle, "Gitmo Trials Rigged," *The Nation*, Feb. 20, 2008; Fox, "Ex-Prosecutor to Serve as Defense Witness in Terror Case," *Washington Post*, Feb. 22, 2008; Ephron, "Gitmo Grievances," *Newsweek*, May 17, 2008. On Hamdan's saga, see J. Mahler, *The Challenge* (London: Picador, 2009).

70 Williams, "U.S. Charges Australian with War Crime," *Los Angeles Times*, Mar. 2, 2007; Elliott, "Hicks Case Rushed to Suit Howard—US," *Herald Sun*, Feb. 25, 2008.

71 "Ex-Prosecutor Calls War Tribunals Tainted," *Los Angeles Times*, Apr. 29, 2008; Glaberson, "Ex-Prosecutor Tells of Push by Pentagon on Detainees," *New York Times*, Apr. 29, 2008; White, "From Chief Prosecutor to Critic at Guantánamo," *Washington Post*, Apr. 29, 2008; White, "Guantánamo Detainee Rejects Court Procedure," *Washington Post*, Apr. 30, 2008.

72 Glaberson, "Judge's Guantánamo Ruling Bodes Ill for System," *New York Times*, May 11, 2008.

73 Williams, "Judge Critical of War Crimes Case Is Ousted," *Los Angeles Times*, May 31, 2008.

74 White, "Colonel Says Speaking Out Cost a Medal," *Washington Post*, May 29, 2008.

75 Williams, "Officer Calls Sept. 11 Cases Tainted," *Los Angeles Times*, June 5, 2008.

76 Davis post from Guantánamo Bay, June 17, 2008.

77 Rosenberg, "Afghan Detainee Claims Abuse at Guantánamo," *Miami Herald*, June 19, 2008.

78 Markon, "Hamdan Guilty of Terror Support," *Washington Post*, Aug. 7, 2008.

79 Finn, "Guantánamo War-Crime Trials Advisor Is Reassigned," *Los Angeles Times*, Sep. 20, 2008.

80 Meyer, "Guantánamo Tribunals Overseer under Investigation," *Los Angeles Times*, Oct. 25, 2008.

81 Davis, "Restoring U.S. Reputation Starts at Guantánamo Bay," *Toronto Star*, Nov. 13, 2008.

82 Davis, "Justice and Guantánamo Bay," *Wall Street Journal*, Nov. 10, 2009.

83 "Fired for Speaking Out," *New York Times*, Dec. 17, 2009.

84 *Davis v. Billington*, DC Circuit, June 1, 2012.

85 Williams, "Canadian's Terrorism Trial Is Expected to Be Rocky," *Los Angeles Times*, Nov. 8, 2007; Williams, "Terror Case Could Turn on Eyewitnesses," *Los Angeles Times*, Nov. 9, 2007; Glaberson, "Decks Are Stacked in War Crimes Cases, Lawyers Say," *New York Times*, Nov. 9, 2007; Williams, "Guantánamo Defense Lawyers See Stacked Deck," *Los Angeles Times*, Nov. 13, 2007; Glaberson, "Witness Names to Be Withheld from Detainee," *New York Times*, Dec. 1, 2007; Glaberson, "Guantánamo Judge Is Urged to Get on with Proceedings," *New York Times*, Apr. 12, 2008; Williams, "Detainee's Lawyer Says Death Was Possibly by Friendly Fire," *Los Angeles Times*, Apr. 12, 2008; Austen, "Lawyer Urges Canada to Try a Citizen Held by U.S. Forces," *New York Times*, Apr. 30, 2008; Glaberson, "Army Judge Is Replaced for Trial of Detainee," *New York Times*, May 31, 2008; Melia, "Defense Lawyer: US Urged Interrogators at Gitmo to Destroy Notes in Case They Had to Testify," *Washington Post*, June 9, 2008; Glaberson, "An Unlikely Antagonist in the Detainees' Corner," *New York Times*, June 19, 2008; Austen, "Citing New Report, Lawyers for Canadian Detainee Denounce Abuse," *New York Times*, July 11, 2008; el Akkad, "Khadr Lawyers Demand Independent Psychiatrist Assessment," *Globe & Mail*, Aug. 13, 2008; Rosenberg, "Judge Delays Omar Khadr War Crimes Trial," *Miami Herald*, Sep. 11, 2008; al Akkad, "Khadr's Lawyers Argue for Trial Delay," *Globe & Mail*, Oct. 22, 2008; CanWest News Service, Apr. 8, 2009; Danzig, "Khadr Case Goes Nowhere at Gitmo (Again)," *HuffPost*, Oct. 7, 2009.

86 Rosenberg, "Army Prosecutor Quits Gitmo War Court Case," *Miami Herald*, Sep. 24, 2008; Melia, "Guantánamo Prosecutor Quits over Detainee Case," *Miami Herald*, Sep. 25, 2008; Meyer, "Guantánamo Prosecutor Quits amid Controversy," *Los Angeles Times*, Sep. 25, 2008; Finn, "Guantánamo Prosecutor Quits, Says Evidence Was Withheld," *Washington Post*, Sep. 25, 2008; Glaberson, "Guantánamo Prosecutor Is Quitting in Dispute over a Case," *New York Times*, Sep. 25, 2008; "Guantánamo Ex-prosecutor Demands Immunity to Testify," *Los Angeles Times*, Sep.

26, 2008; Melia, "Former War Crimes Court Prosecutor Blasts Tribunals," *Miami Herald*, Sep. 27, 2008; Meyer, "Guantánamo Prosecutor Who Quit Had 'Grave Misgivings' about Fairness," *Los Angeles Times*, Oct. 12, 2008; Sullivan, "Confessions of a Former Guantánamo Prosecutor," *Salon*, Oct. 23, 2008. See E. Press, *Beautiful Souls: Saying No, Breaking Ranks, and Heeding the Voice of Conscience in Dark Times* 175–83 (New York: Farrar, Straus & Giroux, 2012).

87 Declaration of Lt. Col. Darrel Vandeveld, U.S. v. Mohammed Jawad, Sep. 22, 2008.

88 "U.S. Drops Charges against 5 Gitmo Detainees," Associated Press, Oct. 21, 2008; Williams, "U.S. Drops Charges against 5 Terrorism Suspects," *Los Angeles Times*, Oct. 22, 2008; Finn, "Charges against 5 Detainees Dropped Temporarily," *Washington Post*, Oct. 22, 2008.

89 See also Smith, *Eight O'Clock Ferry*.

90 "Afghan Detainee's Confession Excluded on Torture Grounds at Guantánamo Trial," *Guardian*, Oct. 29, 2008; Melia, "Former Prosecutor Says Ruling Wrecks U.S. Case," *Miami Herald*, Oct. 29, 2008; McFadden, "Gitmo Judge Tosses Out Detainee's 2nd Confession," Associated Press, Nov. 20, 2008.

91 Corera, "Guantánamo's a stain on US military," BBC News, Dec. 2, 2008.

92 Finn, "Evidence in Terror Cases Said to Be in Chaos," *Washington Post*, Jan. 14, 2009; Wilber, "ACLU Says Government Used False Confessions," *Washington Post*, July 2, 2009.

93 Vandeveld, "I Was Slow to Recognize the Stain of Guantánamo," *Washington Post*, Jan. 18, 2009.

94 250 *Law and Security Digest*, July 10, 2009.

95 Glaberson, "Government Might Allow U.S. Trial for Detainee," *New York Times*, July 24, 2009.

96 Hansen, "The Prosecution Rests: Why Darrel J. Vandeveld left Guantanamo," *America: The Jesuit Review*, Sep. 26, 2011.

97 Vandeveld and Dratel, "Military Commissions: A Bad Idea," *Salon*, Mar. 10, 2010.

98 Epigraph to E. Press, *Beautiful Souls* (New York: Farrar, Straus & Giroux, 2012).

99 H. Melville, *Bartleby, the Scrivener: A Story of Wall Street* [1853].

100 Edmond N. Cahn, *The Sense of Injustice* (Bloomington: Indiana University Press, 1975).

101 Richard Wasserstrom, "Lawyers as Professionals: Some Moral Issues," 5 *Human Rights* 1 (1975).

102 In a letter to William Smith (Jan. 9, 1785), see *Bartlett's Quotations* (14th ed.).

103 Ingo Müller, *Hitler's Justice: The Courts of the Third Reich* (Cambridge, MA: Harvard University Press, 1991).

5

Law's Infamy

Ashker v. Governor of California *and the Failures of Solitary Confinement Reform*

KERAMET REITER

Instead of focusing on overturned and repudiated legal decisions already consigned to legal infamy, in this chapter I zero in on a punitive practice that has (allegedly) been repudiated: solitary confinement. Through the lens of *Ashker v. Governor of California*, a class-action lawsuit filed on behalf of 500 prisoners in California who had each been housed continuously in solitary confinement for ten years or more, I examine whether *Ashker* indeed repudiated the practice of solitary confinement, consigning it to legal infamy. Notably, prison officials maintained the *Ashker* class members in indefinite solitary confinement not because of any crimes committed, or even prison rules violated, but because each class member was alleged to be a dangerous gang member or affiliate. I contend that solitary confinement persists in California, resisting legal infamy, through two underappreciated mechanisms: publicized demonization of agitators and strategic deployment of scientific expertise. While I trace how the practice of solitary confinement has persisted in California, in spite of a seemingly reform-oriented 2015 settlement in the *Ashker* litigation, I also examine how this persistence and its mechanisms might reveal alternative possibilities for reform that might finally render solitary confinement a legally infamous practice.

On August 31, 2015, the parties in the case of *Ashker v. Governor of California* announced that they had reached a sweeping settlement agreement eliminating solitary confinement for periods of more than five years in all California prisons. The settlement also guaranteed the 500 class members, who had each been in continuous solitary confinement for at least ten years, the opportunity to live in the general prison population. At the time, Todd Ashker, the lead plaintiff in the case, had been in solitary confinement at Pelican Bay State Prison for twenty-five years. For more than two decades, his life had consisted of at least twenty-two hours a day locked in a windowless, poured-concrete cell measuring 80 square feet. If he was lucky, and prison officials followed policy, Ashker left the cell three times a week for a fifteen-minute shower, plus a few more times for an hour or two of exercise in an outdoor "dog run." In twenty-five years, Ashker had only two phone calls with his mother. He went years at a time without a social visit.[1]

Ironically, a series of massive, statewide prisoner hunger strikes in 2011 and 2013, protesting the durations and conditions of confinement in the Pelican Bay Security Housing Unit (SHU), had provided Ashker with opportunities for more social contact than he had during two prior decades. Ashker was one of the strike leaders, and one of the lead negotiators, who met more than once face to face with California Department of Corrections and Rehabilitation (CDCR) and other state officials to coordinate an end to the strikes.[2] The weeks-long hunger strikes infused the *Ashker* litigation with a sense of urgency: Would these prisoners starve themselves to death absent a legal resolution? Until the 2015 *Ashker* settlement, Todd Ashker expected to die in the SHU, whether from assault, refusing food, or natural causes. But within a year of the 2015 *Ashker* settlement, Ashker—along with the hundreds of other class members for whom he was the named representative—would be living among the general prison population. In a 2018 letter to a reporter, Ashker wrote: "I'm still amazed at how big the sky looks."[3]

Such hunger strikes and the *Ashker* settlement have been the subject of hundreds of pages of criminological, philosophical, and legal scholarship, largely celebrating the prisoners' brave collective action and the sweeping reforms set into motion by the case.[4] I have been among those writers, albeit one sounding a cautionary tone, suggesting that the reforms may well be limited or unsustainable.[5]

I had already (or so I thought) said all I had to say about *Ashker*: from the beginning, the demands were insufficiently radical to fundamentally reshape either solitary confinement or the prison system into which it is inextricably woven.[6] And the resulting settlement reflected this, providing temporary individual relief for the class members by "unsettling" the practice of solitary confinement but not seriously and sustainably altering the practice, let alone abolishing it. The month the case settled in 2015, I wrote that "one settlement agreement . . . cannot sweep away decades of abusive prison policies," warning that settlements are weaker than judicial decisions as nonprecedential reference points, that prison officials still seemed to be clinging to all their beliefs about dangerous and undeserving prisoners requiring placement in restrictive solitary confinement, and that the settlement did not do enough to promote transparency around solitary confinement practices in the state.[7] I wrote with conviction, but also with a hope that I would be proven wrong and could write something else besides this piece.

But nine years after the first Pelican Bay hunger strike, and nearly five years after the state and the prisoners reached an initial settlement agreement, Todd Ashker and his case continue to appear regularly in the national news. Sometimes the news is good. In spite of my warning that settlements have limited legal relevance compared to judicial decisions and orders, the *Ashker* case and settlement have been touchpoints in the American Civil Liberty Union's "Stop Solitary Campaign," kicked off the same summer as the first hunger strikes centered in and around Pelican Bay.[8] I will return to both alternative interpretations of the broader relevance of legal settlements and the broader implications of the *Ashker* case, outside of California prisons, in the conclusion.

Despite *Ashker's* national (and even international) implications, California prisoners continue to complain about the conditions and durations of solitary confinement in the state. Although the settlement agreement was originally scheduled to sunset in 2017 or 2018, the plaintiffs' lawyers are still arguing that the promises of the agreement are unrealized more than five years later.[9] So I return again to the hunger strikes and the *Ashker* litigation, mining the legal motions and filings, the public commentary, and the scholarship for new insights about when reform works, where it goes wrong, and especially what makes and unmakes infamous cases.

After contextualizing *Ashker* in a pantheon of infamous prisoners' rights and civil rights cases, and providing some brief additional background on the case, I explore how the practice of solitary confinement has continued much as I predicted in 2015: persisting, often beyond public oversight, driven by discretionary administrative decision making.

But I also identify and trace two new mechanisms in the persistence of the practice: publicized demonization of agitators and strategic deployment of scientific expertise. I then discuss the national and international implications of these mechanisms of persistence, suggesting that the patterns have implications for understanding how infamous cases might be unmade, if not avoided in the first place.

Such analyses seem especially important in light of recent shifts in the U.S. federal judiciary. As of 2020, one in four circuit court judges had been appointed by the unusually authoritarian forty-fifth president of the United States. Moreover, of that president's 187 total federal judicial appointees, 78 percent were male and 89 percent were white, entrenching the already exaggerated representation of white male perspectives in the federal courts.[10] In light of this reshaping of the federal judiciary, legal pundits predict a new rash of *Plessys, Lochners*, and *Stanfords* in the coming generations of federal judicial lawmaking, permitting discrimination in service provision and voting access, minimizing workers' rights to organize, and limiting the rights of vulnerable populations such as prisoners and pregnant women.[11] In this context, analyzing disappointing legal results—whether infamous outcomes or failures to establish existing practices as infamous—seems all the more critical, especially in the context of class actions and settlements, where so much legal reform actually happens these days.[12]

Did *Ashker v. Governor of California* Render the Practice of Solitary Confinement Infamous?

Ashker has been treated as a decision that repudiated the practice of solitary confinement, at least of *indeterminate* solitary confinement, and sparked legal, legislative, and administrative reforms across the United States.[13] But did it render the practice infamous? Simply posing the question feels potentially dismissive of the inspiring collective action the Pelican Bay SHU prisoners coordinated, the ongoing creative legal battle their lawyers are waging, and the real day-to-day improvements many prisoners have experienced in the conditions of their confinement as a result of the case. But the question is meant to provoke a deeper engagement with the concepts of infamy and injustice, especially the more subtle legacies of implementations failures.

In the field of prisoners' rights, under the protections of the Eighth Amendment, the consignment of practices to legal infamy is rare. As recently as 1995, prisoners in Alabama were chained to hitching posts for punishment.[14] As recently as 2005, kids as young as sixteen could be executed for their crimes.[15] As recently as 2009, one prisoner a week was dying unnecessarily from inadequate medical care in California.[16] In spite of the repudiation of these specific practices, prisoners continue to die in four-point restraints in prison, are executed for crimes they committed as teenagers, and die daily from inadequate medical care, especially as the COVID-19 pandemic rages through prisons.[17] In light of this institutional resistance to change, prisoners' rights scholars and advocates tend to have a broader conception of infamy beyond actually discredited practices or values. In the prisoners' rights canon, more subtle forms of infamy earn attention as catalyzing, if not always hopeful, reference points. For example, when a court simply acknowledges the horrible treatment a prisoner has received (infamous facts), where a prisoners' claim has been established to have been completely misinterpreted (infamous myths), and when principles that would seem unjust in any nonprison context remain good law in the prison context (infamous principles).

Hope v. Peltzer (2002), one of a small handful of prisoners' rights cases to be heard by the Supreme Court in the past few decades,[18] exemplified infamous facts: an African American prisoner was chained to a hitching post for seven hours straight, not in 1890, 1920, or 1950, but in 1995. The Supreme Court noted the "obvious" brutality of this practice, though the officers imposing the punishment were never held responsible.[19]

"The Peanut Butter Case" exemplifies infamous myths: it was a case in which a prisoner complained about receiving the wrong peanut butter from his commissary order, returning the incorrect item, and never receiving the $2.50 (at best, a day's wages in prison) credit for the return on his prison books. But Senator Robert Dole complained that the prisoner had brought a lawsuit complaining about "being served chunky peanut butter instead of the creamy variety," a sound bite that was repeated again and again in defense of federal legislation sharply constraining the rights of prisoners to bring any lawsuits challenging the conditions of their confinement.[20]

Farmer v. Brennan (1994) exemplifies an infamous principle: a trans woman who had undergone hormonal and surgical treatment was placed in a male federal prison facility, beaten, and raped. The Supreme Court held that in order for Dee Farmer to receive either retrospective relief (damages) or prospective relief (an injunction preventing future harm), she would have to establish "deliberate indifference": proving not only substantial harm she experienced but also that prison officials were subjectively aware of the existence of the risk of that substantial harm—a rather difficult fact for a prisoner to establish.[21]

Ashker v. Governor of California could be infamous by all the standards of prisoners' rights cases. It includes infamous facts about prisoners spending decades in long-term solitary confinement, with limited human contact, missing seeing the moon above, feeling grass under their feet, patting a dog. It arguably includes infamous myths about prisoners whom the prison system asserted (and in some cases continues to assert) are too dangerous to have any human contact whatsoever for the rest of their lives, even though hundreds of these prisoners are released annually into our communities, when their criminal sentences conclude, without incident (unless their ongoing struggles with the psychological effects of solitary confinement count).[22] And, by international law standards, the case even includes an infamous principle: The *Ashker* settlement capped terms of solitary confinement at five years, whereas the United Nations Special Rapporteur on Torture says that more than fifteen days could constitute cruel, inhuman, and degrading treatment, if not torture.[23]

But did it actually render the practice of solitary confinement infamous? Advocates and prisoners celebrated it as a triumph, a central case in coordinated advocacy "efforts to challenge mass incarceration, discrimination, and abusive prison policies."[24] The cap of five years in solitary confinement represents a significant improvement over no cap at all, which left hundreds of people languishing in solitary for decades. Other aspects of the *Ashker* settlement increased procedural protections governing placement in solitary confinement and improved conditions of confinement for those ultimately placed in solitary confinement. At best, these reforms rendered the practice of *indefinite* solitary confinement infamous. At worst, the reforms simply perfected an existing practice, functioning, however counterintuitively, to maintain the status quo.

This is an argument I have made previously about prison conditions litigation, especially solitary confinement litigation: since the 1970s, cases celebrated as reformist have instead contributed to refining solitary confinement and even making it more resistant to litigation. For example, 1970s cases requiring segregation cells to be clean, well-lit, and not overcrowded partially inspired poured-concrete solitary confinement cells equipped with fluorescent lights that never turn off.[25] And again, following litigation challenging the conditions of confinement at Pelican Bay in the 1990s, "practices were streamlined and sterilized, in a rational and superficially compliant response to the legal oversight."[26] These are examples of the concept of legal endogeneity: institutions signal compliance with legal orders through formal and often superficial regulations that then receive deference in future legal challenges.[27] The *Ashker* settlement, in my interpretation, joins this long tradition of legal challenges to solitary confinement ultimately refining and reinforcing the status quo.

In the following sections, I look at the outcomes—a case was litigated; little changed—as well as the mechanisms by which those outcomes are achieved (and infamy resisted). By analyzing the aftermath of the *Ashker* settlement, tracing implementation attempts, roadblocks, and reinterpretations, I explain not only how law-in-action differs from law-on-the-books but also the specific tools of resistance deployed in California by prison officials, their lawyers, and experts.[28] This analysis ultimately reveals that neither the legal principles upholding some forms of solitary confinement nor the social practices of solitarily confining some people have been fully repudiated. And so solitary confinement—arguably even indefinite solitary confinement—has repeatedly avoided legal infamy. Before analyzing this process of avoidance, though, I provide a summary of how the *Ashker* case arose, gradually accruing the markers of a classic civil rights case and seemingly building toward consigning the practice of indefinite solitary confinement to infamy.

Unsettling Solitary Confinement: The Unusual Litigation History of Ashker v. Governor of California

Prisoners' rights cases often begin when enough prisoners file substantively similar pro se (on their own behalf, usually handwritten) petitions to gain the attention of a sympathetic judge, or when civil rights lawyers investigate a series of individual complaints and build a case. Sometimes prisoners' rights cases begin more like other civil rights cases, such as *Brown v. Board of Education* or *Roper v. Simmons*, when lawyers look for sympathetic litigants to represent in order to challenge an unjust legal decision and turn it into an infamous one.[29] The *Ashker* case, however, became relevant through a massive, statewide hunger strike initiated by prisoners who had apparently given up hope of resolving their grievances through the courts.

Todd Ashker, a white prisoner and alleged Aryan Brotherhood (AB) hitman, and Danny Troxell, another alleged AB leader, were two of the hunger strike leaders. Together, the two had filed a pro se petition in 2009 complaining about the conditions of their confinement in the Pelican Bay SHU, but the petition had gone nowhere. In 2009, they had been held continuously in the SHU for nineteen and twenty-three years, respectively, and Ashker had already filed dozens of lawsuits complaining about his treatment and conditions of confinement.[30] So on April 1, 2011, Ashker and Troxell, along with nine other prisoners identifying as African American and Latino, as well as white, and all alleged leaders of different, rival prison gangs (AB, Black Guerilla Family, Mexican Mafia, and Nuestra Familia), signed a letter committing to begin an indefinite hunger strike on July 1 unless the CDCR (state prison officials) acceded to their demands.

Each signatory was serving an indefinite term in the Pelican Bay SHU because he had been labeled as a gang member. At the time, a "gang validation" required only three pieces of evidence: a letter from another known or alleged gang member, drawings or tattoos associated with gang symbols (including otherwise innocuous things like Aztec mandelas or Irish shamrocks), books associated with gang leaders (including *The Autobiography of Malcolm X* and George Jackson's book of letters *Soledad Brother*), and other forms of expression protected—but only for nonprisoners—by the First Amendment.

The signatories' demands were distressingly simple: Punish prisoners with solitary confinement only for specific, individual acts (rather than status-based assumptions about "safety and security" risks); abolish the opaque, discretionary process by which prison administrators permanently labeled prisoners as gang members and sent them to solitary confinement indefinitely; comply with nationally and internationally recognized best practices about conditions of and limitations on periods in solitary confinement; provide "wholesome, nutritional meals"; and provide constructive programming, including specific requests such as allowing prisoners the ability to take one photo of themselves per year, a calendar, a cap to be worn on the cold exercise yards, and participation in proctored exams for correspondence courses.[31] As simple as the demands were, they sounded far-fetched to me, to prisoners' rights advocates, and (I suspect) to the prisoners themselves.

The prisoners' eloquent critiques of confinement conditions as both unfair and unimaginably harsh had already been assessed by an unusually liberal judge and dismissed. Thelton Henderson, a progressive federal district court judge based in San Francisco had recently closed a case initiated in the 1990s, *Madrid v. Gomez*, after finding that conditions of confinement at Pelican Bay had been consistently meeting minimum constitutional standards for years. That case had originally alleged unconstitutional conditions of confinement at Pelican Bay, and especially in the SHU, and generated decades of close monitoring.[32]

Much like the initial demands, the prisoners' outside supporters were also radical, explicitly abolitionist groups (a decade before Black Lives Matter and "defund the police" arguments generated a more mainstream conversation about abolition): California Prison Focus, Critical Resistance, and Legal Services for Prisoners with Children.[33] Ashker and Troxell had sent out multiple copies of their neatly handwritten demand letter to advocates across the state, and those advocates in turn had helped to spread the word about the planned July 1 strike.

The prisoners themselves, though both eloquent and seemingly forsaken, were not, at first glance, especially sympathetic. State prison officials considered SHU prisoners to be the "worst of the worst," the most dangerous prisoners in the sprawling state system of more than 100,000 prisoners and thirty-four state facilities. Among the more than 4,000 people in long-term solitary confinement in the state in 2011, the signatories on the demand letter were some of the most reviled gang leaders in the state, at least according to corrections department officials. Officials had kept seven of the demand letter signatories alone together for years on the "short corridor," a special cellblock within the SHU designated for the extra layer of isolation imposed by being surrounded by enemies. Most of the prisoners signing on to the letter had been detained in the Pelican Bay SHU at least ten years, if not since this archetypal supermax facility first opened in 1989—more than two decades earlier. A corrections department spokeswoman accused the strike leaders of coercing prisoners into refusing food as a publicity stunt to manipulate their way into dangerously lax conditions of confinement for themselves and other gang leaders.[34]

Put simply, in light of the legal landscape in California, the prisoners' radical allies, and their serious criminal histories and alleged gang leadership, Todd Ashker, Danny Troxell, and the others seeking significant improvements in the conditions and indefinite durations of their extreme confinement seemed unlikely to see much change in their lifetimes. At least the strike, and crafting their demands, gave them something to do with the endless hours and perhaps something to live for. On July 1, 2011, more than 5,000 prisoners across the state started refusing meals. The strike went on for three weeks—until the undersecretary of corrections in the state agreed to sit down, in person, with the strike leaders. At that meeting, Undersecretary Scott Kernan agreed to reconsider many of the policies the prisoners were protesting.[35] Major national newspapers covered the prisoners' demands and the coordinated nonviolent action, and Amnesty International and the United Nations Special Rapporteur on Torture started asking questions about the conditions of confinement in the Pelican Bay SHU.[36] Over the next year, the conditions of the prisoners' confinement and their individual stories continued to receive national and international attention.

One story, published by KPCC, a Southern California subsidiary of NPR, on August 23, 2011, exemplifies the power of this increased scrutiny. Julie Small, the author of the story, published a small bar graph online showing how long the 1,111 prisoners then housed in the Pelican Bay SHU has been in solitary confinement: 95 percent had been in the SHU for at least five years; nearly half (513) had been in the SHU at least ten years.[37] This was data I had been asking the Department of Corrections to produce for years; I had been told that the Department "counted beds, not people."[38] Even Julie Small, who finally successfully obtained the aggregated snapshot data on lengths of confinement, noted that "prison officials won't say how long [specific] inmates in the SHU have been there, how long they might stay, or who they are."[39]

Still, Small's KPCC graph of the SHU population broken down by time changed the conversation around long-term solitary confinement in California. First, the graph made public and obvious something I had only accidentally learned through my data requests: Californians knew shockingly little about their prisons—understanding neither how their tax dollars were being spent nor how prisoners were being treated in the most secure and hidden prison in the state. Second, in the context of so little knowledge, a single statistic (513 people for ten-plus years) galvanized change, raising questions about what else was unknown, providing sufficient detail to identify subjects of potentially unconstitutional policies, and establishing benchmarks for reform (capping solitary confinement terms at five years would affect hundreds, if not thousands, of California state prisoners). Indeed, Small's graph and the single statistic about those 513 people in the SHU for more than ten years was the fuel Todd Ashker, Danny Troxell, and their collaborators needed in their public campaign to bring attention to the conditions in solitary confinement and in their legal campaign to assert a violation of their constitutional rights inherent in those conditions. The graph provided proof that a significant number of people (513) were in conditions similar to that of Ashker and Troxell—a critical fact in the class certification process and thus a critical step in prison conditions reform litigation.[40]

By June 2013, the lawyers representing Ashker and Troxell had sought and won class certification on behalf of all 500-plus prisoners who had been in solitary confinement for ten years or more. A federal judge in the Northern District of California agreed that the named plaintiffs had "raised viable questions about the constitutionality of the SHU," which deserved a legal hearing.[41] Litigation (and inside prisoner organizing) continued. In July 2013, the state filed declarations from former gang members claiming that the strike leaders were active gang members, that the SHU successfully stifled gang activity, and that the conditions in the SHU neither constituted torture nor were as bad as the *Ashker* plaintiffs claimed.[42] The declarations punctuated the third, largest, and longest statewide hunger strike orchestrated by the *Ashker* plaintiffs between July and September 2013. The strike went on for more than sixty days, prompting the state to seek and obtain an order "authorizing refeeding."[43] Litigation continued. In March 2015, plaintiffs' lawyers filed ten reports from leading experts (experts-cum-critics, that is) including: correctional leaders from other states condemning the extremity of policies in place in California's Pelican Bay SHU;[44] doctors documenting physical impacts of social isolation, such as brain changes and cardiovascular problems;[45] and psychologists documenting the relationship between conditions in the SHU, such as lack of touch, and physical and mental health symptoms.[46] A few months later, in August 2015, the *Ashker* settlement officially "prohibited the assignment of prisoners to the SHU based solely on their status as gang members, capped all stays in the SHU at five years, made the provisions retroactive, and required prison officials to provide prisoners' lawyers monthly data reports for two years about the characteristics of the SHU population."[47]

In the end, the *Ashker* case accrued all the characteristics of a classic civil rights case. Potentially sympathetic litigants attempted to file a lawsuit pro se on their own behalf and ultimately attracted the attention of judges and lawyers (albeit through a massive, statewide hunger strike), who investigated their claims. This team of advocates then sought to confront—and even abolish—the practice of long-term solitary confinement through litigation. At first, the settlement seemed like a triumph. Todd Ashker and Danny Troxell moved out of the SHU after a quarter-century: they not only got to see the sky, but they had achieved acquiescence to each and every one of the initial demands made in summer 2011 that had touched off the first hunger strikes. A year after the settlement, the Center for Constitutional Rights celebrated the fact that indefinite solitary confinement was down 99 percent, and the overall solitary population (including definite terms) had fallen by 65 percent in California.[48] The Pelican Bay SHU has largely been converted into a minimum-security facility, the doors to the individual cells and isolation pods, including the short corridor, thrown open, letting sunlight stream in from the outside. The blank concrete walls, which prisoners such as Todd Ashker and Danny Troxell spent decades staring at, are now covered in colorful murals. Oprah Winfrey even filmed a *60 Minutes* episode sitting in a now-empty Pelican Bay cell, interviewing former SHU prisoners enrolled as college students within the University of California system.[49] The images make for a feel-good encapsulation of drastic reform. But how much actually changed, below the surface, for unnamed class members?

Settling Solitary Confinement: The Not-So-Unusual Implementation Story of Ashker v. Governor of California

In spite of the clear terms of the *Ashker* settlement, solitary confinement has persisted in California since 2015, carried on behind closed doors, for long durations, with little public oversight. During the peak period of litigation in California, between 2013 and 2015, correctional officials initially sought to avoid the *Ashker* litigation simply by moving prisoners around—that is, out of Pelican Bay, where all of the attention was focused—into other facilities.[50] At the time, I wrote that this attempt to moot the claims of the *Ashker* plaintiffs (along with declarations filed by former prison gang members accusing named *Ashker* class members of "advancing agendas of violence") suggested California prison officials were likely to resist full implementation of the settlement.[51] Indeed, they have.

Members of the *Ashker* class have experienced three new forms of de facto solitary confinement, about which they and their lawyers have complained. First, some class members have been placed in the highest security general population facilities in the state (so-called Level IV facilities), where they have as little as one hour per day outside their cells, less time than they had in the Pelican Bay SHU.[52] Second, some other class members have been placed in a Restricted Custody General Population (RCGP) unit, justified as a place to facilitate transition from the SHU to the general prison population, practically functioning as a highly restrictive indefinite confinement space. Third, still other class members have been placed in administrative segregation pending investigation of confidential information about security threats and potential attacks.

Lawyers in the *Ashker* suit have sought, with limited success, to challenge these new iterations of solitary confinement, repackaged as Level IV lockdowns, RCPGs, and administrative segregation. In October 2017, plaintiffs' lawyers filed an enforcement motion arguing against the first form of de facto solitary confinement. The Level IV conditions of confinement, the *Ashker* lawyers argued, violated the principles of the settlement by "failing to meet the ordinary meaning of general population" conditions assumed by the terms of the settlement, providing formerly segregated SHU prisoners with even fewer privileges in the general prison population, and creating similar risks of serious harm to health as the SHU.[53] The court "declined to intervene" in the matter.[54]

Early in 2018, plaintiffs' lawyers sought to address both the RCGP and the administrative segregation forms of confinement, arguing that California prison officials continued to "violate the due process clause" by (1) "placing and retaining class members in the RCGP without adequate procedural protections" and (2) "systematically misusing confidential information to return *Ashker* class members to solitary confinement."[55] On the basis of reviews of "about 40" files, details of which were (ironically) largely redacted even from the plaintiffs' published motion, lawyers from the Center for Constitutional Rights concluded that prison officials had "fabricated or improperly disclosed confidential information" and repeatedly failed to ensure that "confidential information is accurate [and] reliable."[56] As a remedy, lawyers asked the court to extend the settlement agreement one more year beyond the initial two-year term to allow for further implementation monitoring. Following months of back-and-forth motion-filing about the extension, the court ordered a one-year extension from January 15, 2019, and another from April 9, 2021.[57]

Although settlement implementation monitoring continued into 2022, prison officials successfully stymied attempts to expand the initial *Ashker* settlement to require reforms to RCGP and administrative segregation conditions of confinement. The state attorney general, facilitating prison officials' continued resistance to implementing *Ashker*, appealed the district court's finding that prison officials breached the terms of the settlement agreement by putting class members in units like the RCGP. In late 2020, the United States Court of Appeals for the Ninth Circuit agreed with the attorney general, holding that units like the RCGP did not violate the settlement agreement. The *Ashker* attorneys requested a rehearing *en banc* (before a larger panel of Ninth Circuit judges), but the request was denied. So the 2020 appellate decision, establishing that California prison officials have "substantially complied" with the settlement, stands.[58]

The ongoing litigation in *Ashker* confirms that solitary confinement persists in California because of continued opacity in who experiences solitary confinement, why, and for how long—in addition to continued total administrative control over not only information but also the placement process. Lawyers in the *Ashker* case have now asked for "more long-term remedies that go beyond continued monitoring," including an appointed official who reviews all solitary confinement placements based on confidential information and a procedural right for prisoners to appeal such placement decisions before an independent reviewer (rather than before a prison official).[59] Even these remedies, however, are limited: they amount to incremental checks on both the total opacity and total discretion defining solitary confinement in California (and elsewhere).

Indeed, at each step in the *Ashker* litigation, prison officials and state lawyers have engaged in resistance and obfuscation that is tediously familiar in the context of the history of solitary confinement reform: coming up with new names for old practices, like the RCPG; reasserting the critical importance of the practice; and maintaining discretionary control. As I wrote with my colleague Ashley Rubin while reviewing the history of solitary confinement reform attempts over two centuries in the United States: "In each historical era we examine, prison administrators reinvented solitary confinement, following critiques of the practice as a failed social experiment. . . . [A]dministrators' claims of reinvention, however, imply a kind of novelty aimed at legitimizing the [continued] use of solitary."[60] *Ashker v. Governor of California* has provided just one more historical example of exactly this pattern. However, two new mechanisms of solitary confinement persistence have become visible over the course of the implementation (or nonimplementation) of the *Ashker* settlement.

Ongoing Demonization

The demonization of solitarily confined prisoners is a longstanding correctional tactic for initially justifying and subsequently legitimizing solitary confinement practices. In California, correctional officials, who designed the Pelican Bay SHU (the archetypal American supermax) in the 1980s, explained the facility was a necessary response to the 1970s era of collective organizing in prison. According to prison officials, the 1970s represented an era of uncontrollable violence, led by George Jackson and Black Panther affiliates.[61] External critiques of California's SHUs, leveled by investigative journalists and lawyers in the

1990s, generated new correctional attempts to "prove" how dangerous SHU prisoners actually were: correctional officers set up gladiator fights between rival gang members and orchestrated riots in front of visiting prison monitors.[62] These gladiator fights, while deeply disturbing, were not an isolated example of correctional resistance to external oversight of internal correctional dangerousness assessments. In reality, the gladiator fights were representative of a persistent mechanism of correctional resistance to oversight and reform: when correctional officials disagree with critiques of their tools of control, or do not buy into reform principles like the terms of the *Ashker* settlement, they tend to proactively undermine prisoners' claims and advocates' reform goals through demonization of solitarily confined prisoners.[63] Given the opacity and administrative discretion characterizing solitary confinement practices, such correctional resistance tends to be remarkably successful.

Consigning the practice of indefinite solitary confinement to legal infamy would require addressing the tactic of demonization. The terms of the *Ashker* settlement sought to do exactly this. While the settlement only gingerly addressed other mechanisms of solitary confinement persistence, such as opacity and administrative control, with data collection limited to class members and data details sealed in litigation, it confronted the problem of demonization head-on. The settlement explicitly stated first that the very *Ashker* class members prison officials had asserted were irredeemably dangerous would be released from the Pelican Bay SHU into the general prison population; and second, it stated that prison officials would be trained to better assess the accuracy of confidential information used against prisoners.[64] Together, these provisions clearly communicated that the *Ashker* class members were not all so excessively dangerous as prison officials had asserted. California correctional officials explicitly and publicly admitted this downgrading in their dangerousness assessment, too. For instance, in 2017, then–CDCR director Scott Kernan (who, as undersecretary of corrections, had instituted some small reforms in 2011 following the first Pelican Bay hunger strikes) told Oprah on *60 Minutes* that the state's prior solitary confinement use and policies had been "a mistake."[65]

By the time Kernan made that statement in 2017, California had released thousands of people from long-term solitary confinement. Any correctional official interested in rolling back the reforms would have had every incentive to identify, as publicly as possible, prisoners who had been released from the Pelican Bay SHU and messed up—that is to say, committed a violent act in prison, trafficked drugs within prison, systematically violated other prison rules, or committed a new crime outside of prison. And yet no such stories made headlines or even back-page special-interest stories. Other reforms in the state (around reducing prison sentences, for instance) generated plenty of public comments and complaints from police leadership alleging (with little evidentiary basis) a connection to rising crime.[66] Over the first few years of the implementation of the *Ashker* settlement, though, no such links were publicly made between the initially drastic reductions in the use of solitary confinement within CDCR and any negative consequences for prison or public safety. The one violent incident associated with a release from the Pelican Bay SHU actually took place two weeks before the finalization of the *Ashker* settlement: alleged George Jackson coconspirator Hugo Pinell, who had served the longest period of time in solitary confinement in California as of 2015 (forty-five years), was released from the Pelican Bay SHU and transferred to a general population yard at California State Prison, Sacramento. Within days, fellow prisoners stabbed Pinell to death. Prisoners and prison staff alike had something to prove by enacting or permitting violence against a prisoner as well known as Pinell.[67] Still, Pinell's death neither slowed down the settlement negotiations nor, remarkably, foreshadowed more such violence.

The direct attack on demonization as a mechanism of persistence, through release of demonized prisoners and external oversight of demonization tools (such as the use of confidential information), however, was unsuccessful. Three recent notable examples of demonization have surfaced in the ongoing battle to compel implementation of the *Ashker* settlement: The (mis)use of confidential information in order to return *Ashker* class members to some form of solitary confinement; the (mis)use of "gang validation" information and status to disqualify *Ashker* class members from consideration for parole; and the filing of a formal criminal complaint, relying on the very same questionable confidential information and gang validation evidence challenged in the prior two examples, against Danny Troxell, one of the named *Ashker* class members.

First, in the 2019 order to extend for an additional year the *Ashker* settlement agreement and court-ordered monitoring, the judge noted that "systemic and ongoing due process violations exist—namely, the systemic misuse of confidential information in what appear to be meaningless disciplinary hearings such as to return class members to solitary confinement."[68] Such due process violations directly contradict the *Ashker* settlement's central requirement that prisoners be sent to solitary confinement only for fixed periods of time following specific rule violations, rather than for indefinite periods of time based on their status as alleged gang members. Judge Robert Illman based his finding about systemic misuse of confidential information on individual disciplinary file reviews conducted by the prisoners' lawyers as part of the monitoring of settlement implementation. In fact, the judge reviewed in detail seven different cases in which prisoner class members received rule violation reports stating that confidential information existed or was reliable, when in fact no such information existed, the information had already been determined to be unreliable, or contradictory evidence existed and had not been disclosed to the prisoner.[69] In all, almost half of 110 reviewed disciplinary cases exhibited these sorts of problems. Similarly, the judge reviewed in detail nine cases in which prisoner class members were transferred into the RCGP based on claims that they constituted a general threat to institutional security, essentially restricting a class member's liberty based on their status, rather than based on a specific rule violation as required by the terms of the *Ashker* settlement.[70]

Of course, prisoners' lawyers had access to reviewing the files only of *class members* incurring disciplinary infractions or placement in RCGP, so the small subset of reviewed cases were ones in which prison officials knew their actions would subsequently be scrutinized by an adversarial party. This leaves open the disturbing question of what might have been or be happening in other cases where prison officials know no such scrutiny exists. In sum, even under known close scrutiny, CDCR officials continued to rely on vague, false, and unreliable claims about the unruliness and dangerousness of *Ashker* class members to justify continued placement in highly restrictive conditions of confinement.

Second, in the same 2019 order that extended the *Ashker* settlement agreement and court-ordered monitoring for an additional year, the judge noted that prisoners with disciplinary records indicating that they had previously been housed in the SHU were systematically being denied parole. Even those class members, who avoided the expanding range of mechanisms by which they might have been returned to solitary confinement (especially convictions for disciplinary infractions based on confidential information or placement in the RCGP without disciplinary infraction), remained ineligible for parole based on "gang validation" (through the repudiated, proven to be error-prone, three-pieces-of-evidence policy) records officially discredited and renounced by the terms of the settlement. At parole hearings, when formerly gang-validated prisoners attempted to explain the repudiation of the gang validation process, parole commissioners interpreted these "defenses" as dishonest, lacking both credibility and remorse.[71] CDCR officials maintained gang validation records in prisoners' files (with no acknowledgement of their discrediting) and transmitted the files to the parole commissioners. Thus prisoners claiming the records were discredited, when no such acknowledgement existed in their official files, indeed seemed unremorseful at best. This process provides another example of how CDCR officials continued to assert, defend, and leverage vague, false, and unreliable claims about prior gang membership to justify class members' continued incarceration.

The redeployment of discredited information to redemonize former SHU prisoners at parole hearings reveals the limitations of even the most direct and forceful provisions of the *Ashker* settlement. In order to truly present an existential threat to the practice of indefinite solitary confinement, the litigation will have to guarantee not only the release of demonized prisoners from solitary confinement into the general prison population but also their release from the general prison population onto parole. Indeed, prisoners who have previously spent an extended period in the SHU but are subsequently released to the streets and thrive beyond the prison gate forcefully delegitimize the entire institution of indefinite solitary confinement.

As one example, during her 2017 *60 Minutes* episode, Oprah interviewed the eloquent and poised University of California, Berkeley undergraduate Steven Czifra and the recent Berkeley graduate Danny Murillo about the Pelican Bay SHU reforms. Both Cizfra and Murillo had spent extended periods in the Pelican Bay SHU under the gang validation policy repudiated by the *Ashker* settlement. Czifra and Murillo's postincarceration lives highlight the logical and financial absurdity of confining alleged gang members to solitary confinement indefinitely.

First, Czifra and Murillo—not only by leading nonviolent, law-abiding lives but also by attending and succeeding at an internationally renowned university—conclusively discredit their prior labels as indefinitely (and implicitly irredeemably) dangerous gang members. Second, the annual cost of educating Czifra and Murillo at Berkeley is less than half the annual cost of keeping them locked in the SHU: an estimated $35,000 for tuition, fees, and campus housing compared to an estimated $90,000 for maintaining a prisoner in the SHU. Such dramatic numbers raise an obvious question for taxpayers: How can the cost of $90,000 per person per year to keep someone like Czifra or Murillo locked away in solitary confinement for years on end be justified? If successful release stories such as Czifra and Murillo undermine correctional claims about dangerousness and the necessity of the SHU, they may also galvanize prison officials to generate confidential informants and prison disciplinary records that discourage such releases in the first place. Consigning indefinite solitary confinement to infamy therefore requires not only getting prisoners out of solitary but also releasing formerly solitarily confined prisoners from prison. This continues to be an apparent goal of the *Ashker* litigation and a potential avenue for rendering indefinite solitary confinement infamous, but neither goal has yet been achieved.

Meanwhile, in addition to continuing to misuse confidential information in disciplinary infractions and continuing to misuse prior gang validation information in parole hearings—fairly generalized tactics applied broadly to all *Ashker* class members—California correctional officials have also deployed this information in more individualized cases. On May 21, 2019, the U.S. Attorney's office in Sacramento filed a formal criminal complaint against eleven alleged Aryan Brotherhood prison gang members from across the state prison system, including, most notably, Danny Troxell. Troxell was one of the named plaintiffs in the *Ashker* case and Ashker's cosignatory on the initial 2011 hunger strike demand letter. The 2019 complaint in *United States v. Yandell* alleges that the defendants, including Troxell, had been involved in conspiracies to commit murder and traffic drugs. Conveniently, the investigation began in 2014, just after the hunger strikes led by Ashker and Troxell had raised awareness of the conditions of confinement in the SHU and called into question the gang validation policies justifying indefinite periods of confinement in the SHU. The 2019 complaint makes no attempt to obfuscate the connection.

In fact, in the affidavit supporting the complaint, Brian Nehring, a special agent with the Drug Enforcement Administration, directly connects the hunger strikes and *Ashker* litigation to the criminal conspiracy to murder and traffic drugs, which his investigation purports to uncover: "[B]oth were effective achieving Ashker's goal of changing the confinement conditions of extraordinarily dangerous inmates."[72] The *Ashker* settlement, the complaint goes on to assert, "required CDCR to release extraordinarily dangerous prison gang members from the Pelican Bay SHU into less-stringent California prison environments" and subsequently "created a growth opportunity for the Aryan Brotherhood."[73] The first named defendant, Yandell, the complaint concludes, is "a direct beneficiary of the *Ashker* settlement."[74]

Special Agent Nehring's affidavit provides a battery of details about the alleged conspiracies, from "cooperating witness" evidence to tapped phone call transcripts, "CDCR documentation," and surveillance agents. It reads like a convincing episode of the acclaimed HBO crime drama *The Wire*. But in light of the substantial body of evidence gathered by the *Ashker* plaintiffs in the ongoing litigation regarding settlement implementation, the complaint is, potentially, less convincing. "Cooperating witness" evidence and "CDCR documentation" are both, as Center for Constitutional Rights lawyers have painstakingly argued and local federal court judges have repeatedly agreed, unreliable at best, and in some cases entirely fabricated.

Indeed, one line in Nehring's affidavit calls into question the reliability of the key cooperating witness referred to throughout. According to the affidavit, the "purported hunger strike was mostly an illusion"; according to the key cooperating witness, "striking inmates did not risk their own health." A broad body of evidence—from the United Nations Special Rapporteur on Torture, Amnesty International, and individual interviews with *Ashker* class members to the fact that the state was worried enough about hunger-striking prisoners to publicly seek a controversial "force feeding order"—suggests that the 2011–13 hunger strikes were hardly just an "illusion." Still, the acceptance of the cooperating witness's statement, and the inclusion of the claim that the hunger strikes were an illusion, suggests an about-face from both the *Ashker* settlement and Scott Kernan's acknowledgement on *60 Minutes* to Oprah Winfrey that, even though the policy of validating gang members and keeping them in the Pelican Bay SHU indefinitely "was intended to save lives and make prisons safer across the system," such a policy *was* a "mistake."[75]

In light of the history of criminalization and demonization as mechanisms of persistence surrounding solitary confinement, perhaps this about-face is not surprising. But it does represent a failure of the *Ashker* settlement to achieve even those reforms it explicitly and proactively sought: to humanize the class members and eliminate the misuse of confidential information. Importantly, while litigation in the *Ashker* case is ongoing around misuse of confidential information to reimpose solitary confinement and misuse of gang validation evidence to preclude releases onto parole, confronting the evidence leveraged in the *Yandell* complaint and affidavit is beyond the scope of the *Ashker* litigation. This suggests that California prison officials may well be winning the battle in resisting the consignment of the practice of indefinite solitary confinement to infamy.

Insider Expertise and Social Science Research

If demonization is one critical mechanism perpetuating solitary confinement, opacity is another.[76] The power of Julie Small's single statistic from 2011—513 prisoners had been in solitary confinement for more than ten years in California—exemplifies how little we knew about solitary confinement practices in California ten years ago and what a difference a small amount of knowledge made in thinking about how to reform those practices (at least systematically and incrementally reducing the duration of time people spend in solitary). As with demonization, much of the *Ashker* litigation sought to directly address opacity as a mechanism of persistence: generating new data about the impacts of solitary confinement on individuals as part of the presettlement litigation and requiring collection of data about the use of solitary confinement (albeit limited in scope and public accessibility) as part of the postsettlement implementation. As with demonization, however, these attempts to address opacity met with both direct and indirect resistance, which in turn thwarted any conclusive consignment of the practice of indefinite solitary confinement to infamy. Unlike the resistance to addressing demonization, though, which happened in individual cases and through institutional and state-level policies, the resistance to addressing opacity involved a more diverse set of agents from a broader, more national pool of institutions.

Before a settlement was ever reached in the *Ashker* litigation, lawyers from the Center for Constitutional Rights were working hard to systematically increase knowledge about the practice of solitary confinement (especially for long and indefinite terms) in California and nationally. Prior to the Pelican Bay hunger strikes, the field of solitary confinement studies was finite: It included sensory deprivation studies conducted in labs in the 1960s and 1970s; research conducted largely in the course of litigation by psychologists documenting a constellation of psychological symptoms that arise and are exacerbated in solitary confinement dubbed "SHU syndrome"; and one quasi-experimental and heavily criticized study, funded by the National Institute of Justice and conducted in collaboration with the Colorado Department of Corrections in 2011, which found that "psychological disturbances are not unique" to the solitarily confined population and sometimes even improve over time in solitary confinement.[77]

The prisoners' lawyers in *Ashker*, however, set a new standard for the caliber and role of expertise and research in the context of solitary confinement. They solicited and filed ten detailed expert reports attacking the necessity of long-term solitary confinement for maintaining institutional safety and security as well as documenting the serious mental and physical health consequences of long-term solitary confinement. Three *Ashker* expert reports attacked the necessity of long-term solitary confinement. The authors of these reports included correctional leaders from outside California, including the former director of the Ohio Department of Corrections, who had never before served as an expert in court; a retired prison warden who had overseen prisons in Texas, Kentucky, and Mississippi; and a retired British prison warden.[78] In addition to the three *Ashker* expert reports written by insider correctional experts, three reports brought additional medical and psychological experts into the debate over the effects of solitary confinement: One report documented the increased prevalence of hypertension in solitary confinement; one documented the health problems associated with deprivations of human touch; and a third documented the neuroscientific connection between social and physical pain.[79] The other four reports included two by existing experts in "SHU syndrome" summarizing and updating the state of the knowledge about the psychological impacts of long-term solitary confinement, including drawing on recently updated longitudinal interviews with prisoners at Pelican Bay; a report from a sociologist and nationally recognized expert in "correctional planning and research"; and a report from the United Nations Special Rapporteur on Torture concluding that conditions in the Pelican Bay SHU amounted to cruel, inhuman, and degrading treatment under international law.[80] The case settled within weeks of this barrage of expert evidence.[81]

The filing of the expert reports in *Ashker* also marked the beginning of an explosion of litigation (nationally and internationally) as well as research about solitary confinement.[82] The expert reports seem at first like a forceful blow against opacity around solitary confinement practices in California and a significant step toward rendering the practice of indefinite solitary confinement infamous. After all, the reports include statements that long-term solitary confinement is institutionally unnecessary, causes physical and psychological harm, and constitutes cruel, inhuman, and degrading treatment. However, as the prior two sections on thwarted settlement implementation and demonization revealed, long-term solitary confinement has hardly been abandoned in California. In fact, the practice has persisted, often in ways that are difficult to identify and track.

Perhaps the *Ashker* reports were only a first step toward greater transparency and more robust critiques of long-term solitary confinement; more steps need to be taken to further develop the arguments framed in those expert reports. The *Ashker* settlement itself could have facilitated ongoing transparency by requiring more data collection about prisoners in and out of the SHU and by insisting on provisions that this data would be made public.[83] Even absent such provisions, though, the expert reports in *Ashker*—along with the drastic changes in conditions the settlement did require—seemed at first to provide an ideal opportunity for further research, which would have at least facilitated transparency, if not also contributed to existing critiques of indefinite solitary confinement.

Specifically, CDCR's willingness to commit to at least some reform of solitary confinement practices, as evidenced in their agreement to the *Ashker* settlement, in combination with the fact that carefully planned policy changes can provide opportunities for robust evaluations of the impacts of those changes, seemingly created a natural opportunity for data collection and analysis. A number of experiments ripe for systematic analysis arose. I describe just two of many possibilities. First, some prisoners who would have been placed in solitary confinement just months prior to the *Ashker* settlement (especially prisoners labeled as gang members without having committed specific rule violations) were no longer eligible for placement in solitary confinement. Did those prisoners not placed in solitary confinement after the settlement fare differently, in terms of their rates of violence in prison, rates of recidivism after release, and rates of health problems in and out of prison, from similarly situated prisoners who had been placed in solitary confinement prior to the settlement? Second, *Ashker* class members were released gradually from solitary confinement into different contexts such as the RCPG, Level IV institutions, and lower security general population prisons. How did these similarly situated groups fare in these different conditions of confinement?

Not only were there obvious new opportunities for robust evaluations of solitary confinement practices in California following the *Ashker* settlement; many individuals should have had incentives to pursue these opportunities. While California prison officials had not historically collected robust data on solitary confinement use, doing so following the *Ashker* settlement could have provided opportunities to prove their fears around the implications of the settlement correct and to generate insights about how to mitigate such fears. External researchers also had incentives to pursue research in California prisons. The National Institute of Justice (NIJ) put out the first federally funded application specifically focused on studying solitary confinement in 2015, just after *Ashker* settled, following a conference on solitary confinement at which a number of NIJ-commissioned white papers were presented highlighting just how little was known about the practice.[84] The Langeloth Foundation, a private foundation in New York City, likewise funded large research and policy efforts around solitary confinement.[85] And the Vera Institute of Justice, a major criminal justice policy research organization, made solitary confinement a central area of research, partnering with multiple states across the country to better understand (and reform) the practice.[86] Many researchers approached California seeking research partnerships, but as of yet, no systematic independent analysis of the impacts of solitary confinement and its reform on individuals and institutions, using California corrections data, has been conducted or published.

One of the few reports evaluating any part of California's solitary confinement reform process was conducted by Stanford University's Human Rights in Trauma Mental Health Laboratory (the Stanford Lab), "a multidisciplinary collaboration between Stanford University's School of Medicine, Law School, and the WSD Handa Center for Human Rights and International Justice . . . composed of . . . academic clinicians, lawyers, and policy experts with special knowledge in the area of trauma mental health," at the request of the Center for Constitutional Rights, the public-interest law firm representing the *Ashker* class members. The Stanford Lab interviewed twenty-nine randomly selected members of the *Ashker* class and found that "most of the men experienced severe psychological disturbances with lasting detrimental sequelae."[87] The fact that the Center for Constitutional Rights requested this report suggests that legal pressure was required to gain even enough access for this litigation-oriented, small-scale, qualitative study. This ongoing resistance to research within CDCR is yet another example of the persistence of opacity and administrative control around solitary confinement in the state.

Neither the expert reports initially filed in *Ashker* nor the terms of the settlement facilitated the kind of research around solitary confinement reform in California that might have signaled either a move away from opacity and toward transparency or a willingness on the part of CDCR to objectively reconsider the fundamental justifiability of the practice of long-term solitary confinement. The expert reports and litigation in *Ashker*, however, did mark the beginning of an explosion of research about solitary confinement practices outside California. This research has included articles about the medical and public health implications of solitary confinement,[88] criminological implications in terms of institutional effects on violence and recidivism,[89] and even metanalyses about the impacts of the practice.[90]

The expert reports in *Ashker*, which highlighted clear knowledge gaps in our understanding of solitary confinement, from its medical and psychological to its criminological effects, at least partially inspired this explosion of social science research. (Additional funding opportunities, such as the 2015–16 National Institute of Justice program solicitation described above, certainly also contributed to the creation of what amounts to a new subfield of research on the effects of solitary confinement.) For instance, my own work in public health journals was certainly influenced by the arguments in the *Ashker* expert reports (and funded by the Langeloth Foundation, referenced above); the metanalysis referenced above has been cited in multiple subsequent expert reports filed by the coauthor himself (who also testified as an expert for the state in *Ashker*) in cases considering the legality of solitary confinement,[91] and a number of other social science analyses cited above were collected in a 2019 anthology coedited by Jules Lobel, president of the Center for Constitutional Rights and lead counsel in the *Ashker* case.[92]

This increased research attention to evaluating the practice of solitary confinement seems at first like a mechanism for greater transparency. More data collection, analysis, and dissemination of results about the effects of solitary confinement seems intuitively like it would at least hinder the kind of administrative obfuscation described in the preceding two sections. And to the extent research findings confirm the claims of the *Ashker* expert reports, they seem likely to contribute to consigning the practice of solitary confinement to infamy. But every new study seems to bring more debate about just how harmful solitary confinement is and whether it works or not. In fact, although solitary confinement policies, post-*Ashker*, are facing challenges across the United States in individual and class-action lawsuits, through legislative reforms, and by administrative oversight bodies such as Protection and Advocacy Systems, social science evidence is being leveraged not only by prisoner plaintiffs to condemn the practice of solitary confinement but also by prison official defendants to vindicate the practice.

The explosion of attention in social science to the impacts of solitary confinement may in turn be contributing to legal and policy debates that ultimately legitimize the practice. First, to the extent solitary confinement becomes a central area of study, researchers might be indirectly legitimizing the practice by treating it as a neutral subject of evaluation rather than as an ethically unacceptable practice to be abandoned—whether or not its theoretically negative impacts can be confirmed empirically.[93] Alternatively, to the extent that research, as in the expert reports, is generated in the service of litigation, otherwise objective empirical analyses might be colored by policy agendas, such as the goals of solitary confinement abolition or its maintenance. Second, researchers might accept the data they collect from correctional officials at face value, even if the data was generated on the basis of flawed assumptions about, for instance, the inherent violence, riskiness, or criminality of prisoners confined in solitary (i.e., the kinds of flawed assumptions established in the *Ashker* litigation). Analyzing this flawed data might produce findings that focus on individuals and distract from institutional practices (focusing on individual measures of misbehavior rather than on institutional patterns of punishment, for instance).[94]

My argument is not one against solitary confinement research; the footnotes in this piece alone suggest that would be hypocritical at best. Rather, my argument is that, although social science research may mitigate opacity, it may also interact with administrative discretion and become another mechanism to perpetuate the practice, serving a variety of legitimizing roles, even when critical.

Resettling Solitary Confinement: *Ashker v. Governor of California* as an Archetype of Reform Challenges

While this chapter has focused in excruciating detail on the implementation of the *Ashker* settlement, the litigation arising from the Pelican Bay hunger strikes was only one of dozens of attempts to reform, and to constrain the use of, solitary confinement across the United States. Many of these reform efforts have been inspired by the litigation and settlement in *Ashker* and thwarted by the same mechanisms of persistence identified in the *Ashker* implementation efforts: opacity, administrative discretion, ongoing demonization, and legitimizing expertise and social science.

Even if *Ashker* failed to consign the practice of indefinite solitary confinement to infamy in California, it certainly contributed to the initiation of litigation challenging the practice of long-term solitary confinement in jurisdictions across the United States. In a recent article, for instance, Judith Resnik lists systemwide settlements limiting solitary confinement use in New York, Illinois, Arizona, Pennsylvania, and Virginia.[95] While these settlements represent a changing consensus against solitary confinement, they do not necessarily represent a changing practical experience for prisoners. In New York, officials report that many vulnerable populations, such as juveniles, continue to end up in solitary confinement in spite of clear prohibitions on incarcerating such vulnerable people in this manner. In Arizona, a case with provisions for limiting the placement of mentally ill prisoners in solitary confinement and for implementing other fundamental improvements to the conditions of solitary confinement was settled in 2014.[96] But as in *Ashker*, Arizona prisoners continue to complain of reforms being superficially implemented.

Examples of prison systems creatively avoiding implementation of policy reforms and settlement agreements, much as California prison officials have done in the *Ashker* case, abound. For instance, in the federal prison system, prisoners with disabilities are precluded from solitary confinement placements, but prison officials still "find ways to disappear disabilities, coerce people not to identify as disabled or make it dangerous for people to identify as disabled," such as removing mentally ill prisoners from their medications in order to neutralize their mental health diagnoses. The American Civil Liberties Union is seeking to preclude anyone with an official Serious and Persistent Mental Illness from placement in solitary confinement, but Talila Lewis, a local disability rights attorney, pointed out "systems have figured out ways around federal disability rights laws and legal judgments."[97] Indeed, Rhode Island is placing prisoners in solitary confinement for thirty-one days or more for disciplinary violations, contradicting a thirty-day cap that had been in place in state regulations for almost fifty years.[98] Likewise, Texas in 2014 created a "a mental health therapeutic diversion program" as part of a statewide initiative to reduce solitary confinement use. But in 2019, the *Texas Tribune* reported that "the program largely operates as a rebranded version of the isolated conditions they were already living in," not unlike the new RCPG unit at Pelican Bay functioning as a rebranded SHU.[99] As with California prison officials, Texas prison officials resist collecting and sharing data about solitary confinement practices. A more recent *Texas Observer* investigation concluded that Texas prison officials "track . . . very little about the effects of this extreme practice," not even the frequency of suicide attempts and tear-gassings in solitary confinement.[100]

In other countries, solitary confinement persists in spite of reform efforts. In Canada, where courts in Ontario and British Columbia have declared solitary confinement unconstitutional and the federal government has passed legislation claiming to abolish solitary confinement, practical conditions of solitary confinement persist, simply with more robust procedural protections preceding placement in those conditions. As Canadian legal scholar Lisa Kerr noted: "It is the end stage of solitary, but the question is what will arrive in its place."[101] Likewise, historian and criminologist Peter Scharff Smith has documented how solitary confinement has persisted in Denmark, in pretrial and postconviction settings, in spite of reform efforts designed to abolish the practice.[102]

Conclusion

The analysis here has been unrelentingly critical of the *Ashker* settlement and its implementation failures, arguing that indefinite solitary confinement in California has not yet achieved the legal infamy the case sought (and has been heralded for achieving). But I do not mean to suggest (1) that the prisoners and lawyers could have done a better job with the tools they had at the time of litigation or (2) that reform is hopeless. Rather, I hope that by tracing the patterns of resistance to reform— repackaging discredited practices under new names; demonizing the beneficiaries (and instigators) of reforms; and co-opting knowledge production into a tool of legitimation—new mechanisms of reform, and even abolition, might become more visible. Tracing these patterns provides a better of idea where to look for resistance in the future, the need to identify new tools for counteracting demonization, and the risks of conducting policy-relevant social science research without a critical eye to its legitimizing power.

In the 2020s, with a conservative and increasingly politicized federal judicial bench in place, the list of unjustly decided cases from which American democracy has somehow recovered—*Plessy v. Ferguson, Lochner v. New York, Stanford v. Kentucky*—to name just a few overturned and repudiated decisions—provide some comfort. There is hope that cases now being decided—limiting a woman's right to abortion, permitting discrimination in voting, minimizing rights to organize in labor and litigation—will eventually be overturned. There is hope as well that cases such as *Ashker* will eventually stand for a policy (solitary confinement) that has become infamous not just on paper but in practice.

NOTES

The author would like to thank Austin Sarat, Lawrence Douglas, and the partici-
pants in the Law, Jurisprudence, and Social Thought workshop for their inspiring
and critical engagement with an initial draft of this chapter; Judith Resnik for reading an earlier draft and pushing me to think less cynically about the implications
of *Ashker*; and the prisoners and lawyers who continue to seek repudiation of the
practice of solitary confinement with such focused intensity.

1 "Exhibit A: Declaration of Todd Ashker in Support of Plaintiff's Motion for Class
   Certification," Ashker v. Brown [Governor of California], No. 4:09-cv-05796-CW
   (N.D. Cal. May 2, 2013), https://ccrjustice.org.
2 Keramet Reiter, "The Pelican Bay Hunger Strike: Resistance within the Structural
   Constraints of a U.S. Supermax Prison," *South Atlantic Quarterly* 113, no. 3 (2014):
   579–611.
3 Victoria Law, "'As Long As Solitary Exists, They Will Find a Way to Use It'" *The
   Nation*, July 14, 2018, www.thenation.com.
4 *See, e.g.*, Angelica Camacho, "Unbroken Spirit: Pelican Bay, California Prisoner
   Hunger Strikes, Family Uprisings, and Learning to Listen," Dissertation, https://
   escholarship.org; Chris S. Earle, "Just Violence? California's Short Corridor Hunger Strikes and Arguments Over Prison Legitimacy," *Argumentation and Advocacy*
   51, no. 3 (2015): 185–99; Lisa Guenther, "Political Action at the End of the World:
   Hannah Arendt and the California Prison Hunger Strikes," *Canadian Journal of
   Human Rights*, 4, no. 1 (2015): 33–56; Jules Lobel, "Litigation to End Indeterminate
   Solitary Confinement in California: the Role of Interdisciplinary and Compara-
   tive Experts," in *Solitary Confinement: Effects, Practices, and Pathways Toward
   Reform*, ed. Jules Lobel and Peter Scharff Smith (Oxford: Oxford University Press,
   2019): 353–71; Zafir Shaiq, "More Restrictive than Necessary: A Police Review of
   Secure Housing Units," *Hastings Race and Poverty Law Journal* 10, no. 2 (2013):
   327–78; Azadeh Shahshahani and Priya Arvind Patel, "From Pelican Bay to
   Palestine: The Legal Normalization of Force-Feeding Hunger-Strikers," *Michigan
   Journal of Race & Law* 24, no. 1 (2018): 1–14.
5 Reiter, "The Pelican Bay Hunger Strike"; Keramet Reiter, "(Un)Settling Solitary in
   California," *Social Justice*, Sept. 28, 2015, www.socialjusticejournal.org; Keramet
   Reiter, "Lessons and Liabilities in Litigating Solitary Confinement," *University of
   Connecticut Law Review* 48, no. 4 (2016): 1167–89; Keramet Reiter, "The International Persistence & Resilience of Solitary Confinement," *Oñati International
   Series in Law & Society*, 8, no. 2l (2018): 247–66.
6 Reiter, "The Pelican Bay Hunger Strike."
7 Reiter, "(Un)Settling Solitary Confinement."
8 J. Ridgeway and J. Casella, "New Video: ACLU Launches 'Stop Solitary' Campaign," *Solitary Watch*, Sept. 30, 2011, https://solitarywatch.org.
9 See Center for Constitutional Rights, "*Ashker v. Governor of California*" list of
   legal motions and briefs, https://ccrjustice.org.

10 Carrie Johnson, "Trump's Impact on Federal Courts: Judicial Nominees by the Numbers," NPR, Aug. 5, 2019, www.npr.org; Federal Judicial Center, "Demography of Article III Judges, 1789–2017," www.fjc.gov.

11 *See, e.g.*, Amelia Thomson-Devaux, "Is the Supreme Court Heading for a Conservative Revolution?" *FiveThirtyEight*, Oct. 7, 2019, https://fivethirtyeight.com.

12 See Judith Resnik, "Reorienting the Process Due: Using Jurisdiction to Forge Post-settlement Relationships Among Litigants, Courts, and the Public in Class and Other Aggregate Litigation," *New York University Law Review* 92 (2017): 1017–67.

13 See Keramet Retier, "After Solitary Confinement: A New Era of Punishment?" *Studies in Law, Politics, and Society* 77: 1–29.

14 Hope v. Pelzer, 536 U.S. 730, 742 (2002).

15 Roper v. Simmons, 543 U.S. 551 (2005).

16 Brown v. Plata, 563 U.S. 493 (2011).

17 On deaths in restraints, *see, e.g.*, Josh Kovner, "Inmate Who Died After Restraint at New Haven Jail Had Rigor Mortis by the Time He Was Brought to the Hospital," *Harford Courant*, Oct. 21, 2019, www.courant.com; Christopher Zoukis, "$5 Million Settlement After Mentally Ill Prisoner Dies in Restraint," *Prison Legal News*, Mar. 6, 2018, www.prisonlegalnews.org. On executions of people who were teenagers at the time of their crime, *see, e.g.*, Death Penalty Information Center, "Alabama Prisoner Seeks Stay, Reprieve to Challenge the Death Penalty for 19-year-old offenders," May 14, 2019, https://deathpenaltyinfo.org. On COVID-19, *see, e.g.*, Cary Aspinwall and Joseph Neff, "These Prisons Are Doing Mass Testing For COVID-19—And Finding Mass Infections," Apr. 24, 2020, www.themarshallproject.org.

18 Margo Schlanger, "Inmate Litigation," *Harvard Law Review* 116, no. 6 (2003): 1555–1706, 1570–73.

19 Hope v. Pelzer, 536 U.S. 730, 742 (2002).

20 Robert Dole, "Hearings on 'Prisoner Litigation Reform Act,'" *Congressional Record*, Sept. 27, 1995, quoted online at http://jthomasniu.org; Jon O. Newman, "Not All Prisoner Lawsuits are Frivolous," *Prison Legal News*, Apr. 1996, 6, www.prisonlegalnews.org; Keramet Reiter, *Mass Incarceration* (New York: Oxford University Press, 2017).

21 Farmer v. Brennan, 511 U.S. 825 (1994); Sharon Dolovich, "Forms of Deference in Prison Law," *Federal Sentencing Reporter* 24, no. 4 (2012): 245–59; Keramet Reiter, "Supermax Administration and the Eighth Amendment: Discretion, Deference, and Double-Bunking, 1986–2010," *University of California Irvine Law Review* 5, no. 1 (2015): 89–152.

22 See Center for Constitutional Rights, "*Ashker v. Governor of California*" list of legal motions and briefs, https://ccrjustice.org; Keramet Reiter, *23/7: Pelican Bay Prison and the Rise of Long-Term Solitary Confinement* (New Haven: Yale University Press, 2016).

23 United Nations General Assembly, 2016. United Nations Standard Minimum Rules for the Treatment of Prisoners (the Nelson Mandela Rules). A/RES/70/175 [online]. Resolution adopted by the UN General Assembly on 17 December 2015 on the report of the Third Committee (A/70/490). Available at www.penalreform. org.

24 Center for Constitutional Rights, "*Ashker v. Governor of California,*" https://ccrjustice.org.

25 Keramet Reiter, "The Most Restrictive Alternative: A Litigation History of Solitary Confinement in U.S. Prisons, 1960–2006," *Studies in Law, Politics and Society* 57 (2012): 69–123.

26 Reiter, *23/7*, 5.

27 Lauren B., Edelman, Christopher Uggen, and Howard S. Erlanger, "The Endogeneity of Legal Regulation: Grievance Procedure as Rational Myth," *American Journal of Sociology* 105, no. 2 (1999): 406–54.

28 For more general discussions of the forces that produce the "transformation of law and the state over time" in law and society scholarship, see L. Mather, "Law and Society," in *The Oxford Handbook of Political Science*, ed. Robert E. Goodin (published online Sept. 2013), www.oxfordhandbooks.com; Bryant Garth and Joyce Sterling, "From Legal Realism to Law and Society: Reshaping Law for the Last Stages of the Social Activist State," *Law & Society Review* 32, no. 2: 409–72 (1998).

29 Brown v. Board of Education, 347 U.S. 483 (1954); Roper v. Simmons, 543 U.S. 551 (2005).

30 Reiter, *23/7*, 11.

31 Prisoner Hunger Strike Solidarity, "Prisoners' Demands," Apr. 3, 2011, https://prisonerhungerstrikesolidarity.wordpress.com.

32 Madrid v. Gomez, 889 F. Supp. 1146 (1995); Reiter, *23/7*.

33 Reiter, *23/7*.

34 Reiter, *23/7*.

35 Reiter, "The Pelican Bay Hunger Strike."

36 Reiter, "After Solitary."

37 Julie Small, "Under Scrutiny Pelican Bay Officials Say They Target Only Gang Leaders," KPCC, Aug. 23, 2011, www.scpr.org.

38 Reiter, *23/7*, 167.

39 Ibid.

40 Order Granting in Part Motion for Class Certification; Denying Motion to Intervene, *Ashker v. Brown*, Case No. 09-5796CW, June 2, 2014, https://ccrjustice.org.

41 Reiter, *23/7*, 197.

42 *See, e.g.*, Declarations of J. Zubiate and J. Bryan Elrod, Ashker v. Brown, Case No. 09-5796CW, Jul. 18, 2013. On file with author.

43 Reiter, SAQ, 603.

44 Expert Reports of Terry J. Collins, and Emmitt L. Sparkman, Ashker v. Brown, Case No. 09-5796CW, Mar. 2015, https://ccrjustice.org.

45 Expert Report of Louise C. Hawkley, Ashker v. Brown, Case No. 09–5796CW, Mar. 2015, https://ccrjustice.org/home.

46 Expert Reports of Dacher Keltner, Matthew D. Lieberman, Craig Haney, and Terry Kupers, Ashker v. Brown, Case No. 09–5796CW, Mar. 2015, https://ccrjustice.org.

47 Reiter, 23/7, 202.

48 Center for Constitutional Rights, "California Solitary Confinement Settlement: Year One after landmark settlement," Oct. 18, 2016, https://ccrjustice.org.

49 CBS News, "Oprah Winfrey Goes Inside Pelican Bay State Prison," Oct. 18, 2017, www.cbsnews.com.

50 Order Granting Motion for Leave to File a Supplemental Complaint at 2, 16, Ashker v. Brown, No. 4:09-cv-05796-CW (N.D. Cal. Mar. 9, 2015), https://ccrjustice.org. See also Reiter, "Lessons and Liabilities in Litigating Solitary Confinement," 1187.

51 Reiter, "Lessons and Liabilities in Litigating Solitary Confinement," 1187.

52 Victoria Law, "As Long as Solitary Exists, They Will Find a Way to Use It," *The Nation*, Jul. 13, 2018, www.thenation.com.

53 "Plaintiffs' Enforcement Motion Regarding Violation of Settlement Agreement Provision Requiring Release of Class Members to General Population," Ashker v. Brown, Case No. 09–5796CW, Nov. 28, 2017, https://ccrjustice.org.

54 Center for Constitutional Rights, "Ongoing Isolation in CA Prisons Not Governed by Settlement, Judge Rules," Mar. 28, 2018, https://ccrjustice.org.

55 Motion for Extension of Settlement Agreement Based on Systemic Due Process Violations, *Ashker v. Brown*, Case No. 09–5796CW, Feb. 6, 2018, https://ccrjustice.org.

56 Ibid., 7.

57 Order, Ashker v. Brown, Case No. 09–5796CW, Jan. 25, 2019, https://ccrjustice.org. Order Extending the Settlement Agreement, Ashker v. Newsom, Case No. 09–5796CW Apr. 9, 2021, https://ccrjustice.org.

58 Maria Endicott, "A 2015 Case Was Supposed to Overhaul California's Solitary Confinement. The Reality Is Much More Complicated," *Mother Jones*, Feb. 13, 2019, www.motherjones.com. Ashker v. Newsom, Case No. 18–16427, 9th Cir., Aug. 3, 2020, http://cdn.ca9.uscourts.gov.

59 Ibid.

60 Ashley T. Rubin and Keramet Reiter, "Continuity in the Face of Penal Innovation: Revisiting the History of American Solitary Confinement," *Law & Social Inquiry* 43, no. 4 (2018): 1604–32, 1606. See also Reiter, "The International Persistence & Resilience of Solitary Confinement."

61 Reiter, 23/7, 34–58.

62 Reiter, 23/7, 121–44.

63 See Rubin and Reiter, "Continuity in the Face of Penal Innovation."

64 Notice of Joint Motion, Case No. 09–5796CW, Sept. 1, 2015 (on file with author).

65 Law, "As Long As Solitary Exists."

66 *See, e.g.*, Tim Johns, "Are California's Criminal Justice Reforms Actually Working?" *Bakersfield Now*, Feb. 20, 2019, https://bakersfieldnow.com.

67 Reiter, "(Un)Settling Solitary in California."

68 Endicott, "A 2015 Case."

69 Order, Ashker v. Brown, Jan. 25, 2019, 7–10.

70 Order, Ashker v. Brown, Jan. 25, 2019, 11–12.

71 Order, Ashker v. Brown, Jan. 25, 2019, 15.

72 Affidavit in Support of Criminal Complaint, U.S. v. Yandell, Case No. 2:19-MJ-0080-CKD, May 21, 2019, 24.

73 U.S. v. Yandell Affidavit, 25.

74 U.S. v. Yandell Affidavit, 26.

75 Oprah Winfrey, "Reforming Solitary Confinement at an Infamous California Prison," Jul. 22, 2018, www.cbsnews.com.

76 *See generally* Reiter, 23/7; Rubin and Reiter, "Continuity in the Face of Penal Innovation."

77 The NIJ study quoted is Maureen O'Keefe et al., *One Year Longitudinal Study of the Psychological Effects of Administrative Segregation*, Document No. 232973 (Washington, DC: National Criminal Justice Research Service, National Institute of Justice, 2011), www.ncjrs.gov. On sensory deprivation studies, see Richard E. Brown and Peter M. Milner, "The Legacy of Donald O. Hebb: More Than the Hebb Synapse," *Nature Reviews: Neuroscience 4* (Dec. 2003): 1013–19; Alfred W. McCoy, "Science in Dachau's Shadow: Hebb, Beecher, and the Development of CIA Psychological Torture and Modern Medical Ethics." *Journal of the History of the Behavioral Sciences* 43, no. 4 (2007): 401–17; and Reiter, 23/7, 180–82 (discussing these and other studies). On SHU Syndrome, see Stuart Grassian, "Psychiatric Effects of Solitary Confinement," *Washington Journal of Law and Social Policy* 22 (2006): 325–83; Craig Haney, "Mental Health Issues in Long-Term Solitary and 'Supermax' Confinement," *Crime and Delinquency* 49, no. 1 (Jan. 2003): 124–56.

78 Expert Reports of Terry J. Collins, Emmitt L. Sparkman, and Andrew Coyle, Ashker v. Brown, Case No. 09-5796CW, Mar. 2015, https://ccrjustice.org; Lobel, "Litigation to End Indeterminate Solitary," 363.

79 Expert Reports of Louise C. Hawkley, Dacher Keltner, and Matthew Lieberman, *Ashker v. Brown*, Case No. 09-5796CW, Mar. 2015, https://ccrjustice.org; Lobel, "Litigation to End Indeterminate Solitary," 360–62.

80 Expert reports of Craig Haney, Terry Kupers, James Austin, and Juan Mendez, Ashker v. Brown, Case No. 09-5796CW, Mar. 2015, https://ccrjustice.org.

81 Lobel, "Litigation to End Indeterminate Solitary," 369.

82 Keramet Reiter, "The International Persistence & Resilience of Solitary Confinement," *Oñati International Series in Law & Society* 8, no. 2 (2018): 247–66; Judith Resnik et al., "Punishment In Prison: Constituting the 'Normal' and the 'Atypical' in Solitary and other Forms of Confinement" (forthcoming; on file with author).

83 Reiter, "(Un)Settling Solitary Confinement."

84 National Institute of Justice, "Exploring the Use of Restrictive Housing in the U.S. Issues, Challenges, and Future Directions," NCJ Number 250523, Nov. 2016, https://nij.ojp.gov.

85 See Langeloth Foundation, "Grants: Justice Reform," www.langeloth.org.

86 "Rethinking Restrictive Housing," Vera Institute of Justice, May 2018, www.vera. org.

87 Jessie Brunner, Katie Joseff, Ryan Matlow, Jessica Rahter, Daryn Reicherter, and Beth Van Schaack, *Mental Health Consequences Following Release from Long-Term Solitary Confinement in California Consultative Report Prepared for the Center for Constitutional Rights* (Stanford: Human Rights in Trauma Mental Health Lab, Stanford University, 2017), https://ccrjustice.org.

88 *See, e.g.*, L. Brinkley-Rubinstein, J. Sivaraman, and D. L. Rosen et al., "Association of Restrictive Housing During Incarceration with Mortality After release," *JAMA* 2, no. 10 (2019); B.O. Hagan et al., "History of Solitary Confinement Is Associated with Post-traumatic Stress Disorder Symptoms Among Individuals Recently Released from Prison," *Journal of Urban Health* 95, no. 2 (2018): 141–48; Keramet Reiter et al., "Psychological Distress in Solitary Confinement: Symptoms, Severity, and Prevalence in the United States, 2017–2018," *American Journal of Public Health* 110, no. S1 (2020): S56–S62.; C. Wildeman and L. H. Andersen, "Solitary Confinement Placement and Post-release Mortality Risk Among Formerly Incarcerated Individuals: A Population-based Study," *The Lancet Public Health* 5, no. 2 (2020): 107–13; B. A. Williams et al., "The Cardiovascular Health Burdens of Solitary Confinement," *Journal of General Internal Medicine* 34, no. 10 (2019): 1977–80; M. J. Zigmond and R. J. Smeyne, "Use of Animals to Study the Neurobiological Effects of Isolation. Solitary Confinement: Effects, Practices, and Pathways Toward Reform," in *Solitary Confinement: Effects, Practices, and Pathways toward Reform*, ed. Jules Lobel and Peter Scharff Smith (Oxford: Oxford University Press, 2019).

89 *See, e.g.*, H. D. Butler, B. Steiner, M. D. Makarios, and L.F. Travis III, "An Examination of the Influence of Exposure to Disciplinary Segregation on Recidivism," *Crime & Delinquency*, 0011128719869194 (2019); M. F. Campagna et al., "Understanding Offender Needs Over Forms of Isolation Using a Repeated Measures Design," *Prison Journal* 99, no. 6 (2019): 639–61; R. M. Labrecque, D. P. Mears, and P. Smith, "Gender and the Effect of Disciplinary Segregation on Prison Misconduct," *Criminal Justice Policy Review*, 0887403419884728 (2019); R. M. Labrecque and P. Smith, "Assessing the Impact of Time Spent in Restrictive Housing Confinement on Subsequent Measures of Institutional Adjustment Among Men in Prison," *Criminal Justice and Behavior*, 46, no. 10 (2019): 1445–55; J. W. Lucas and M. A. Jones, "An Analysis of the Deterrent Effects of Disciplinary Segregation on Institutional Rule Violation Rates," *Criminal Justice Policy Review* 30, no. 5 (2019): 765–87; L. M. Salerno and K. M. Zgoba, "Disciplinary Segregation and Its Effects on In-Prison Outcomes," *Prison Journal*, 0032885519882326 (2020); C. Wildeman and L. H. Andersen, "Long-Term Consequences of Being Placed in Disciplinary Segregation," *Criminology* 58, no.3 (Aug. 2020): 423–53.

90 *See, e.g.*, R. D. Morgan et al., "Quantitative Syntheses of the Effects of Administrative Segregation on Inmates' Well-being," *Psychology, Public Policy, and Law* 22, no. 4 (2016): 439–61.

91 *See, e.g.*, expert reports and testimony in Vermillion v. Levenhagen, Case No. 1:15-CV-0605-RLY-TAB (S.D. Ind. May 21, 2019); Brazea v. Atty. Gen. of Canada, Court File No. CV-15-53262500-C (Ontario Sup. Ct., Dec. 12, 2017).

92 See Jules Lobel and Peter Scharff Smith, eds., *Solitary Confinement: Effects, Practices, and Pathways Toward Reform* (Oxford: Oxford University Press, 2019).

93 For an elaboration of this argument, see K. Reiter, "Does a Public Health Crisis Justify More Research with Incarcerated People?" *Hastings Center Report* (Mar.–Apr. 2021): 10–16.

94 For an analysis of this claim, see D. Lovell et al., "Opening the Black Box of Solitary Confinement Through Researcher-Practitioner Collaboration: A Longitudinal Analysis of Prisoner and Solitary Populations in Washington State, 2002–17," *Justice Quarterly* 37.7 (2020): 1303–21.

95 Judith Resnik et al., "Punishment in Prison" (forthcoming; on file with author); Peoples v. Annucci, 180 F.Supp.3d 294 (S.D.N.Y. 2016); Davis v. Baldwin, 1:2019cv02270 (S.D. Ill. 2017); Parsons v. Ryan, 16–17282 (9th Cir. 2018); Reid et al. v. Wetzel, 1:18-CV-00176-JEJ (M.D. Pa. 2018); Porter v. Clarke, 923 F.3d 348 (4th Cir. 2019), rehearing en banc denied (Jul. 26, 2019); Reyes v. Clark, 2019 WL 4044315 (E.D. VA 2019); Reynolds v. Arnone, 402 F. Supp 3d 3 (D. Conn. 2019) (appeal pending).

96 "Parsons v. Ryan," www.safealternativestosegregation.org.

97 Ella Fassler, "Disabled People Are Tortured in Solitary Confinement, but Tides May Be Turning," *Truthout*, Jan. 25, 2020, https://truthout.org.

98 Katie Mulvaney, "U.S. District Court Chief Judge John J. McConnell Rules That 15 Years Ago the Rhode Island Department of Corrections Unilaterally Raised the Limit on Punitive Solitary Confinement from 30 Days to a Year," *Providence Journal*, Jan. 29, 2020, www.providencejournal.com.

99 Jolie McCullough, "Solitary Confinement Worsens Mental Illness," *Texas Tribune*, Apr. 23, 2019, www.texastribune.org.

100 Michael Barajas, "The Prison Inside Prison," *Texas Observer*, Jan. 2020, www.texasobserver.org.

101 Lisa Kerr, "The End Stage of Solitary Confinement," 55 C.R. (7th) 382 (2019).

102 Peter Scharff Smith, "Punishment Without Conviction? Scandinavian Pre-trial Practices and the Power of the Benevolent State," in *Scandinavian Penal History, Culture and Prison Practice: Embraced By the Welfare State?*, ed. Peter Scharff Smith and Thomas Ugelvik (New York: Palgrave Macmillan, 2017), 129–56.

6

Fame, Infamy, and Canonicity in American Constitutional Law

PAUL HORWITZ

Introduction

American lawyers are crazy about canons.[1] They are also obsessed with greatness—great men and women, great judges, great cases. With that, of course, comes the obverse: an interest in identifying and reviling bad judges and bad cases. This is particularly true of constitutional law, which offers a repository of the aspirations and failings of our legal and political cultures.

In our own age—which is perhaps less comfortable with tradition and more inclined to often spurious quantification—the obsession with the great and terrible can take the form of lists and rankings.[2] So there are top-25 lists and the like, academic[3] and popular,[4] identifying the "greatest" constitutional decisions. And there are similar efforts to identify an "anticanon," a list of cases whose holdings "all legitimate constitutional decisions must be prepared to refute."[5] The ability to properly identify and praise the "good" canonical cases, and to identify and reject the "bad" anticanonical cases, remains a must for "admission to polite legal circles."[6]

It is not that surprising that lists of great cases and judges are longer than lists of terrible ones. The common-law method of judging is, after all, one of adaptation and error correction. Given that American constitutional law is a record of our nation's ups *and* downs, however, it is striking just how disparate the number of anticanonical cases is compared to the number of "great" cases. Chief Justice John Marshall's Supreme Court (1801–35) alone supplies three of the cases that most people place on the list of the greatest or most important decisions, despite (or because of) their antiquity. But a leading article on the constitutional anticanon contains only four cases in *total*, ranging over some 230 years. Even so, the article's author suggests that one of those decisions may not belong on the list,[7] and I question the status of another one below. Why is this? The Supreme Court may be "final" but is far from "infallible."[8] What explains the disproportion of famous canonical decisions to infamous anticanonical decisions?

In this chapter, I explore a number of explanations for this disparity. Some of them, like the common-law nature of much of American constitutional law,[9] are obvious. Others, having to do with the nature of modern legal and political culture generally and contemporary legal academic culture in particular, are less frequently remarked upon.

The disparity between the constitutional canon and anticanon is a jumping-off point. Ultimately, the goal in this chapter is to consider not only the disparity itself but also the implications of that disparity for the continuing vitality of a constitutional canon or anticanon altogether. I consider what this disparity says about changes in the nature of some fundamental cultural concepts, legal and otherwise. Central to that inquiry is the changing nature and prominence of fame and infamy, as well as their effect on the possibility of famous or infamous, and thus properly canonical or anticanonical, cases.[10]

In brief, I argue that changes in our culture are likely to affect the hardihood of our canon and anticanon. Truly infamous decisions are hard to come by, and their infamous status harder to sustain, in a culture in which a full and, I would say, proper understanding of fame itself is on the wane. I discuss proper or "good" fame, and infamy, below.[11] For now, we can say that fame in this conception is a spur to and reward for greatness of a lasting kind, judged by posterity and closely tied to virtue and the public good. Fame understood in this sense is distinct from something such as celebrity, which is divorced from virtue and tied to the current moment. It is, at least ideally, evaluated according to higher and more lasting standards of virtue and honor than merely taking the "right" side of some transient controversy. Fame—and its obverse, infamy—are "part of the social technology that encourages truly noble individuals to strive for virtue and by so doing to serve the state" and the public good.[12] Although this conception of fame has long been in decline, the qualities that make it legible have been further undermined by contemporary cultural conditions.

I acknowledge forthrightly at the outset that the diminishment or disappearance of a culture of fame and infamy, much like our society's move over time from a more aristocratic honor culture to a more democratic culture of dignity, has many positive aspects.[13] It is surely true that concepts like fame or honor are contestable, potentially dangerous, and carry much historical baggage. Here, however, I focus more on what is lost than on what is gained.

Just as the loss of a "proper Sense of Honor"[14] has its costs,[15] the same is true of the loss of an older and particularly defined sense of fame and infamy. Without them, we are left without stable ground on which to mount and maintain an anticanon of dishonorable and infamous legal decisions—or, for that matter, a canon of honorable and famous ones. There can be few decisions that admit or debar entry into polite legal circles when many of the shared premises and values that underwrite the very notion of polite legal circles have been fractured and undermined. Of course, there is great value in questioning and democratizing the notion of polite legal circles altogether. But the contemporary landscape also demonstrates the value of a common vocabulary and the dangers of its absence. What is true for politics and public discourse is also true for professional culture and discourse, which requires a common vocabulary and some shared premises in order to operate at all.

The first part of this chapter is largely definitional. I discuss some terms—"fame" and "infamy," "canon" and "anticanon"—that feature prominently here. After briefly re-presenting my foundational premise—that the constitutional canon is much larger than the constitutional anticanon—I canvass some reasons why this may be so. I then return to the fundamental terms with which the chapter begins, examining the changing nature and role of qualities such as fame and infamy over time and the effect of those changes on our ability to agree on what constitutes a "famous" or "infamous" judicial decision.

Some Working Definitions

We must first consider what we mean by a constitutional "canon" and "anticanon," as well as what it means for something to be famous or infamous. Here, I look briefly at academic discussions of the constitutional canon and anticanon. I then draw on dictionaries and history to define "fame" and "infamy," examining the earlier meanings of these terms and their changing and fallen or failing meanings. Although I do not define "honor" in this chapter,[16] we will see suggestions that this value is closely related to fame and infamy.

Canon—and Anticanon

A canon is "a set of standard texts, approaches, problems, examples, or stories" that the members of a discipline "repeatedly employ or invoke, and which help define the discipline *as* a discipline."[17] It goes to the core not only of disciplinarity but also of a society and its culture. It suggests and invokes "certain ways of thinking, talking, and arguing that are characteristic of a culture."[18] English professors who argue for or against the inclusion of Shakespeare in the literary canon are arguing at a disciplinary level about whether one can join the discipline of the study of English literature without reading and studying Shakespeare; but those who argue for a broader cultural canon may still think that exposure to Shakespeare is a necessary part of "cultural literacy" and, ultimately, of the production and encouragement of an "edified" and "virtuous" citizenry.[19] Debates about what should make up that canon—whether it should focus on "classic literature" narrowly defined, or whether it should include newer works dealing with issues such as race or gender and written by a more diverse group of authors—are themselves moved not only by questions about who *belongs* in a literary canon but also about the canon's role in "edify[ing] and enlighten[ing]" those who read it.[20]

An important difference between law and other disciplines, one that reflects law's close connection to history, politics, and culture, is that law, much like culture, focuses on the bad as well as the good. Professors and students of literature may argue about what constitutes a great poem or novel, but they do so to define greatness, not to enshrine the terrible. They "do not usually offer badly written or badly reasoned literature in their courses"; there is no *Norton Anthology of Awful English Poetry*.[21]

By contrast, in our larger culture, we remember both terrible and great leaders, the tragic and the foolish as well as the wise and the virtuous. We remember slavery as well as emancipation and read *Mein Kampf* and the Gettysburg Address. Doing so has cautionary purposes: it teaches us to avoid mistakes. But it is also formative. It is part of what it means to be an acculturated member of society at all, not just a good member.

So it is in law. In constitutional law, we commemorate "examples of the worst errors in its field as well as the finest moments."[22] As Richard Primus writes: "Constitutional law . . . has not only a canon composed of the most revered constitutional texts but also an anti-canon composed of the most reviled ones."[23]

One understanding of the role of a constitutional anticanon is prudential. The anticanon consists of cases whose "errors are susceptible to repetition by otherwise reasonable people."[24] It is as important as the list of great constitutional decisions, but it consists of "cautionary tales rather than heroic ones."[25] The anticanon "map[s] out the land mines of the American constitutional order" to enable us to avoid stepping on them in the future.[26]

But the constitutional anticanon serves more than just precautionary purposes. Like the broader cultural canon (and anticanon), it is formative.[27] Lawyers operate within a shared community of culture and meaning. Their arguments about constitutional law "must be understood and ratified within the relevant community, for [them] to make any legitimate assertion of constitutional meaning."[28] Constitutional canonicity is part of our "ethos"—our "community's self-conception of its values and commitments, and the stories it tells about itself to itself."[29] Anticanonical cases "symbolize a set of generalized ethical propositions that we have collectively renounced."[30] Learning what counts as a canonical or anticanonical case is part of what it means to be "indoctrinate[d] . . . in the norms of professional legal practice."[31] It is important to know what can be cited and how: what is exemplary versus what should be mentioned only with a fitting show of shame or anger. That knowledge is "an admission ticket for entry into mainstream constitutional dialogue."[32]

That mainstream does not treat all mistakes equally. One may be forgiven for forgetting the date on which the Treaty of Versailles was signed, but not for ignorance of what December 7 or September 11 signify within our culture. Conversation between new acquaintances can manage a disagreement over the relative merits of Helen Mirren versus Judi Dench, but it can collapse when someone asserts that the works of Steven Seagal are the pinnacle of cinematic achievement. Such questions do not turn alone on the fact of error or questionable opinion but on the nature of the error, the occasion on which one offers the opinion, and other more or less subtle factors.

Similarly, it is not error alone that marks out the difference between an opinion that may be wrong and one that is anticanonical. Neither the "presence" nor the "magnitude" of error defines an anticanonical opinion. Its status depends on "the attitudes the constitutional community takes toward the ethical proposition that the decision has come to represent."[33] Our constitutional language must "match the outcomes deemed essential by the legal community at large."[34] Within conventional legal circles, a "good [constitutional] theory must yield *Brown v. Board, Griswold v. Connecticut* (though not necessarily *Roe v. Wade*), and *Baker v. Carr*; it must disapprove *Dred Scott v. Sandford, Plessy v. Ferguson,* and *Lochner v. New York*."[35]

Thus, what marks out a canonical or anticanonical decision is not its legal wrongness or even its arguable *moral* wrongness. Rather, it is that it has come to be understood as emblematic of *fundamental* ethical wrongness.[36] Lawyers and others may not even agree on what a particular decision means.[37] But they agree that it is and must be indisputably right or indisputably wrong. To reach any other conclusion is unacceptable.[38]

Fame and Infamy

In chapter 3 in this volume, Robert Tsai asks two questions: "[W]hat makes a precedent no longer worthy of respect—infamous, even—and therefore something that ought to be rejected?"[39] And how can a precedent "become 'infamous'—that is to say, irrelevant to decision making and vulnerable to repudiation"?[40] He draws on the constitutional anticanon, calling it "a collection of despised rulings and unfortunate events that serve as negative lessons for a polity."[41] His chapter offers an instructive analysis of the ways in which various communities can convince us that a judicial precedent is "an exemplar of public regret."[42] Tsai ranges over a number of well-known and controversial cases, from *Roe v. Wade*[43] to *Gobitis*[44] to *Korematsu*.[45] He closes with *Trump v. Hawaii*,[46] writing that "[t]ime will tell whether [it] is perceived by the people as a legitimate ruling or instead one that, as Justice Sonia Sotomayor contends in her scathing dissent, 'def[ies] our most sacred legal commitments.'"[47]

For current purposes, two things are striking about Tsai's approach and his definitions. The first is that, going by standard accounts, at least some of the precedents he discusses may be controverted or disfavored—even, in the case of *Gobitis*, one that was swiftly overturned by the Supreme Court—but they are not *anticanonical*. The second is the degree to which this approach elides potential differences between a precedent that is unworthy of respect, one that is weak and vulnerable, one that is cause for regret—and one that is unmistakably "infamous."

Insofar as Tsai is asking what is required to render a precedent ripe for "repudiation," this elision may not matter. Perhaps not every infamous decision is anticanonical: *Prigg v. Pennsylvania*[48] probably counts as one but not the other.[49] But is *every* decision that is "no longer worthy of respect," or that is "irrelevant to decision making and vulnerable to repudiation," truly "infamous?" Surely not. We need a clearer and stronger definition of "infamy" and its antonym "fame" to examine the kinds of issues raised by infamy in law and its connection to the constitutional canon and anticanon.

I begin with infamy rather than fame. One reason to do so is that we are much more accustomed to talking about fame than about infamy. Infamy has stayed closer to its core meaning, whereas fame has become a protean term, mostly unmoored from moral connotations. In ways that support my thesis about the small number of infamous or anticanonical decisions and the unlikelihood that the number will grow, our common understanding of infamy has remained clearer even though—or precisely because—the frequency of the word's use has diminished. That being said, the meaning of and attachment to both terms has changed over time in ways that bode ill for the broader project of constitutional canonicity or anticanonicity.

The *Oxford English Dictionary* defines "infamy" as follows: "Evil fame or reputation; scandalouse repute; public reproach, shame, or disgrace." An alternative definition describes it as "[t]he quality or character of being infamous or of shameful vileness" or "an infamous or utterly disgraceful act."[50]

That infamy denotes more than mere notoriety is evident from its historical illustrations, which also suggest its close connection to honor and dishonor. Thus, William Caxton's *Eneydos*, a 1490 translation of Virgil's *Aeneid*, contains the phrase "Thou hast dyuerted my honour in-to dishonest infamye."[51]

The same connection to honor—and to public office, which is one source of and reward for honor—is equally evident in its historical root: the ancient Roman status of *infamia*. Infamia was a "lack of public honor."[52] It was a consequence of condemnation for acts treated as particularly gross or shameful, such as prostitution, "ignominious . . . expulsion from the army," crimes and some civil wrongs undertaken with deliberate evil intent, and "appearing on the public stage as an actor."[53] The infamous person "lost the capacity for certain so-called public rights," including the right to hold some public offices.

The modern definition of "infamy" has not lost its sense of exceptional ill-repute. Merriam-Webster's online dictionary defines it as an "evil reputation brought about by something grossly criminal, shocking, or brutal" or "an extreme and publicly known criminal or evil act."[54] This is the sense in which the word was used in President Franklin Roosevelt's description of December 7, 1941, as "a date which will live in infamy." That has not stopped it from being used more casually, as in Merriam-Webster's citation to a United States men's soccer team as fated "always [to] live in American soccer infamy for failing to make the World Cup."[55] But a search of Ngram Viewer on Google Books suggests that the word is characterized more by disuse than alteration or misuse.

The trajectories of the words "fame" and "famous," by contrast, are characterized by a dramatic change in *meaning* without a drop-off in frequency of *use*. The change is nicely illustrated by Andy Warhol's ironic adage that in the future everyone will be famous for fifteen minutes. It suggests the broadening and thinning out of the word, its "lack of discrimination."[56] As the pioneering student of fame and the Founders, Douglass Adair, wrote in 1965—after the advent of the Hollywood celebrity but before the birth of Twitter's blue checkmark—fame "has been vulgarized and democratized."[57]

The alteration in the *application* of the word "fame" is perhaps less apparent in its dictionary meaning. There, its connection to public approbation of one's virtues and deeds remains, if in attenuated form, in definitions such as "[t]he character attributed to a person by thing or report or generally entertained; reputation. Usually in a good sense"; and "[t]he condition of being much talked about. Chiefly in good sense:

Reputation derived from great achievements; celebrity, honour, re-nown."[58] So, too, with "famous," which is to be "[c]elebrated in fame or public report; much talked about, renowned."[59]

A number of qualities set the classic definition of fame apart from its promiscuous modern usage. The first is its connection to virtue and honor. To untangle the complex relationship between fame and virtue or honor is too great a task for this space. But the fact of such a relation-ship, as well as its complicated, shifting nature, can be seen in examples from the sixteenth and seventeenth centuries—a period during which the relationship between fame and honor "fascinated successive generations of moralists, artists, preachers, politicians, playwrights, soldiers, and poets."[60] Connecting fame to virtue and honor, Fulke Greville's 1633 *In-quisition Upon Fame and Honour* "characterize[d] the search for personal fame as an effort for men to find a 'frame' beyond themselves that should be equivalent to religious and civic virtue."[61] And Thomas Hobbes, who influenced the Founding generation but did not convince them on this point, assimilated fame into an undifferentiated quest for reputation, "turn[ing] classical honor into modern fame by removing any justifica-tion beyond an inner demand to be appreciated."[62] Even this effort to cut honor down to size shows that fame and honor are closely connected.

An important difference between the two is the audience for one or the other, as well as the public or private nature of the concept. Adair describes honor as "primarily a private ethic that links a person's identity with social stratification or occupational specialization."[63] It is linked in this sense with the "honor group," the small and selective group that supplies a person with an "honor code" to observe and provides or with-holds approval.[64] Adair overstates the point. But he is right that honor can be internalized.[65] Although it is generally associated with public honors, as a spur to virtue it is more closely connected to *deserving* such honors than to receiving them. This is the point of Thomas Jefferson's letter advising his nephew, Peter Carr, to "ask yourself how you would act if all the world were looking at you, and act accordingly."[66] In con-trast, fame "is more public, inclusive, and looks to the largest possible human audience, horizontally in space and vertically in time."[67] Even if, as was once the case, fame was tied to character and achievement, it nevertheless required an approving audience. One can have a personal "sense of honor" but not a "sense of fame."

Another key aspect of fame is its connection to worthy achievements and good character. Although one can now be famous for feats of hot dog eating or spectacular crimes, fame in its original and still extant sense is tied to "achievement," particularly achievement "oriented toward public behavior."[68] A proper desire for fame involves the desire to be known for doing something truly memorable and praiseworthy.

This sense of fame is what led Adair to remark on the "almost obsessive desire for fame" of the leading figures of the Founding generation.[69] Evidence of this obsession can be seen across their public and private writings, as in Alexander Hamilton's description in *Federalist No. 72* of fame as "the ruling passion of the noblest minds."[70] It is visible in its more and less attractive aspects—from a commendable motivation for public-spiritedness to a curdled envy and bitterness—throughout John Adams's long correspondence with Benjamin Rush.[71]

The orientation of fame toward public ends is one key to its value. As Adair notes, a common trope of the classical authors studied by the Founding generation, and of that generation itself, was "the metaphor of the 'spur,' or the 'goad,' when *fame* is discussed."[72] They were fully aware that it was a potentially dangerous motivation. As the mixed stories of virtuous leadership and villainous tyranny in Plutarch's *Lives* taught them, the desire to "impose" one's "will, his ideas, . . . upon history in such a way that [one] will always be remembered" can lead as easily to "superlative wickedness" as to private virtue and public greatness.[73]

Still, "the great tradition of Fame" was "neither ethically blind nor morally neutral."[74] The key safeguard was the relevant audience for fame. Fame aimed at recognition by an idealized version of *posterity*: "The audience that men who desire Fame are incited to act before is the audience of the wise and the good in the future—that part of posterity that can discriminate between virtue and vice."[75] Just as honor involves "the agreed approval of *good* men,"[76] so fame, properly understood, requires the time-extended approval of the good and great.

Thus, although fame was subject to the dangers and need for restraint that are implicated in any "passion," it was ultimately seen as conducive to good character and great deeds by channeling the passion for recognition toward worthy ends. The Founding generation believed that "[t]he pursuit of fame . . . was a way of transforming egotism and self-aggrandizing impulses into public service," of using "ambition and self-interest" to spur a "dedicated effort for the community."[77] At crucial moments, it provided "a *personal* stake in creating a national system dedicated to liberty, to justice, and to the general welfare."[78]

It is obvious that, whatever the dictionaries say, the common usage of "fame" has strayed far from this sort of definition. This is not to suggest that it was ever an uncontested or uncomplicated value.[79] To the contrary, both fame and honor were subjected to criticism (as in Hobbes), and fame was understood—even by those who pursued it to salutary effect—as a potentially corrupting "passion."[80] In its modern form, however, it applies to almost anyone and anything. One reason the meaning of "infamy" has changed little, and that it is used less often, is that "fame" has become a catch-all term. It is used as much for celebrity as for public achievement, and it is as applicable to notoriety—or what used to be considered infamy or *ill* fame—as to publicly approved behavior.

It is worth making a few points about how and why fame has changed, points that bear on the topic of infamy in constitutional law. First, the connection between fame and posterity has weakened considerably. As Leo Braudy observes, posterity "used to be the place where true fame was judged," and "one intriguing difference between the star and the saint is that the greatest power of the saint tends to come after death."[81] But posterity has become "shrunken and attenuated."[82] In "our culture of immediacy[,] the contemporary saint . . . must still be alive."[83] That move encourages the urge toward fame as mere celebrity, and it untethers the "love of fame" from the constraining effect of a desire to win the approval of an imagined audience of virtuous men and women, who can distinguish between mere glitter and true gold.

Second and relatedly, one possible reason for the disappearance of a sense of posterity, and for the indiscriminate nature of fame today, is the plurality of views and ideas that characterize modern society. To the extent that fame or honor were connected to a shared sense of what constitutes virtue and vice, and of which acts are praiseworthy and which are deserving of condemnation, they could be internalized and lead to what Benjamin Franklin called a form of "self-monitoring."[84] Although that sense has not disappeared, and may be stronger in small or specialized communities, on the whole it is true that "there is no obvious national consensus about proper behavior."[85]

Finally, when one is acting on a public stage that is already crowded, one may seek fame as much in destruction as in creation. The point was made powerfully by Abraham Lincoln in 1838. Lincoln worried about the "manner in which some of the forces essential for sustaining the American Revolution and the new regime that it had produced were now turned against that very regime."[86] The Founding generation had been given a bare stage on which to build. "All that sought celebrity and fame, and distinction expected to find them in the success of that experiment. Their all was staked upon it:—their destiny was inseparably linked with it."[87]

They *did* succeed, "and thousands have won their deathless names in making it so."[88] But for their successors, the "field of glory is harvested, and the crop is already appropriated."[89] Since the desire for fame and glory had hardly disappeared from human nature, this left the question whether the "gratification [of the desire for fame could] be found in supporting and maintaining an edifice that has been erected by others."[90] Lincoln answered himself: "Most certainly it cannot."[91] This created risks for any "towering genius" who sought to carve out something genuinely new rather than preserve the work of others. Although that person might "as willingly, perhaps more so, acquire [distinction] by doing good as harm; yet, that opportunity being past, and nothing left to be done in the way of building up, he would set boldly to the task of pulling down."[92]

Lincoln's concern remains relevant today. It has mundane yet important applications. But at a grander level, it suggests that the desire for fame can produce the greatest results when one has the chance to write on a blank page. The more filled-in the map is, as Alexander wept to discover, the fewer new worlds there are to conquer. To win fame for building something new, one must perforce tear down what already exists.

The Puzzle Stated and Examined

This brings us back to the basic question. I restate it here before considering some possible explanations.

Constitutional scholars have compiled lists of cases that appear in all the major casebooks. Limiting it to cases that are widely praised or treated as essential, one such list includes nine decisions:[93] *Brown v. Board of Education*,[94] *Gibbons v. Ogden*,[95] *Griswold v. Connecticut*,[96] *Marbury v. Madison*,[97] *McCulloch v. Maryland*,[98] *New York Times Co. v. United States* (the Pentagon Papers case),[99] *Roe v. Wade*,[100] and *Youngstown Sheet & Tube Co. v. Sawyer* (the Steel Seizure case).[101] Adding cases omitted from an outlier casebook would add two or three cases: *Heart of Atlanta Motel, Inc. v. United States*,[102] *New York Times v. Sullivan*,[103] and *NLRB v. Jones & Laughlin Steel Corp*[104] or *Wickard v. Filburn*.[105] A more recent study, based on citations by courts, might persuade some to add others such as *Yick Wo v. Hopkins*[106] or *West Virginia State Board of Education v. Barnette*.[107] For reasons I discuss below, one might be reluctant to include newer cases, but there have surely been recent additions to the list of canonical cases. The strongest candidate is the same-sex marriage decision *Obergefell v. Hodges*.[108]

This list is not perfectly stable and won't command unanimous consent. If our focus is on "fame" as defined above, some will disagree with, say, the inclusion of *Roe v. Wade*. Others might be inclined to add additional cases: *Loving v. Virginia*,[109] *United States v. Nixon*,[110] perhaps *Texas v. Johnson*[111] or *Lawrence v. Texas*.[112] The curricular separation in legal education between "constitutional law" and "constitutional criminal procedure" leaves out some decisions that certainly have a strong claim to canonical status, including *Miranda v. Arizona*.[113] Let us assume that there is a relatively stable constitutional canon of around fifteen cases.

The constitutional anticanon is much shorter. Jamal Greene's leading article on the subject suggests that the list is "both narrower and less contested."[114] Greene names only four cases: *Dred Scott v. Sandford*,[115] *Plessy v. Ferguson*,[116] *Lochner v. New York*,[117] and *Korematsu v. United States*.[118] This is not the entire list of cases widely considered to be wrong or thought to be immoral. Other cases are widely condemned but do not make it onto the list of anticanonical cases.[119]

And the anticanon "may comprise just *three*: *Dred Scott, Plessy*, and *Lochner*."[120] *Korematsu*, Greene argues, "presents the weakest case for anticanonicity" of the four cases he lists, although it is also "the hardest of the four to defend using conventional constitutional arguments."[121] Unlike the other cases, however, *Korematsu* "has been cited positively far more than negatively" by federal courts,[122] albeit only for its requirement of strict judicial scrutiny for legal restrictions categorized by race.

Greene concludes that *Korematsu* retains its place in the anticanon.[123] As he notes, however, the case for *Lochner*'s anticanonicity has weakened. It was once "famously anticanonical," and it still is for judges. With respect to *academic* canonicity, however, "*Lochner* revisionism has become something of a cottage industry."[124] Greene argues that *Lochner* "remains firmly within the anticanon, and its defenders must always remain self-conscious about their iconoclasm."[125] But it is less true than it once was that reviling *Lochner* is an essential membership requirement for the mainstream legal academy. Indeed, even *Dred Scott* and *Plessy*, while remaining firmly anticanonical, have been subjected to a growing number of scholarly treatments arguing that neither of them "is unusually wrong, either by contemporaneous legal standards or by the conventional forms of legal argument that remain popular today."[126] For now, we can conclude that a good case can be made for a constitutional canon consisting of some ten to fifteen cases and a constitutional anticanon of four cases at most and perhaps only three.[127]

Why the disparity? I offer several possible explanations. Some have been amply discussed. Other, more speculative explanations have received less attention and deserve more. Their effects on the canon vary. Some aspects, such as the fixation on "novelty" in modern legal scholarship, help explain the disparity and also chip away at the size of the existing anticanon. Others, such as the loss of a consensus style in legal scholarship, do not change the size of the canon or anticanon but make new additions less likely. Still others, such as polarization, destabilize canonicity altogether. As I argue in the next section, it is evident that a number of these explanations are related to the changing status of fame and infamy.

Common Law Correction. It is a commonplace observation that American constitutional law operates in a common law–like way.[128] On this account, courts approach existing readings of the constitutional text and constitutional precedents with a deference born out of humility and a preference for judgments that are "grounded in experience" rather than "abstract."[129] They prefer refining those precedents over rejecting them wholesale. But they also appreciate that sometimes "a tradition should be rejected on the ground that it is morally wrong."[130] The judge-made law of the Constitution is thus subject to both "evolutionary" and "revolutionary" change.[131] "If one is quite confident that a practice is wrong," or if "one believes, even with less certainty, that it is *terribly* wrong," common-law constitutionalism "permits the practice to be eroded or even discarded."[132]

On this view, the common-law constitutional tradition is responsible for some of the most important, often canonical, decisions addressing and remedying infamous cases.[133] Whether the Supreme Court acts later in one bold stroke or puts a period on the sentence after allowing the infamous decision to fall into disfavor and desuetude,[134] the result is that the prior decision is no longer good law.

Common-law correction obviously does not mean that a repudiated decision cannot remain anticanonical. A fundamentally ethically wrong decision that has been rejected through common-law methodology can remain notorious for its wrongness. But common-law correction makes that fate less likely, in several ways. The rejection of such a precedent may orphan it, depriving it of a strong hold on cultural memory. The common-law "erosion" of a precedent may sap it of its strength as an influential exemplar of unjust and immoral legal decision making. And a decision that has been orphaned or repudiated decisively, and thus comes to seem like an aberration, may be less "susceptible to repetition by otherwise reasonable people."[135] If the anticanon "map[s] out the land mines of the American constitutional order,"[136] common-law correction can defuse or bury a potential mine and thus consign it to obscurity.

Changes in Legal Scholarship. The legal academy is only one part of a larger structure in American constitutional law.[137] But it is still a key site of canon and anticanon formation. Balkin and Levinson argue that the legal canon actually consists of *three* canons: the pedagogical canon, consisting of materials that are key to legal education; the academic theory canon, or those cases that "serve as benchmarks for testing academic theories about the law"; and the cultural literacy canon, including the cases (and other constitutional texts) that any cultured citizen ought to know.[138] Law professors help to shape all three.

Legal scholarship is not static in its approach. This is obviously true with respect to the subjects it discusses and the trends, theories, and methodologies that occupy its attention. But more than that is at work. Its *style* has changed. So have the structural incentives that drive and influence it. All these changes may affect canonicity in constitutional law. I focus on two changes here.[139]

The first is the neophilia of the modern legal academy: its love of the ostensibly "novel" or "counterintuitive." That impulse is not wrong in itself. Scholarship is meant to make original and significant contributions to a field of knowledge. Jamal Greene argues that scholarship within "the best traditions of academic argument" offers claims that are "interesting precisely because and to the degree to which they are counterintuitive, exposing our hunches to the rigors of principle."[140] And even if some legal problems are enduring, new cases, doctrines, statutes, and problems arise that demand new ideas or at least new discussions.

But academic neophilia can be taken to an extreme. Rather than be impelled by scholarly imperatives, it can be driven and sometimes distorted by the structures of professional advancement in a field, by the flaws of that field's gatekeepers, and by a lack of clear professional standards of judgment that might distinguish the truly original and useful from mere flash. It is conceivable that some legal scholars might recognize the presence of some of these factors in their own discipline.

The result is a scholarly fixation on the "novel," the "brilliant," and the "counterintuitive." Readers of law review articles will be well aware of the increasing number of articles claiming to be the first to discuss some issue; offering neologism-laden taxonomies that purport to reframe an entire legal field; providing "counterintuitive" accounts of some subject; "rethinking" something; and so on.

This is not new, to be sure. Thomas Ulen worried in 2004 that legal scholarship was infected by "an almost unseemly striving after fads and fancies."[141] In 1986, Daniel Farber suggested that law review "articles defending the status quo are much less likely to be published than articles attacking the status quo. The more sensible a legal rule, the less will be published supporting it, while articles cleverly attacking it will be taken as brilliant insights."[142] Law review editors note that their lack of knowledge may lead them to "disadvantage[e] articles that participate in conversations in fields where small moves mean a lot" and "systematically advantage maverick ideas."[143] But the trend continues at an accelerated pace. The occasional palliative measure has been as effective as King Canute's order to hold back the tide. Such measures are overwhelmed by other factors and incentives, which are often internalized by young and even established scholars. The wave of claimed "firsts" has become a tsunami.

This hyper-neophilia has a direct effect on the canon and anticanon and on the status of famous and infamous decisions. Scholarship defending a canonical case on canonical grounds will draw less attention than scholarship questioning its canonical status or challenging the taboo status of an anticanonical case. Of course, there are still conventional invocations of canonical and anticanonical cases. But there is also a growing volume of revisionist history and analysis devoted to the canon and anticanon.

The short list of anticanonical, "infamous" decisions may be especially vulnerable to this treatment. Their infamy lies in their fundamental *moral* and ethical wrongness, not necessarily their legal analysis. From an *intellectual* perspective, there is good reason to argue that "none of the [major] anticanon cases is unusually wrong, either by contemporaneous legal standards or by the conventional forms of legal argument that remain popular today."[144] In each case, the fame or infamy of those decisions will attract attention, and the incentive to say something "novel" about them will attract revisionist scholarship.

That has indeed been the result. *Dred Scott* has been "defended," not in the sense that the author favors the result but on the grounds that "the majority was armed with a set of interpretive resources that made its claims just as plausible as the dissent's."[145] *Plessy* has been said to be "consistent with the original understanding of the Fourteenth Amendment"[146] as well as with constitutional text and judicial precedent.[147] *Lochner*, in particular, which once was "famously indefensible," has been the subject of a "cottage industry" of "iconoclas[tic]" reconsideration.[148] Similarly, most if not all of our canonical cases have been subject to reconsideration.[149]

I am not suggesting these treatments are wrong or unnecessary. But they affect our sense of a canon and anticanon of famous and infamous cases. In such an environment, a canonical or anticanonical case is not an occasion for didactic praise or condemnation. It is a subject for reexamination, reconsideration, and revision. It is a text for explication—preferably in a contrarian vein—and not for ethical invocation and reaffirmation.[150] One finds echoes of Lincoln's concern that the "gratification" of the desire for fame cannot be achieved by "supporting and maintaining an edifice that has been erected by others" and must instead be sought by "set[ting] boldly to the task of pulling down."[151]

The second factor involves more ineffable changes in the culture and style of the legal academic community, perhaps driven by larger cultural changes. Consider first a question of timing. Greene's important article observes that the status of three of the four anticanonical cases—*Dred Scott*, *Plessy*, and *Lochner*—did not really firm up until "the Warren Court era."[152] The fourth, *Korematsu*, was equally bound up with the Warren Court, in that it "could not . . . emerge as anticanonical" until the Warren Court justices who had "played a significant role in the decision . . . had left the Court."[153]

The same is true of many cases commonly viewed as canonical. Some of them, such as *Brown*, are actually products of the Warren Court. Others did not achieve full canonical status until that period or until the Progressive Era that was in some ways a forerunner to it. *McCulloch*, for example, became canonical first "as part of a John Marshall revival movement designed to protect the Court's assertion of judicial supremacy in anticipation of Populist political attack," then later to buttress Progressive and New Deal arguments in favor of broad federal power to address national problems, eventually including modern civil rights legislation.[154] Similarly, *Marbury* was invoked as a canonical case first to defend the aggressive exercise of judicial review in the *Lochner* era and then to defend its use by the Warren Court.[155]

These arguments locate canonization or anticanonization in a political-historical context, one that addresses both judicial and scholarly work during a particular period. I argue here that this historical period matters in a different way, in that it involves the culture and sociology of the American legal academy. Much of the work of forming or entrenching these cases as canonical or anticanonical occurred during a period of relative liberal consensus. Despite areas of internal disagreement, and despite significant changes as the community grappled with civil rights during the 1960s, the liberal consensus did not truly founder until the end of that decade. This was a period, moreover, in which the scholarly active legal academy was smaller and in some respects more restrictive than it is today.

This period was characterized by an "unacknowledged dependence on homogeneity of outlook and values."[156] Legal scholars shared a "widespread consensus on the fairness and legitimacy of the institutions and procedures through which law is made, administered, and applied."[157]

The "respectable band" of the legal academy and its elite figures, much like those of elite or professional society generally, held a set of social and political views that placed them within "a narrow band between mild liberalism and mild conservatism."[158] In this period of "relative social stability and ideological consensus," historical change was understood in a "meliorist" fashion that "equated change with progress" and "privileg[ed] the present where it had been shown to diverge from the past" and its errors.[159]

The position and views of these scholars inevitably affected their approach to scholarship, their voice or style, and ultimately their treatment of canonical and anticanonical cases. Although (or because) they shared many of the same broadly liberal political positions, they were committed to the belief that scholarship should be moved more by "professional judgment" than "personal preferences" and that their scholarship should focus on "process rather than substance" and avoid "being result-oriented with respect to scholarly criticism."[160]

At the same time, the belief that the standard liberal positions were fundamental to a well-ordered and well-governed society and its "structure and procedures" allowed them to champion those positions in their scholarly work, ostensibly without violating the principle that this work should be driven by professional judgment and not personal preference.[161] Substantive "liberal democratic values" like freedom and toleration were understood not as ideological preferences but as natural and necessary components of a "rational consensus."[162] That consensus was rationally grounded as well as "morally good," and its rejection "courted destruction of democracy."[163] The scholarly voice of the consensus thinker was thus characterized by a "rhetoric of reasonableness"[164] that channeled moral argument through proceduralism and conveyed it in a register of calm exposition of settled values.

One sees something of this in Mark Tushnet's retrospective description of articles by two leading scholars, Harry Kalven and Kenneth Karst, who were writing in the *Supreme Court Review* in 1960. The questions these scholars examined are still discussed today. But they were treated "in a style—simultaneously detached from and engaged with the Justices—that has been lost to us."[165] Their method was unabashedly doctrinal, not theoretical or explicitly political. They wrote with "urbane detachment," a voice they thought appropriate to the scholar and not the judge, but with a "detached sympathy" for the role of the judge and the difficulties he or she faces.[166]

Although Tushnet did not put it in these terms, one might argue that the tone of these midcentury scholars was possible because their work was grounded in an untroubled sense of the availability of rational analysis and of reasonable judgment. This included the possibility of reasonable disagreement, which made possible their detached sympathy for the doctrinal work of courts.[167] Their confidence in the rightness of widely shared values allowed them to speak in this register and to employ a doctrinal approach that could take for granted the possibility of reasonable resolution of contested issues through legal doctrine. It did not require them to treat those who fell within the band of reasonable disagreement as "fools or knaves."[168]

One effect of the fact that this consensus allowed scholars to voice their (narrow, moderately liberal, proceduralist) values confidently, without feeling that they were resorting to moral or political rather than scholarly argument, and of the calm and confident register in which they spoke, was to reinforce the constitutional canon and anticanon. It made those cases available for invocation as signposts of greatness or failure—moral *and* doctrinal. The degree of consensus within what was a fairly small and narrow legal academic community reduced the likelihood of forceful contestation and contradiction. And the doctrinal nature of their academic work, as opposed to work drawing on other disciplines, left historical revisionism off the menu. To be sure, their process orientation and political perspective meant that they cited the canonical and anticanonical cases in their own way and for their own reasons. *Lochner*, for example, was "evil" not for its "substantive and ethical" wrongs but for the procedural wrong of engaging in judicial activism in an area belonging to the legislature.[169]

This admittedly speculative discussion is not meant to deny all the differences within this generation of scholars. Those differences, along with broader social, political, and generational changes, would reveal and produce major cleavages. I have elided many important complications and intramural arguments. In this account, however, what matters is that this generation of scholars shared important commonalities of *style*; of attitude and approach; and of cultural and political consensus.

This extended even to important subjects on which there was disagreement. The Supreme Court's *decision* in *Brown* opened up rifts within the process-oriented generation of legal scholars and between it and later generations of scholars.[170] But there was agreement about its *outcome*. The view that segregation was a fundamental wrong and that the Court had a key role to play in ending it was widely shared across those divides.[171] That consensus—and the voice of "detached sympathy" that accompanied it—made available a confident invocation of canonical and anticanonical cases as signal moments of judicial greatness or failure. Just as *Lochner* was invoked as an evil, so *Brown*, whatever jurisprudential debates surrounded it, was "presented . . . not simply as a fact of equal protection doctrine, but, beyond that, as a key symbol of the open and democratic character of American society" and of law's ability "to respond to legitimate claims for freedom and liberty."[172]

In short, this was still a period in which a small fraternity of elite public law scholars spoke with a relatively common voice and set of assumptions. Epigones of a select group of equally elite judges and other mentors, they operated within an elite tradition and confidently conveyed a view of that tradition that spotlighted particular cases as indisputably good or bad in a moral and doctrinal sense.

That tradition—and the sense of consensus underlying it—shattered toward the end of the 1960s as a new generation of scholars entered the legal academy. They were greater in number, more often trained in nonlegal disciplines such as history and political science, more drawn to novelty and controversy, and less firmly attached to the view of the scholar as adjunct judge. Once things changed, it would be more difficult for the canon or the anticanon to grow further, and the desire to "rethink" moral and legal commonplaces—for political and jurisprudential reasons, to be sure, but also to make names for themselves—would ultimately make revisiting the anticanon increasingly attractive.

Pluralism and Polarization. The 1960s thus marked the beginning of a period in which legal scholarship was less likely to be hospitable to the confident maintenance of a constitutional canon and anticanon, let alone to the addition of new cases to that list. Conditions have become even less hospitable since then. Some of those conditions, as we have seen, are professional, such as the growth of interdisciplinary work that can reexamine a canonical or anticanonical decision from an outside perspective. But two broader social forces are also at work. Both affect the state of the canon and anticanon, making it likelier that the list of canonical and anticanonical decisions will be reduced than expanded.

One is that the United States has become an "increasingly culturally diverse nation."[173] It is home to a vast array of different political views, religious commitments, racial and ethnic backgrounds, and so on. We may share the view that "this variety of perspective[s] makes life more interesting" and that pluralism is a classic American good worthy of celebration.[174] But pluralism also makes it harder to rely on shared values, a shared tradition, a shared ethos or set of sacred symbols—including a constitutional canon or anticanon. Pluralism makes it less likely that we will maintain the canonical symbols built in the past or that we will achieve consensus about new cases belonging in that category.

The other social force is cultural and political polarization, a topic that "dominates discussions of contemporary American politics" and culture.[175] Polarization consists not of ordinary disagreement but of "excessive partisanship and deep ideological divisions," especially among "political elites and officeholders."[176] In a polarized political environment, "ideological convergence within parties and divergence between parties" leads to "hyperpartisanship."[177] As Ezra Klein puts it: "We are so locked into our political identities that there is virtually no candidate, no information, no condition, that can force us to change our minds. We will justify almost anything or anyone so long as it helps our side, and the result is a politics devoid of guardrails, standards, persuasion, or accountability."[178]

Within and beyond elite circles, we find today "a larger cultural phenomenon of 'incivility,' namely the erosion of norms that historically constrained the discourse and actions of political actors or the mass public."[179] As politics and political disagreement become defining elements of individual identity, our culture is marked by "an escalation of conflict" characterized by "prejudice, anger, and activism on behalf of that prejudice and anger."[180]

There is disagreement about how polarized the general population is, but there is a broad consensus that polarization is a significant phenomenon among elites—a category that surely includes lawyers and legal academics.[181] Elite polarization affects constitutional law as well. When "mutual suspicions and animosities increasingly define our politics," constitutional law can be "infect[ed]" by polarization and be understood and practiced as "a continuation of political conflict by other means."[182]

Polarization may also affect the stability of precedent given the strain that our "polarized moment" places on "shared institutional commitments."[183] Even if judges and scholars value stare decisis, cultural and political polarization are likely to lead to "divergent views on when the Court is being partisan and results-driven as opposed to neutral and objective."[184] Those views will be heavily influenced by motivated reasoning.[185] Professional training provides some constraint on motivated reasoning. But it does not confer immunity, particularly on issues that are less capable of strictly "legal" resolution. Indeed, some of the qualities lawyers and academics tend to associate with the capacity to resist biased or motivated reasoning, such as a capacity for "critical thinking," can actually exacerbate the tendency to engage in "ideologically motivated reasoning."[186] While it will be hard (and impolitic) to identify particular examples, it is fair to say that the broader presence of hyperpartisanship and the absence of guardrails will encourage some deliberately strategic and disingenuous uses of law and precedent by legal scholars.

These phenomena do not absolutely preclude an ongoing constitutional canon and anticanon. Indeed, Jamal Greene argues that they are especially consistent with the anticanon. Anticanonical cases, he writes, are characterized by agreement that they are wrong but by "disagreement, even irreconcilable disagreement, as to why. This feature of anticanon cases is indispensable, as it enables multiple sides of contemporary constitutional arguments to use the anticanon as a rhetorical trump."[187] Thus, *Lochner* can be invoked by different "sides" as an example of courts improperly intruding into the sphere of policy; of the dangers of substantive due process doctrine; of the application of substantive due process to the wrong kind of issue; or of the substantive wrongness of ignoring the reality of inequality between capital and labor. To take a canonical rather than an anticanonical case, the competing opinions in the *Parents Involved* case all invoke, and fight fiercely over the meaning of, *Brown*.[188]

Greene has a point. He is right, too, in noting that this makes the anticanon "*normatively* unstable."[189] But his argument depends on background conditions of stability and relative consensus. It draws on Cass Sunstein's account of "incompletely theorized agreements," which "allow a pluralistic society with disparate views to produce some semblance of political and legal consensus."[190] For incompletely theorized agreements to function, and for a canon or anticanon to remain meaningful, there must be some degree of general consensus on values or specific consensus on results, not to mention some degree of confidence in each other and in our deliberative and cultural institutions. We must believe that the canon invoked by all sides—however differently they do so— represents a common culture maintained by reasonably trustworthy cultural gatekeepers. We must believe that disputes over the meaning of canonical cases are conducted more or less in good faith and in a common tongue and that the institutions that mediate these struggles are relatively stable and relatively trustworthy. Even if the *meaning* of our canon remains normatively unstable, the canon as an *institution*, and the many institutions that tend it, must remain relatively stable and credible.

These things are possible under conditions of *reasonable* pluralism. But when pluralism meets hyper-partisanship, polarization, incivility, and the merger of politics with identity, these conditions become untenable. This has at least two possible effects, which will either prevent additions to the canon or anticanon, thereby maintaining the existing disparity between the number of canonical and anticanonical cases, or undermine the idea of canonicity altogether, with the same or greater effect.

One possibility is that, under conditions of polarization, different camps will develop different and increasingly divergent canons. Cases already entrenched as canonical will either remain that way, subject to different readings for each separate community, or will be dropped from different canons for substantive or revisionist reasons. Drawing on newer as well as older decisions, each community will establish its own list of canonical or anticanonical cases that are emblematic of the moral and political propositions these separate groups see as essential to law—libertarian, natural law–oriented, progressive, and so on. Although constrained by the ultimate effects of Supreme Court review, lower federal courts and state court judges may invoke these different cases for canonical purposes in their own, more politicized work. Some newly canonical cases may adventitiously overlap across groups. None of these groups will abandon the idea of canonicity. But absent a sufficient cultural and legal consensus, the project of a *common*, universal canon will come to an end.

This is a vision of a fissiparous legal community that breaks into separate cultures but still believes that some cases stand as moral landmarks, as monuments to fame or infamy. But there is another possibility. As we saw, polarization can lead to a state of mutual suspicion and cynicism, in which "[w]e will justify almost anything or anyone so long as it helps our side, and the result is a politics devoid of guardrails, standards, persuasion, or accountability."[191] The invocation of a decision as canonical will be unrestrainedly rhetorical and strategic. Despite the tendency to hold on to the idea that one's *own* community is acting in good faith, belief in the bad faith of others may lead to a suspicion of the possibility of good faith itself. In the absence of the norms that make canon formation possible and relatively stable, albeit contested, and given the tendency of a hyper-partisan society to see every cultural dispute as a legitimate occasion for cunning political maneuvers, canonicity itself will collapse under the strain. Divided by its differences, our society will in a broader sense be united by cynicism and disenchantment. The existing canon and anticanon may remain but with a more vestigial status and without the same power to conjure.

Posterity and Media Immediacy. Recall the discussion above of the connection between fame, properly or classically understood, and posterity, which "used to be the place where true fame was judged."[192] In her account of struggles over the content of American history textbooks, Frances FitzGerald writes that they "contain the truths selected for posterity."[193] In the legal field, the constitutional canon aids the legal profession, the "keeper of the nation's constitutional memory," in "sustaining our constitutional tradition."[194] The canon's vision of fame and infamy is thus time-extended, looking to posterity and not just the immediate moment.

Long before the rise of new media, Leo Braudy worried that, in our "culture of immediacy," posterity had become "shrunken and attenuated."[195] Social-media platforms and other forms of online communication have exacerbated those concerns. They have in common "the sense of immediacy they foster [and] the polarization that they encourage."[196] Newspapers' shift from a once-daily physical object to a constantly

238 | PAUL HORWITZ

updated online presence, along with their online competitors and the twenty-four-hour news cycles of cable networks, have "facilitated ever greater immediacy in the delivery of news."[197] Our standards of immediacy themselves have become foreshortened and accelerated. Not long ago, a blog seemed high-speed—even *too* high-speed.[198] Compared to Twitter, blog posts seem positively plodding and reflective.[199]

Our obsessive attachment to the latest micro-moment, combined with a more polarized and uncivil culture,[200] decreases the power of the existing canon and the likelihood that new canonical or anticanonical cases will take root in an evanescent culture. A consensus that some action merits the label of "fame" or "infamy" emerges only with time. It requires patience and perspective. These qualities are absent in our culture. A decision has barely been announced before commentators rush to celebrate or execrate it in the strongest terms. Decisions are instantly deemed not sound but heroic, not mistaken but disastrous. Advocacy groups quickly seize on decisions in equally strong terms, not least because a sense of urgency is essential to fundraising and publicity in a competitive market. The kinds of praise or obloquy that were once given only to a few potentially canonical or anticanonical decisions will be thick on the ground before most people—even the commentators themselves—have had a chance to finish reading that decision, let alone to ponder it calmly. Some of this will be a matter not of reaction but of strategy: of the desire to be heard over the noise, or for attention and status, or to shape the narrative.

In such a society, invocations of a constitutional canon or anticanon will be frequent, insincere, and meaningless. The old canon will lose force, and arguments that a new case should be treated as canonical or anticanonical will be met with deep skepticism. The invocation of canonicity will be to past invocations what celebrity is compared to fame: a fallen-off shadow of its former self.

Canon and Anticanon in an Age of False Fame and Infamy

What becomes of a constitutional canon or anticanon under such conditions? I answer that question by posing a prior question: What are the underlying cultural qualities or concepts required for a stable constitutional canon or anticanon—qualities that may now be frail or absent?

To be sure, canonical cultural texts—whether literary or legal—are never absolutely fixed. The numbers of canonical or anticanonical texts, and even their received meanings, are always in a state of flux. But just as we distinguished between fame and infamy properly understood in light of posterity and the more evanescent quality of celebrity or notoriety, we can say the same thing about the constitutional canon. It is true that the canonicity of a decision such as *Marbury* had as much to do with later developments and needs as with some immediate sense of greatness. But without *any* stability or lasting quality, without any embeddedness in even an *invented* tradition, there is no canonicity. There is merely a brief moment of celebrity or notoriety. Fame and infamy are closely connected to the canon and anticanon. Both should be understood in their proper and not adulterated senses, and both share many of the same prerequisites.

One prerequisite, it follows, is a relative degree of stability. An important part of that stability is the idea of posterity. A sense of posterity as the imagined audience for one's actions and as the ultimate judge of fame and infamy is necessary to encourage bold and virtuous conduct that may win one true, lasting fame. Likewise, the conclusion that a case is truly canonical or anticanonical requires an expanded time horizon. The shared ethos on which the existence of the constitutional canon depends, and that in turn is shored up by that canon, must represent something more than a snapshot of the transient sentiments of the profession. It must have some meaningful temporal continuity.

A viable constitutional canon also requires some degree of consensus within the interpretive community of lawyers, scholars, and other legal elites—and probably beyond. Consensus is not unanimity. There are always disagreements within an interpretive community. But some degree of agreement on fundamentals may be necessary for a case to be understood as famous or infamous, canonical or anticanonical. For *Brown* to be *Brown*, we do not need agreement on whether it stands for color-blindness or antisubordination—whether "[t]he way to stop discrimination on the basis of race is to stop discriminating on the basis of race" or whether "to get beyond racism, we must first take account of race."[201] But we do need agreement on the importance of attacking legal segregation itself. For *Plessy* to be *Plessy*, we need not agree on its precise legal error,[202] but there must be agreement on its fundamental *ethical* wrongness. A canon requires a shared *nomos* through which the status of an opinion can be settled (as much as anything can be settled). There must be a set of "generalized ethical principles" that have been "collectively" embraced or "renounced."[203]

A basic level of agreement is one prerequisite for canonicity; another is as or more important. Canonical and anticanonical cases often have that status precisely because they are capable of being invoked by "multiple sides of contemporary constitutional arguments."[204] These arguments may involve fierce contestation. But each side's argument must be *legible* to the other side. Agreement that a case is canonical or anticanonical—that it is deserving of fame or infamy and thus that there are some poles around which argument must proceed without knocking them out of place—is part of that legibility.

Put simply, there must be a common culture that allows different members of the interpretive community to share a common language. Shakespeare's stock may rise or fall over time, and there will be arguments over the meaning of his works. But there must be an interpretive community that reads and is capable of reading Shakespeare for his work to be canonical. It must be able to read and speak together, sharing some fundamental views but also able to air disputes in the same tongue and through the same texts. This is as true for fame and infamy as it is for canonicity and anticanonicity. The ethical and political disagreements that divided federalists from antifederalists in the Founding era were nevertheless conducted in a common tongue in which both had recourse to the models of fame and infamy provided by Plutarch's *Lives*.[205]

Stability, consensus, and a legible common culture allow us to conduct our discussions and arguments in a particular kind of voice or spirit, one that I have suggested was present in consensus-era legal scholarship despite intramural disagreements. It provides a kind of taken-for-granted quality in the terms and language of our discussions. The agreement that certain texts or actions are deservedly famous or infamous—that they are emblematic of a broad shared ethos—allows disagreement about particulars to move forward without stumbling at the first step or devolving immediately into pure hostility.

One might even say that canonicity, understood in terms of the older meanings of fame and infamy, requires a kind of naïveté—not a lack of wisdom and experience but the sort of artless simplicity of vision that a belief in shared values permits.[206] That sort of confidence and innocence has its dangers. It is often blind, easily shaken by events, and capable of curdling into hypocrisy and cynicism. But its virtues are real. It allows for a belief in qualities—heroism or villainy, morally straight or bent behavior, good and bad role models—that are essential to the love of fame and the civic engagement it encourages, an engagement that is tied to both fame and infamy and, ultimately, to a constitutional canon and anticanon.

This is not the sort of quality that is trumpeted from the rooftops by sophisticates.[207] But there is surely some truth to James Hankins's assertion that "all human societies need heroes, or at least decent, well-educated people of goodwill who can serve as models for later generations."[208] This quality is present in the confident assumptions and assertions of the consensus-era legal scholars, who were neither unworldly nor lacking in technical skill but who did possess a confidence in a shared ethos, an undisturbed sense of the possibility of heroism or villainy, and a common vocabulary in which to express it. And it was present, in all its tensions, in the writings of the founding generation, who lacked neither experience nor a sense of the imperfection of human nature but were not merely adding decoration to strategy when they invoked the Plutarchian exemplars that had long figured in their reading and self-searching.

It is this kind of naïveté that makes it possible for virtuous and public-regarding action to be "actuated by just praise for merit and fine examples of conduct"[209] and scorn for their opposite—by "the spur of praise and the whip of blame."[210] It is necessary in order for fame and infamy, properly understood, to have any purchase. The same holds true for a constitutional canon or anticanon. Without that "naïve" belief in greatness and its opposite, those cases may stand as coordinating precedents, serving an essentially technical stabilizing function in law, but they will not function as exemplars of a shared constitutional ethos and its triumphs or failures.

Finally, in keeping with the need for both a sense of posterity and a naïve belief in fame and infamy properly understood, a healthy system of constitutional canonicity and anticanonicity must believe that greatness and its opposite are relatively exceptional. A culture in which every good judicial decision is acclaimed as great, and every bad one is condemned as appalling, is one in which fame and infamy are rendered meaningless. If everything is a spur or whip, nothing will be.

Now compare these prerequisites with the academic, legal, political, and public culture described above. That culture is characterized by various uneasily coexisting traits. They include a love of the novel and counterintuitive; relentless scholarly revisionism; a lack of the capacity to confidently invoke common values and judgments; hyper-polarization and the breakdown of guardrails, accompanied by an increase in incivility and the strategic rhetoric it encourages; a heavy focus on the present and away from posterity; and a focus on celebrity rather than fame properly understood.

It should be evident that few, if any, of the prerequisites I have identified exist in such a culture. The constitutional canon and anticanon will thus be increasingly unlikely to command consent or maintain stability under such conditions, let alone grow. Consider the requirement of posterity and its relationship to stability. A culture that is obsessed with the current moment, defined in ever smaller increments, and that is combined with an academic culture obsessed by novelty and drawn to revisionism, loses any serious attachment to posterity. Far from "transcending the present moment" and thereby being immune to the caprices of good and bad fortune,[211] it rejects the past and has little meaningful sense of futurity.[212] Fame and infamy as features of an extended tradition have little power within a culture that insists on being born anew with each micro-sized news cycle. Judgments about new actions that deserve praise or obloquy can have little power to persuade, or to become entrenched, within a culture that is unwilling to take the long view.[213]

Neither is such a culture conducive to serious consensus. That is true both in the narrower sense of substantive consensus on particular issues and in the more general—and more important—sense of a shared language in which disagreements can proceed with relative calm. Polarization and hyper-partisanship make it hard to agree on what is praiseworthy or disgraceful.[214] More than that, their tendency to encourage self-sorting into separate epistemic communities reduces the ability of these communities to speak to one another in a common tongue, with relatively shared premises, and without those discussions being stifled by mutual suspicion or simple incomprehension.

Polarization and hyper-partisanship are important causes of a self-reinforcing cycle of suspicion. Suspicion of the statements and motives of one's adversaries leads to cynicism. That in turn supports the view—especially in the absence of a strong sense of posterity as the ultimate judge of virtuous conduct—that the guardrails of politics and of political civility are misplaced and that one ought to defeat one's opponents cleanly or otherwise. The reciprocation of those views and tactics encourages cynicism not only about one's opponents but also, ultimately, about politics and public and political discourse altogether.[215] This is hardly a healthy breeding ground for the sort of naïve faith in virtue or heroism that a shared ethos permits, one that makes possible the ingenuous invocation and maintenance or expansion of an ethically freighted constitutional canon or anticanon. Compounding this general problem is the specific problem of academic cynicism and the academic preference for novelty that—not without reason, but to an excessive extent—sees any monument as an object to be chipped away at and analyzed for its clay content.

Conclusion: Prospects, Losses, and Gains

If the conditions for a proper sense of canonicity, with its associated values of fame and infamy properly understood, are absent from contemporary culture, then one possibility is that invocations of canonical or anticanonical cases will wither away. Those cases will be cited, to be sure. But they will lack the weighty *ethical* quality that distinguishes an approving invocation of a canonical case or a cautionary invocation of an anticanonical text from something more mundane and mechanical. The system of precedent will continue. But the constitutional canon properly understood will not grow larger. If anything, it will shrink.

Another possibility worth considering is that we will see a flourishing of what we might call "false" canonicity and "false" fame and infamy. The legal academy is not immune from the tendencies toward polarization, partisanship, and motivated reasoning that affect others. Law professors are natural translators and sought-after "experts," are ambitious, have political views, and are active and hotly followed in traditional and social media. Their partisan views, combined with the lack of a sense of history and posterity and a desire for more immediate celebrity, will encourage them to see every battle as having the highest stakes. They will feel driven to be heard above the din and to shape the narrative of public discussion. This will lead to extravagant and promiscuous celebration or censure. They will describe every decision they support as canonically great—and every decision they oppose as anticanonically wicked and deserving of infamy.

On this account, the population of ostensibly "famous" and "infamous" judicial decisions will grow as quickly as the population of ostensibly "famous" or "infamous" people. In place of genuine canonicity, we will have *hyper*-canonicity and *hyper*-anticanonicity, invoked with strategy rather than naïveté. Every hot-button constitutional decision will have its Warholian fifteen minutes of fame or infamy. Despite being labeled "famous" or "infamous," "canonical" or "anticanonical," few decisions will be remembered longer than we remember anything else in our frenetic news cycle.

Bush v. Gore[216] may serve as an example. The decision was rightly criticized, albeit in the most vituperative terms and with an immediate eye to labeling it even before the ink on the advance sheets had dried, as a "latter-day *Dred Scott*, *Plessy v. Ferguson*, or *Lochner v. New York*."[217] The high stakes and questionable reasoning of the case make the level of attention devoted to it understandable. But the effort to baptize it as anticanonical at birth suggests a kind of strategic effort to pre-form a "judgment of history" in service of more immediate and political goals. In any event, *Bush v. Gore* has occupied an ever-shrinking amount of space in constitutional law casebooks and assessments of the Rehnquist Court and has become more neglected than anticanonical.[218]

A more recent example—less of the strategic labeling of a new decision as "canonical" or "anticanonical" and more of the strategic invocation of existing canonical or anticanonical cases—involves scholarly responses to recent First Amendment decisions in the areas of religious exercise and speech. Those developments were greeted with a host of invocations of "First Amendment *Lochner*ism," with *Lochner* serving here "as a legal hobgoblin."[219] Although I disagree with the substance of many of these views, and there are grounds to question the accuracy of this rubric,[220] I am interested here in the approach and not the merits of their arguments. (And despite my disagreements, the arguments certainly have some merit.) What is striking is that the decisions to which these criticisms are applied—many of them, not incidentally, highly politically salient and the subject of culture-war polarization—are not simply criticized as wrong. The invocation of *Lochner* means, rather, that they are vilified as the rebirth of one of the most disfavored eras of the Supreme Court.

Leaving aside the merits of specific scholarly invocations of *Lochner* in this area, this *approach* illustrates what a hyper-canonicity approach might look like in a hyper-polarized age. It uses anticanonicity as a frame, one that speaks more to current and highly political concerns than to the ultimate evaluation of a decision in light of posterity. Its power lies less in the substance of the arguments than in its political force: in its potential capacity to preemptively and negatively classify the opposed decision in the mind of the interpretive community.

It is not, I think, accidental that the approach is an act of "branding," in its newer as well as older senses. "We know these cases by their petitioners," Greene writes of the anticanon: we need only hear the single name *Plessy* or *Lochner* for all its negative associations to come to mind.[221] Hyper-canonicity as a branding approach fits well with the media and professional environment I have discussed. It is attractive to young law review editors and thus conducive to article placement and professional advancement, and it marries well to media and social-media strategies. The same arguments put differently, even if entirely correct, would not have the same power to simplify, provoke, forestall second thoughts, and rally one's compatriots.[222] In that sense, hyper-canonicity or hyper-anticanonicity may be a substitute for (even if it does not entirely replace) reasoned argument.

It is not clear that there is a great difference between the possibility of a strongly rooted constitutional canon or anticanon vanishing and the possibility of hyper-canonicity. In the first case, the lack of consensus about what is commendable or shameful will rob the canon of its power to conjure within the wider interpretive community. In the second, the lack of restraint provided by a sense of posterity, along with the move from common consensus into warring camps, will lead to the same end.[223] In neither case will we have the shared ethos, naïve belief in great or shameful models, and sense of posterity that a genuine constitutional canon or anticanon needs to survive. If a canonical or anticanonical case serves as an exemplar of the "generalized ethical propositions that we have collectively renounced" or embraced,[224] then the state of the canon in either case will betray the lack of a shared ethos.

If this assessment of the state of the constitutional canon and its likely prospects under current conditions is accurate, much of the reason for this state of affairs has to do with the related state of the concepts of fame and infamy—the way in which their invocation has proliferated even as their meaning has thinned out. Many of the same factors are at work in both cases. It is not clear in the long run that there can be a true constitutional canon and anticanon without true fame and infamy.

Despite the general tone of lament in this chapter, there is room for some ambivalence about that prospect. There have been gains as well as losses. The diversification (along some lines) of the legal academy, and its professionalism and use of other disciplines' sharper tools, have led to many benefits.[225] The rise of greater pluralism and sharper disagreement ultimately showed that the confident tone of the consensus-era scholars—which allowed them to engage in a kind of morally suffused technical discussion—ignored or obscured as much as it revealed. Insights into the incentive- or interest-driven aspects of human conduct may breed cynicism, but they are real insights. "Moralistic romanticism"[226] is attractive *and* troubling. No case, however long it has served as a form of ethical exemplar, should be immune from reconsideration. Closer examination may reveal that its beloved or reviled status is questionable—and perhaps suggestive of an ethical community whose views and assumptions are indeed in need of "rethinking." More broadly, the loss of the constraining power of fame and infamy is both a cause and a product of broader democratizing and egalitarian impulses that reformed or removed unjust and fixed hierarchies, institutions, and behaviors.[227] Even in our own time, the heroes that remain or emerge are still often the products of a relatively closed elite culture—of an ostensible "meritocracy" that is its own hierarchy, more diverse along some lines but a hierarchy nonetheless.[228]

Our reflections on the state and prospects of fame, infamy, and the constitutional canon and anticanon must acknowledge these gains. As this chapter suggests, however, those gains come with losses of their own. It is no act of infamy to give those losses their due.

NOTES
1 For leading commentary on the topic of canonicity in American constitutional law, *see, e.g.*, J. M. Balkin and Sanford Levinson, "The Canons of Constitutional Law," 111 *Harvard Law Review* 963 (1998); Symposium, "The Canon(s) of Constitutional Law," 17 *Constitutional Commentary* 187 (2000).

2 *See, e.g.*, Frank B. Cross and James F. Spriggs II, "The Most Important (and Best) Supreme Court Opinions and Justices," 60 *Emory Law Journal* 407 (2010). I mean no disrespect in citing this article as an example. Cross and Spriggs defend their attempt to "[i]dentify . . . the most important cases decided by the Supreme Court" as "more than an interesting parlor game," arguing that "the process [of identifying these cases] illuminates the function of the law." *Ibid.*, 409.

3 See ibid., 432–41; Balkin and Levinson, 971–72 (identifying ten Supreme Court cases that appeared in all of the major constitutional law casebooks the authors surveyed).

4 *See, e.g.*, Michael Gibson, "The Most Important Supreme Court Cases," Ranker, www.ranker.com.

5 Jamal Greene, "The Anticanon," 125 *Harvard Law Review* 379, 380 (2011). See also Richard A. Primus, "Canon, Anti-Canon, and Judicial Dissent," 48 *Duke Law Journal* 243 (1998). For a version aimed at general audiences, see Joel D. Joseph, *Black Mondays: Worst Decisions of the Supreme Court* (Inprint, Kindle 4th ed., 2013 [National PressBooks, 1987]).

6 Paul Horwitz, "The *Hobby Lobby* Moment," 128 *Harvard Law Review* 154, 188 (2014); see also Laura Kalman, *The Strange Career of Legal Liberalism* (New Haven: Yale University Press, 1996), 59, 90.

7 Greene, "The Anticanon," 383.

8 *Brown v. Allen*, 344 U.S. 443, 540 (1953) (Jackson, J., concurring in the judgment) ("We are not final because we are infallible, but we are infallible only because we are final.").

9 *See generally* David A. Strauss, *The Living Constitution* (Oxford: Oxford University Press, 2010); David A. Strauss, "Common Law Constitutional Interpretation," 63 *University of Chicago Law Review* 877 (1996).

10 This is a key distinction between this chapter and Jamal Greene's article on the constitutional anticanon. That article offers a descriptive and theoretical account of the anticanon. It examines it as "a contingent professional practice" (ibid. at 385) but does not, as this chapter does, explore contemporary cultural and professional factors that might weaken or kill that practice. That said, I draw heavily on Greene's account in this chapter and am greatly indebted to his work.

11 See James Hankins, *Virtue Politics: Soulcraft and Statecraft in Renaissance Italy* (Cambridge, MA: Harvard University Press, 2019), 198–200 (discussing Boccaccio's conception of the worthy ambition for "Good Fame" and situating it as part of the Renaissance "humanist program of moral rearmament").

12 *Ibid.*, 200.

13 *See, e.g.,* Peter Berger, "On the Obsolescence of the Concept of Honour," in *Liberalism and its Critics,* ed. Michael J. Sandel (New York: New York University Press, 1984), 149; Charles Taylor, *Sources of the Self: The Making of the Modern Identity* (Cambridge, MA: Harvard University Press, 1989). Although the concept of honor is obviously relevant to the concept of "good fame" and makes numerous appearances below, a complete discussion of that concept is beyond the scope of this chapter. For a fuller discussion of honor and its relationship to law, see Paul Horwitz, "Honour, Oaths, and the Rule of Law," 32 *Canadian Journal of Law & Jurisprudence* 389 (2019).

14 Caroline Cox, *A Proper Sense of Honor: Service and Sacrifice in George Washington's Army* 40 (Chapel Hill: University of North Carolina Press, 2004) (quoting George Washington).

15 For discussion, see Horwitz, 394–98 (canvassing common criticisms of honor but arguing for the value of a modernized sense of honor). For an influential discussion of the value of a revised form of honor in a modern liberal democratic society, see Sharon Krause, *Liberalism with Honor* (Cambridge, MA: Harvard University Press, 2002). For an examination of both the benefits and the dangers of the concept of honor, see Kwame Anthony Appiah, *The Honor Code: How Moral Revolutions Happen* (New York: W. W. Norton, 2010).

16 Elsewhere, I have drawn on Julian Pitt-Rivers's definition of honor as a quality of character having both internal and external aspects: "[T]he value of a person in his own eyes, but also in the eyes of his society." See Horwitz, 391–94; Julian Pitt-Rivers, "Honour and Social Status," in *Honour and Shame: The Values of Mediterranean Society,* ed. J. G. Péristiany (London: Weidenfeld & Nicholson, 1994), 19, 22.

17 J. M. Balkin and Sanford Levinson, "Preface," in *Legal Canons,* ed. J. M. Balkin and Sanford Levinson (New York: New York University Press, 2000), ix.

18 Balkin and Levinson, *Legal Canons,* 3, 15.

19 *Ibid.,* 12.

20 *Ibid.*

21 *Ibid.*

22 Primus, 245.

23 *Ibid.*

24 Greene, 384.

25 Primus, 245.

26 Greene, 381.

27 *See, e.g.,* Sanford Levinson, "Is *Dred Scott* Really the Worst Opinion of All Time? Why *Prigg* Is Worse Than *Dred Scott* (But Likely to Stay Out of the 'Anticanon')," 125 *Harvard Law Review* F. 23, 23 (2011) (calling the canon and anticanon "an important aspect of the socialization process" of lawyers).

28 Ian C. Bartrum, "The Constitutional Canon as Argumentative Metonymy," 18 *William & Mary Bill of Rights Journal* (2009): 327, 392. I would be more inclined to say "effective" or "shared" than "legitimate," although Bartrum, in fairness, is us-

ing legitimacy in a sense that emphasizes "usage and acceptance within a specific community and context." *Ibid.*, 328.

29 Jack M. Balkin, "'Wrong the Day It Was Decided': *Lochner* and Constitutional Historicism," 85 *Boston University Law Review* (2005): 677, 706–07.

30 Greene, 384; see also Bartrum, 329 (arguing that each canonical or anticanonical text "serves as a placeholder—a metonym—for a larger set of associated ideas or principles").

31 Greene, 381.

32 Louis Michael Seidman, *"Brown* and *Miranda,"* 80 *California Law Review* (1992): 673, 675.

33 Greene, 381.

34 Michael C. Dorf, "Whose Ox Is Being Gored?: When Attitudinalism Meets Federalism," 21 *St. John's Journal of Legal Commentary* (2007): 497, 521.

35 *Ibid.*, 520.

36 See Greene, 464 ("[I]mmorality is neither a necessary nor a sufficient feature of the anticanon. Inconsistency with ethos, by contrast, is an affirmative feature of anticanonical cases.").

37 Jamal Greene argues that this is a necessary feature of the anticanonical case. See ibid., 384: "There is consensus within the legal community that these cases are wrongly decided but . . . there is disagreement, even irreconcilable disagreement, as to why. This feature of anticanon cases is indispensable, as it enables multiple sides of contemporary constitutional arguments to use the anticanon as a rhetorical trump."

38 See Balkin, 709–10: ("To believe [*Plessy* was ever an acceptable constitutional interpretation] would be to accept facts about our country that are painful to accept. We do not want *Plessy* to have been right—regardless of the constitutional common sense of the period in which it was decided—because we do not want to be the sort of country in which *Plessy* could have been a faithful interpretation of the Constitution.").

39 Robert L. Tsai, chapter 3 in this volume.

40 *Ibid.*

41 *Ibid.*

42 *Ibid.* (abstract).

43 Roe v. Wade, 410 U.S. 113 (1973).

44 Minersville Sch. Dist. v. Gobitis, 310 U.S. 586 (1940), reversed by W. Va. Sch. Bd. v. Barnette, 319 U.S. 624 (1943).

45 Korematsu v. United States, 323 U.S. 214 (1944).

46 138 S. Ct. 2392 (2018).

47 Tsai, chapter 3 in this volume (quoting Trump v. Hawaii, 138 S. Ct. at 2448 (Sotomayor, J., dissenting)).

48 Prigg v. Pennsylvania, 41 U.S. (16 Pet.) 539 (1842).

49 See Levinson, 29–32; Greene, 388–95, 428–29, 464 (discussing *Prigg*, which he writes "could easily be called the worst Supreme Court decision ever issued," but arguing that the data place it outside the constitutional anticanon).

50 "Infamy," *The Oxford English Dictionary*, phrases 1, 2.
51 *Ibid.*
52 Catherine Edwards, "Unspeakable Professions: Public Performances and Prostitution in Ancient Rome," in *Roman Sexualities*, ed. Judith P. Hallett and Marilyn B. Skinner (Princeton: Princeton University Press, 1997), 66, 69.
53 William Smith, *A Dictionary of Greek and Roman Antiquities* (1875), 634–36, http://penelope.uchicago.edu; Edwards, 69.
54 "Infamy," Merriam-Webster Online, www.merriam-webster.com.
55 Merriam-Webster Online.
56 Leo Braudy, *The Frenzy of Renown: Fame and Its History* (New York: Vintage Books 1st. ed., 1997 [orig. publ. (in somewhat different form) New York: Oxford University Press, 1986]), 599.
57 Douglass Adair, "Fame and the Founding Fathers," in *Fame and the Founding Fathers: Essays by Douglass Adair*, ed. Trevor Colbourn (Indianapolis: Liberty Press reprint, 1998 [New York: W. W. Norton, 1974]), 3, 11. See also Braudy, 3 ("[T]he concept of fame has been grotesquely distended, and the line between public achievement and private pathology [has] grown dimmer as the claims grow more bizarre.").
58 "Fame," *Oxford English Dictionary*, phrases 2, 3.
59 "Famous," *Oxford English Dictionary*, phrase 1.
60 Adair, 12.
61 Braudy, 13.
62 *Ibid.*
63 Adair, 14.
64 *See generally* Appiah. See also Horwitz, 395–96 (arguing that, despite its alleged obsolescence, honor remains relevant and useful as a motivation for judges, "a small, narrowly defined peer group, in which collegial esteem is an important motivating factor").
65 See Horwitz, 391–94 (discussing internal and external honor).
66 Adair, 14 (quoting Thomas Jefferson).
67 *Ibid.*
68 Braudy, 17.
69 Adair, 9. For a rich collection of critical essays on the subject, see Peter McNamara, ed., *The Noblest Minds: Fame, Honor, and the American Founding* (Lanham, MD: Rowan & Littlefield, 1999). See also William Michael Treanor, "Fame, the Founding, and the Power to Declare War," 82 *Cornell Law Review* 695 (1997).
70 *Federalist No. 72.*
71 See generally *The Spur of Fame: Dialogues of John Adams and Benjamin Rush, 1805–13* (Indianapolis: Liberty Fund ed. [orig. publ. San Marino, CA: Huntington Library, 1966]).
72 Adair, 15.
73 *Ibid.*
74 *Ibid.*

75 *Ibid.*, 15–16.

76 Cicero, *Tusculanae Disputationes*, at III.3–4, quoted in Peter Olsthoorn, *Honor in Political and Moral Philosophy* (New York: State University of New York Press, 2015), 24.

77 Adair, 10, 16.

78 *Ibid.*, 33.

79 For a history of the changing meanings of fame over time, see generally Braudy.

80 On both points, see Paul A. Rahe, "*Fame, Founders, and the Idea of Founding in the Eighteenth Century*," in McNamara, 3; Treanor.

81 Braudy, at 604.

82 *Ibid.*

83 *Ibid.* See esp. 605: ("Although the urge to fame originally was the aspiration for a life after death in the words and thoughts of the community, it has evolved over the centuries into the desire for fame in one's own lifetime.").

84 *Ibid.*, 608.

85 *Ibid.*

86 Rahe, 3.

87 *Ibid.*, 3–4 (quoting Abraham Lincoln).

88 *Ibid.*

89 *Ibid.*

90 *Ibid.*

91 *Ibid.*

92 *Ibid.*

93 See Jerry Goldman, "Is There a Canon of Constitutional Law?," *American Political Science Association Newsletter* (Law and Courts Section of the American Political Science Association), Spring 1993, at 2–4.

94 347 U.S. 483 (1954).

95 22 U.S. (9 Wheat.) 1 (1824).

96 381 U.S. 479 (1965).

97 5 U.S. (1 Cranch.) 137 (1803).

98 17 U.S. (4 Wheat.) 316 (1819).

99 403 U.S. 713 (1971).

100 410 U.S. 113 (1973).

101 343 U.S. 579 (1952).

102 379 U.S. 241 (1964).

103 376 U.S. 254 (1964).

104 301 U.S. 1 (1937). See Balkin and Levinson, at 974 n.43.

105 317 U.S. 111 (1942).

106 228 U.S. 356 (1886).

107 319 U.S. 624 (1943). See Cross and Spriggs, 431–37. I have been sparing in taking cases from this list because it is clear that many of the cases most frequently cited by the courts, especially lower courts, are cited not because of their fame but because of their relevance to everyday matters in the federal courts. See, e.g., McDonnell

Douglas Corp. v. Green, 411 U.S. 792 (1973) (setting out a burden-shifting frame-work in Title VII employment discrimination cases); and Chevron U.S.A., Inc. v. National Resources Defense Council, Inc., 467 U.S. 837 (1984) (setting out a two-part test for whether deference is due an agency interpretation of its enabling statute).

108 135 S. Ct. 2584 (2015).
109 388 U.S. 1 (1967).
110 418 U.S. 683 (1974).
111 491 U.S. 397 (1989).
112 539 U.S. 558 (2003).
113 384 U.S. 436 (1966).
114 Greene, 382.
115 60 U.S. (19 How.) 393 (1857).
116 163 U.S. 537 (1896).
117 198 U.S. 45 (1905).
118 323 U.S. 214 (1944).
119 Greene, 383, 427–34. See esp. 388–91 (listing fifteen cases identified in different subsets of various law review articles as anticanonical).
120 Ibid., 383 (emphasis added).
121 *Ibid.*, 422–23.
122 *Ibid.*, 398.
123 Greene, 456–60. *Korematsu*'s recent treatment in Trump v. Hawaii, 138 S. Ct. 2392 (2018), which declares that it "was gravely wrong the day it was decided, has been overruled in the court of history, and . . . has no place in law under the Constitu-tion" (ibid., 2423), arguably buttresses the case for its anticanonical status. As I contend below, however, the common-law correction worked by the overruling may also limit its future invocation and thus incidentally support Greene's argu-ment that *Korematsu* lacks full anticanonical status.
124 Greene, 417.
125 *Ibid.*
126 *Ibid.*, 405.
127 Or even just two, if one both accepts the argument that *Lochner* has lost truly anticanonical status and rejects Greene's conclusion that *Korematsu* ultimately deserves its place in the anticanon despite presenting the weakest case for antica-nonical status.
128 *See, e.g.,* David A. Strauss, "Foreword: Does the Constitution Mean What it Says?," 129 *Harvard Law Review* 1, 4 (2015).
129 David A. Strauss, "Common Law Constitutional Interpretation," 63 *University of Chicago Law Review* 877, 891 (1996).
130 *Ibid.*, 894.
131 *Ibid.*, 895.
132 *Ibid.* (emphasis added).

133 Saying that the common-law approach *can* address infamous prior decisions is not, of course, the same as saying that it inevitably does so or that it never involves the evolution of bad or unjust doctrine. See Michael C. Dorf, "The Undead Constitution," 125 *Harvard Law Review* 2011 (2012): 2046–47.

134 See Strauss, 906.

135 Greene, 384.

136 *Ibid.*, 381.

137 *Ibid.*, 473; Tsai.

138 Balkin and Levinson, 970.

139 My perspective is impressionistic and may not be widely shared. I would add, though, that not all law professors are especially reflective about the nature of scholarship or (except in a strategic way) about the means of production that affect it, and not all of them have a sense of institutional history about legal scholarship.

140 Jamal Greene, "Thirteenth Amendment Optimism," 112 *Columbia Law Review* 1733, 1736 (2012).

141 Thomas S. Ulen, "The Unexpected Guest: Law and Economics, Law and Other Cognate Disciplines, and the Future of Legal Scholarship," 79 *Chicago-Kent Law Review* 403, 403 (2004).

142 Daniel A. Farber, "Gresham's Law of Legal Scholarship," 3 *Constitutional Commentary* 307 (1986): 309. See also Daniel A. Farber, "The Case Against Brilliance," 70 *Minnesota Law Review* 917 (1986): 917 (arguing that legal scholarship shows a "bias in favor of brilliant, 'paradigm shifting' work" and advocating greater recognition of the value of a "more pedestrian activity of 'normal science'"); Suzanna Sherry, "Too Clever by Half: The Problem with Novelty in Constitutional Law," 95 *Northwestern University Law Review* 921 (2001).

143 Note, "Originality," 115 *Harvard Law Review* 1988, 2008 (2002).

144 Greene, 405.

145 *Ibid.*, 408 (discussing Mark. A. Graber, Dred Scott *and the Problem of Constitutional Evil* (Cambridge: Cambridge University Press, 2006)).

146 *Ibid.*, 415 (citing Lawrence Lessig, "Fidelity in Translation," 71 *Texas Law Review* 1165, 1247 (1993)).

147 *Ibid.*, 417.

148 *Ibid.*, 417.

149 For an exemplar, see Michael J. Klarman, "How Great Were the 'Great' Marshall Court Decisions?," 87 *Virginia Law Review* 1111 (2001).

150 *Cf.* Balkin, 707–08 (discussing the role of canonical cases in forming a constitutional ethos).

151 Rahe, 3–4 (quoting Abraham Lincoln).

152 Greene, 383–84, 436.

153 *Ibid.*, 384.

154 *See, e.g.*, David S. Schwartz, "The Spirit of the Constitution: John Marshall and the 200-Year Odyssey of *McCulloch v. Maryland*" (Oxford: Oxford University Press, 2019), 8–9.

155 *See generally* Davison M. Douglas, "The Rhetorical Uses of *Marbury v. Madison*: The Emergence of a 'Great Case,'" 38 *Wake Forest Law Review* 375 (2003); Kermit Roosevelt III and Heath Khan, "McCulloch *v.* Marbury," 34 *Constitutional Commentary* 263 (2019).
156 Richard A. Posner, *Overcoming Law* (Cambridge, MA: Harvard University Press, 1995), 75–76.
157 Austin Sarat, "The 'New Formalism' in Disputing and Dispute Processing," 21 *Law & Society Review* 695 (1988): 704 and n.13.
158 Richard A. Posner, "The Decline of Law as an Autonomous Discipline, 1962–1987," 100 *Harvard Law Review* 761 (1987): 766.
159 G. Edward White, "The Arrival of History in Constitutional Scholarship," 88 *Virginia Law Review* 485 (2002): 516–17.
160 Gary Peller, "Neutral Principles in the 1950s," *University of Michigan Journal of Law Reform* 561 (1988): 572.
161 *Ibid.*, 586.
162 Neil Duxbury, "Faith in Reason: The Process Tradition in American Jurisprudence," 15 *Cardozo Law Review* 601 (1993): 642–43.
163 Edward A. Purcell, Jr., *The Crisis of Democratic Theory: Scientific Naturalism and the Problem of Value* (Lexington: University Press of Kentucky, 1973), 256.
164 Duxbury, 643 (quoting Michael P. Rogin, *The Intellectuals and McCarthy: The Radical Specter* (Cambridge, MA: MIT Press, 1967)), 278.
165 Mark Tushnet, "Harry Kalven and Kenneth Karst in the *Supreme Court Review*: Reflections After Fifty Years," 2010 *Supreme Court Review*, 35, 36.
166 *Ibid.*, 55, 57.
167 See ibid., 53–57.
168 *Ibid.*, 56.
169 Peller, 563 (discussing how scholars in the 1950s "interpreted and identified the evils of the *Lochner* era of constitutional jurisprudence"), 594–95.
170 For accounts, *see, e.g.*, Peller; Duxbury; Laura Kalman, *The Strange Career of Legal Liberalism* (New Haven: Yale University Press, 1998). The classic article around which these disagreements reached a boiling point was Herbert Wechsler's "Toward Neutral Principles of Constitutional Law," 73 *Harvard Law Review* 1 (1959).
171 For an argument that Wechsler "advocated legal neutrality not to thwart racial justice, but to achieve it," see Anders Walker, "'Neutral' Principles: Rethinking the Legal History of Civil Rights, 1934–1964," 40 *Loyola University Chicago Law Journal* 385 (2009): 386. And for the suggestion that even Wechsler's primary critics regarding *Brown* and neutral principles belonged within the general family of "legal-process oriented liberals," see John Henry Schlegel, "Those Weren't 'the Good Old Days,' Just the Old Days: Laura Kalman on Yale Law School in the Sixties," 32 *Law & Social Inquiry* 841 (2007): 843.
172 Peller, at 562.
173 Jill Norgren and Serena Nanda, *American Cultural Pluralism and Law*, 3rd ed. (New York: Praeger, 2006), at xiii.

174 John D. Inazu, *Confident Pluralism: Surviving and Thriving Through Deep Difference* (Chicago: University of Chicago Press, 2016), 5.
175 Nathaniel Persily, "Introduction," in *Solutions to Political Polarization in America*, ed. Nathaniel Persily (Cambridge: Cambridge University Press, 2015), 3.
176 Michael J. Barber and Nolan McCarty, "Causes and Consequences of Polarization," in Persily, 15.
177 Persily, "Introduction," in Persily, 4.
178 Ezra Klein, *Why We're Polarized* (New York: Simon & Schuster, 2020), xiv.
179 Persily, "Introduction," in Persily, 4.
180 Lilliana Mason, *Uncivil Agreement: How Politics Became Our Identity* (Chicago: University of Chicago Press, 2018). *See also* Alan I. Abramowitz, *The Great Alignment: Race, Party Transformation, and the Rise of Donald Trump* (New Haven: Yale University Press, 2018), 2.
181 See Nolan McCarty, *Polarization: What Everyone Needs to Know* (Oxford: Oxford University Press, 2019), chs. 3–4.
182 Zachary S. Price, "Symmetric Constitutionalism: An Essay on *Masterpiece Cakeshop* and the Post-Kennedy Supreme Court," 70 *Hastings Law Journal* 1273 (2019): 1274, 1280.
183 Zachary S. Price, "Precedent in a Polarized Era," 94 *Notre Dame Law Review* 433 (2018): 444 (reviewing Randy J. Kozel, *Settled Versus Right: A Theory of Precedent* (Cambridge: Cambridge University Press, 2017)).
184 *Ibid.*, 439.
185 *See generally* Dan M. Kahan, "Foreword: Neutral Principles, Motivated Cognition, and Some Problems for Constitutional Law," 125 *Harvard Law Review* 1 (2011); Dan M. Kahan et al., "'Ideology' or 'Situation Sense'? An Experimental Investigation of Motivated Reasoning and Professional Judgment," 164 *University of Pennsylvania Law Review* 349 (2016).
186 Kahan et al., 414.
187 Greene, 384.
188 Parents Involved in Community Schools v. Seattle School District No. 1, 551 U.S. 701 (2007). For discussion, *see, e.g.*, Scarlet Kim, Note, "Judicial Opinion as Historical Account: Parents Involved and the Modern Legacy of *Brown v. Board of Education*," 23 *Yale Journal of Law & Humanities* 159 (2011); Mark A. Graber, "The Price of Fame: *Brown* as Celebrity," 69 *Ohio State Law Journal* 939 (2008).
189 Greene, 461 (emphasis added).
190 *Ibid.* (citing Cass R. Sunstein, "Incompletely Theorized Agreements," 108 *Harvard Law Review* 1733 (1995)).
191 Klein, xiv.
192 Braudy, 604.
193 Frances FitzGerald, *America Revised: History Schoolbooks in the Twentieth Century* (Boston: Little, Brown & Co., 1979), 47.
194 Bruce Ackerman, *We the People, Volume 3: The Civil Rights Revolution* (Cambridge, MA: Harvard University Press, 2014) 7, 121.
195 Braudy, 604.

196 Lyrissa B. Lidsky, "Incendiary Speech and Social Media," 44 *Texas Tech Law Review* 147 (2011): 161.

197 Philip M. Napoli, "What if More Speech Is No Longer the Solution? First Amendment Theory Meets Fake News and the Filter Bubble," 70 *Federal Communications Law Journal* 55 (2018): 85–86.

198 For ambivalent discussions, *see, e.g.*, Orin S. Kerr, "Blogs and the Legal Academy," 84 *Washington University Law Review* 1127 (2006); Randy Barnett, "Caveat Blogger: Blogging and the Flight From Legal Scholarship," 84 *Washington University Law Review* 1145 (2006).

199 Discussing his preference for blogging over social media *more than a decade ago*, one writer lamented: "[B]y constantly micro-broadcasting everything, we've ended up macro-remembering almost nothing." "Thnks Fr Th Mmrs: The Rise of Microblogging, the Death of Posterity," TechCrunch, Aug. 22, 2010, https://techcrunch.com.

200 No doubt these are not unrelated phenomena.

201 Parents Involved, 551 U.S. at 748 (first quote); Regents of the University of California v. Bakke, 438 U.S. 265, 407 (1978) (separate opinion of Blackmun, J.) (second quote).

202 See Greene, 412–17 (canvassing views on the case).

203 *Ibid.*, 384.

204 *Ibid.*

205 *See, e.g.*, Josh Chafetz, "Impeachment and Assassination," 95 *Minnesota Law Review* 347 (2010): 353–54 (collecting sources on the influence of Plutarch's *Lives* on the founding generation and noting that great Romans were chosen as *noms de plume* by federalists and antifederalists alike).

206 One might borrow a phrase from Nelson Lund, who refers to a vision of presidential lawyers owing professional loyalty to "the office of the presidency" and not the individual president they work for as "moralistic romanticism." Nelson Lund, "Lawyers and the Defense of the Presidency," 1995 *BYU Law Review* 17, 21. Lund's point—that such a vision "obscures the economy of incentives that actually determines much of what presidents and their lawyers actually do"—reminds us that too much naïveté has its dangers. Repurposing Lund's phrase for more positive purposes does not so much reject this view as insist that an exclusively Machiavellian view of politics has its own potential dangers. See Hankins, 490–94, 513–14.

207 See Hankins, ibid., 493 ("Historians these days tend to be cynics. . . . Modern academic historians shrink from creating heroes out of flawed human beings; we fear our colleagues will think us sanctimonious or naïve.").

208 *Ibid.*

209 *Ibid.*, 514.

210 *Ibid.*, 141.

211 Hankins, 200 (discussing Boccaccio's account of "Good Fame" as a hedge against "the power that Fortune wields over mere temporal goods").

212 For the connection that the concept of posterity draws between the past and futurity, *see, e.g.*, Aviam Soifer, "Protecting Posterity," 7 *Nova Law Review* 39 (1982): 51.

213 *Cf.* David Brooks, *"The Power of Posterity," New York Times*, July 27, 2009, www.nytimes.com ("Without posterity, there are no grand designs. There are no high ambitions. Politics becomes insignificant. Even words like justice lose meaning because everything gets reduced to the narrow qualities of the here and now.").

214 See Jeffrey Rosen, "I-Commerce: Tocqueville, the Internet, and the Legalized Self," 70 *Fordham Law Review* 1 (2001): 7.

215 *Cf.* Matthew Nisbet and Dietram Scheufele, "The Polarization Paradox," Breakthrough Journal (Winter 2013), https://thebreakthrough.org. See also Hankins, 476 (chapter epigraph quoting *The Spectator*, in July 1711, for the concern that a "furious party-spirit" will "naturally break[] out in falsehood, detraction, calumny and a partial administration of justice. In a word, it fills a nation with spleen and rancor, and extinguishes all the seeds of good-nature, compassion and humanity").

216 531 U.S. 98 (2000).

217 Sanford Levinson, "Was the Emancipation Proclamation Constitutional? Do We/ Should We Care What the Answer Is?," 2001 *University of Illinois Law Review* 1135 (2001): 1157.

218 *Cf.* Jack M. Balkin, *"Bush v. Gore* and the Boundary Between Law and Politics," 110 *Yale Law Journal* 1407 (2001): 1447–50 (speculating about how the decision would be remembered, including both the possibility that it would become anticanonical and the possibility that it would be forgotten).

219 Marc O. DeGirolami, "The Sickness Unto Death of the First Amendment," 42 *Harvard Journal of Law and Public Policy* 751 (2019): 793. For examples of this trope across First Amendment and related scholarship, *see, e.g.*, Ellen D. Katz, "Election Law's Lochnerian Turn," 94 *Boston University Law Review* 697 (2018); Amy Kapczynski, "The Lochnerized First Amendment and the FDA: Toward a More Democratized Political Economy," 118 *Columbia Law Review Online* 179 (2018); Elizabeth Sepper, "Free Exercise Lochnerism," 115 *Columbia Law Review* 1453 (2015); Amanda Shanor, "The New *Lochner*," 2016 *Wisconsin Law Review* 133.

220 For arguments from different parts of the political and jurisprudential spectrum that the "new *Lochner*" writers are wrong in the specifics of their invocation of *Lochner*, see DeGirolami; Genevieve Lakier, "The First Amendment's Real *Lochner* Problem," 87 *University of Chicago Law Review* 1241 (2020).

221 Greene, 380.

222 Since hyper-canonicity in a hyper-polarized environment is likely to occur on both sides of the polarization divide, one can easily imagine similar examples on the right. *See, e.g.*, Louise Melling, "Will *Obergefell* Be the New *Roe*?," Slate, June 5, 2018, https://slate.com (writing, from the left, that "anti-LGBT civil rights activists have vowed to make [*Obergefell*] the new *Roe v. Wade*").

223 *Cf.* Rosen, 2 ("Law is like an antibiotic—when we use the courts too much, they lose some of their power to stigmatize, shame, and usefully restrain behavior"). As

the examples of the "new *Lochner*" and "new *Roe*" labels suggest, hyper-canonicity is most likely to offer solidaristic and public-relations value for the side invoking some older canonical or anticanonical decision or arguing that a new one is canonical or anticanonical, but little power to persuade the other side, which will be busily invoking and labeling its own cases.

224 Greene, 384; see also Bartrum, 329 (each canonical or anticanonical text "serves as a placeholder . . . for a larger set of associated ideas or principles").

225 That case is made well, but with some ambivalence, by Posner.

226 Lund, 21.

227 *Cf.* Rosen, 7; Krause; Appiah.

228 *See* Hankins, 513: ("[W]hen meritocracy diminishes the capacity to see ourselves as sharing a common fate, when it leaves little room for solidarity between ruler and ruled, it becomes a kind of tyranny."). For related reflections on the veneration of federal judges by their former law clerks, and the elite institutions that abet this tendency, see Paul Horwitz, "Clerking for Grown-Ups: A Tribute to Judge Ed Carnes," 69 *Alabama Law Review* 663 (2018).

ACKNOWLEDGMENTS

We are grateful to our Amherst College colleagues David Delaney, Mona Oraby, and Adam Sitze for their intellectual companionship and our students in Amherst College's Department of Law, Jurisprudence & Social Thought for their interest in the issues addressed in this book. We thank Ryan Kyle for her research assistance. We also would like to express our appreciation for generous financial support provided by Amherst College's Corliss Lamont Fund.

ABOUT THE CONTRIBUTORS

RICHARD L. ABEL, Emeritus, School of Law, UCLA

JUSTIN COLLINGS, School of Law, Brigham Young University

PAUL HORWITZ, School of Law, University of Alabama

SHERALLY MUNSHI, School of Law, Georgetown University

KERAMET REITER, Criminology, Law and Society and School of Law, University of California, Irvine

ROBERT L. TSAI, American University College of Law

ABOUT THE EDITORS

LAWRENCE DOUGLAS, Department of Law, Jurisprudence and Social Thought, Amherst College

AUSTIN SARAT, Departments of Law, Jurisprudence and Social Thought and Political Science, Amherst College

MARTHA MERRILL UMPHREY, Department of Law, Jurisprudence and Social Thought, Amherst College

INDEX

AB. *See* Aryan Brotherhood

Abel, Richard, 8–10

abolitionists, 104

abortion rights, 107–8

Abraham, Stephen, 9, 141–43, 166, 167

Abu Ghraib, 131, 137

academic cynicism, 243

academic theory canon, 227

achievement: fame and, 222–23; reputation and, 221

ACLU. *See* American Civil Liberty Union

activism: grassroots, 106, 107; judicial, 107, 232; *Korematsu* and, 122; peace, 159; public repudiation and, 97

Adair, Douglass, 220, 222

Adams, John, 222

Addington, David, 133

Aeneid (Virgil), 220

Ahmed, Sarah, 85

Alaska Territory, 73

Allegheny Mountains, 56

Allotment Act, 71

Allred, Keith J., 150

ambition, 223

American Bar Association, 135, 137

American Civil Liberty Union (ACLU), 131, 153, 178, 204

American Judicature Society, 136

American Revolution, 56, 60, 224

American Samoa, 68

Amnesty International, 132, 185, 196

antiabortion politics, 102

anticanon, 16, 40, 51; in age of false fame and infamy, 238–43; authority and, 41;

Greene list of cases, 74–75; legitimacy and, 41; moral orientation and, 85; precedent and, 41; revisionism and, 38–39; role of constitutional, 217; shadow, 38; United States Constitution and, 38–39. *See also* constitutional anticanon

anti-canonical decision, 2

antiprecedents, 38, 40

anti-Semitism, 34

apex courts: in Germany, 16–17; legitimacy and, 14

Article 131 (Germany), 23–24

Aryan Brotherhood (AB), 183, 195, 196

Ashcroft, John, 132

Ashker, Todd, 177, 178, 183–87, 195

Ashker v. Governor of California, 9, 176, 177; demonization and, 190–97; expert reports, 199, 201; implementation story, 188–90; infamy of solitary confinement and, 179–90; litigation history, 182–87; as reform challenges archetype, 203–5; settlement terms, 188, 191–93

Associated Press, 140

authority: anticanon and, 41; Convening, 146–49, 155, 159–60, 169; history and, 6, 37; judicial review and, 61; over immigration, 67, 70; over Indians, 55, 68, 69, 72; overseas territories and, 72; Presidential, 83–84; public opinion and, 118; symbols of judicial, 13

The Autobiography of Malcolm X, 183

www.ingramcontent.com/pod-product-compliance
Lightning Source LLC
Chambersburg PA
CBHW030457210326
41597CB00013B/696